£12-50

Violet Jacob

*Diaries and letters
from India
1895 – 1900*

Violet Jacob
Diaries and letters
from India
1 8 9 5 – 1 9 0 0

Edited with an Introduction by
Carol Anderson

CANONGATE

First published in Great Britain in 1990
by Canongate Publishing, Edinburgh

The publishers acknowledge subsidy from the
Scottish Arts Council towards the publication of this volume

British Library Cataloguing in Publication Data
Jacob, Violet, 1863–1946
Diaries and letters from India 1885–1900.
1. India. Social life, 1858–1947 – Biographies
I. Title II. Anderson, Carol
954.035092

ISBN 0-86241-224-2

Typeset by Hewer Text Composition Services, Edinburgh
Printed and bound by Butler and Tanner, Frome

Contents

Acknowledgements

I am grateful to Mrs Marjorie Lingen-Hutton for permission to edit and publish this work, and for her kind assistance with information about Violet Jacob and her family. I am also very grateful to Mr Ronald Garden, who found Violet Jacob's manuscript 'Four Good Years' and generously shared his knowledge. To Mr Tom Crawford, who first encouraged me to work on the diaries and letters and has given me unstinting help and support, I owe a special debt. Thank you to him; also to Mrs Jean Crawford, and to Mr John Riddy, who made some useful suggestions. I must express my appreciation of the understanding and enthusiasm shown by the publishers, especially Stephanie Wolfe Murray, and of the valuable contribution made by Stewart Sanderson's ideas and corrections.

Shinwa Women's College, Kobe, Japan, gave me financial assistance to visit the U.K. for research purposes while I was in their employment, and I am indebted to my former colleagues in the English Department for their interest and support.

Staff of the National Library of Scotland and the India Office in London were helpful in answering my questions, sometimes at a distance, and to them, many thanks.

Finally, I feel immense gratitude to the many friends, in several countries, who have given invaluable help of different kinds. Special thanks to them; to my parents Margaret and Nigel Anderson; and to Orazio Ragni for his particular support.

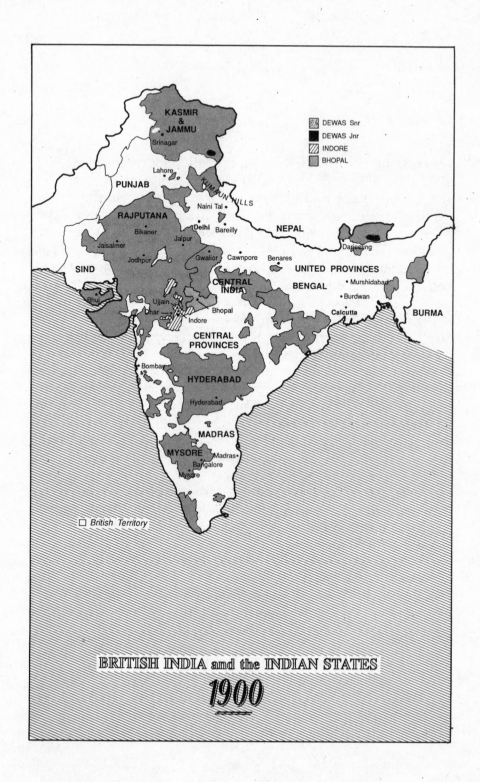

DEWAS Snr
DEWAS Jnr
INDORE
BHOPAL

KASMIR
&
JAMMU
Srinagar

Lahore

PUNJAB

KUMAUN HILLS

Naini Tal

RAJPUTANA

Bikaner

Jaisalmer

Jodhpur

Jaipur

Delhi

Bareilly

NEPAL

Darjeeling

Gwalior

Cawnpore

Benares

UNITED PROVINCES

• Murshidabad

SIND

Bhuj

Ujjain

Dhar

Indore

CENTRAL
INDIA

Bhopal

BENGAL

• Burdwan

Calcutta

BURMA

CENTRAL
PROVINCES

Bombay

HYDERABAD

Hyderabad

MADRAS

MYSORE

Madras•

Bangalore

Mysore

□ British Territory

BRITISH INDIA and the INDIAN STATES

1900

Introduction

Recognised in her own time as a skilled poet and fiction writer, Violet Jacob has been allowed to slip into relative obscurity. Apart from a handful of Scots lyrics which still appear in anthologies of Scottish poetry, her work, especially her prose, is little known. Her diaries and letters, however, recording the late days of the British *Raj* in India with great vividness and humour, act not only as valuable historical documents, but as a reminder of this neglected writer's considerable talents.

Violet Jacob was born Violet Augusta Mary Fredericka Kennedy-Erskine, on September 1st 1863, at the House of Dun (now owned by the National Trust for Scotland) near Montrose in Angus. She was educated at home and spent most of her early life there. Her poetry, like the best of her fiction, is rooted in her native region, and is often skilful and moving in its use of the vernacular Scots tongue. When asked how the aristocratic Violet Jacob could have such a lively command of Scots, a native of Dun apparently replied: 'as a bairn she was aye in and oot amo' the ploomen's feet at the Mains o' Dun'[1], and many of her better known poems, such as 'Tam i' the Kirk' or 'The Gowk', present the personae of rural farming folk. Much of her fiction, too, evokes the farms, landscapes, towns and above all the people of this part of Scotland, especially *Tales of My Own Country* (1922), and several of her novels.

Violet herself came of an ancient landed family, the Kennedy-Erskines, whose history she relates in her book *The Lairds of Dun* (1931). Her ancestors included some notable figures. Sir John Erskine, the 5th Laird of Dun, rose in the Scottish Church to be Moderator of the General Assembly in 1564, and was friendly with John Knox, who stayed at Dun for a month addressing the local people; but Erskine also maintained good relations with Mary, Queen of Scots. Another interesting character, David Erskine (1670-1758), the 13th Laird, became an eminent Scottish judge, and fiercely opposed the Union with England. It was he who built the House of Dun, which dates to 1730 and was designed by William Adam. Violet's grandmother, Augusta, was an illegitimate daughter of William,

Duke of Clarence (later King William IV), and Dorothy Jordan the actress. Augusta died in 1865, and Violet thought of her as the last 'historical' figure in her family.

Tragedy struck several times in her own immediate family, and this may account in part for the darker notes discernible in almost all Violet Jacob's work. Her father, the 18th Laird of Dun, William Henry Kennedy-Erskine (known as 'Willy'), died when Violet was to still a child, and her younger sister Millicent died suddenly and shockingly, probably of appendicitis, at the age of sixteen. A brother born the year after Violet herself lived only three days, and her older brother Augustus, the 19th Laird, died at sea aged forty-two. It was to her Welsh mother, the former Catherine Jones of Carmarthenshire and the 'C.K.E.' of the Indian letters, that Violet wrote when she went overseas — for, like many Scots, she was to travel far from home.

On October 27th 1894, Violet married Arthur Otway Jacob, an Irishman born (August 28th 1867) in Maryborough (now Portlaoise), who was serving as an officer in the British Army. At the time of their marriage he was a lieutenant in the 20th Hussars, a cavalry regiment; he rose while in India to the rank of captain, and later major. Their son, Arthur Henry, or Harry as he was called, was born on August 25th 1895 in Colchester, where Arthur's regiment was based at the time. In the same year Arthur Jacob departed with his regiment, and Violet followed a little later; their destination was India, where they were to spend 'Four Good Years' and more.[2]

Violet recorded her experiences of these years (1895-1900) in letters to her mother. She also kept diaries for her own benefit: she loved India and wanted to remember it, writing in 1899: 'If I live to be old I should like to be able to look back on the sights and sounds of this — to me — beloved country and the good days we had in it, and even on its trivialities.'[3] Much later — in 1932 — she gathered together all the surviving letters and journals and had them typed and bound, illustrating them with her own drawings, paintings and photographs of India, and including a quaint frontispiece stating 'Violet Jacob: Her Book', with a motto in French, 'être et ne pas avoir'.

These lovingly compiled volumes disappeared for years, having passed through several hands after Violet Jacob's death in 1946, and were not rediscovered until the 1980s.[4]

Today, Violet Jacob's Indian letters and diaries make engaging reading, despite being intermittent. The years of her residence in

India were probably the happiest in Violet's life, and her vitality and enthusiasm shine through the writing. Her marriage to Arthur Jacob seems to have been very successful. Referred to usually in these pages just as 'A', he is a rather shadowy figure, but evidently he was a congenial man with whom Violet could share her many interests; nearly thirty years later she wrote of him with obvious love and sympathy: 'No one is more observant than he, or has a more unerring eye for the humours of every episode, and few are more intelligently interested'.5 She dedicated one of her historical novels, *The History of Aythan Waring* (1908), to 'A.O.J.'. Violet's young son Harry was a source of joy to her, too: the diaries contain a touching little photograph of the small boy in action with his beloved leather football, and she notes his love of Indian folklore, which she seems to have encouraged, and his habit of chattering in a mixture of English and Hindi.

Yet Violet Jacob's relationships remain essentially in the background. This may be partly a convention of the time; one critic has pointed out that many nineteenth-century women's diaries 'remained very impersonal throughout the diarist's lifetime'.6 Certainly, although her family and friends were a source of security and pleasure to Violet, the chief subject of the pages that follow is something else; it might be described as India itself.

Violet's letters and diaries are packed with detail, with her rich and sensuous perceptions of India. We read of the colours, smells and sounds of the land, the birds and wildlife, the plants, trees and flowers, perhaps above all the people, their everyday life and lore. Both Indians and Europeans are evoked with much humour and affection, and not a little shrewd wit.

During their 'Four Good Years' Violet and Arthur Jacob were stationed in the hot, dusty plains of Central India. Violet's first and many subsequent letters home to her mother at Dun were addressed from Mhow, an army cantonment town in the large state of Indore, fourteen miles from the British Residency at the city of Indore, in an area historically known as Malwa. This was situated in the Central India Agency, which contained about one hundred and thirty officially recognised states and estates of varying sizes, and now forms part of the large modern state called Madhya Pradesh.

Here, the flat landscape, girded by mountains, stretches for miles, criss-crossed by *nullahs*, or watercourses, often dry; but reservoirs (known as 'tanks') offer cool relief, and, despite the intense heat which starts around March and continues for several months until the monsoon breaks, it is, according to Violet's account, a place with varied wildlife and vegetation: fields of opium poppies, *dak* trees, vultures, panthers and crocodiles.

It is a region of great cultural diversity, too, rich in history. The majority of people in Violet Jacob's time, like today, were Hindus, and Hindi the major language of the area, but many people spoke instead Urdu, or local languages such as Malwi. Violet could visit the sites of struggles down the centuries between Hindus and Muslims (for instance at the ancient hilltop city of Mandu, not far from Mhow), and see everywhere the still significant presence of Muslim culture. She attended both Hindu and Muslim festivals, such as the *Mohurrum* (Muslim) and the *Dusera* (Hindu), which she describes with delight. It is an area where many different powerful forces have in turn held sway — the mighty Mughals and the warlike Marathas — and where, as Violet noted, there were (and are) still pre-Aryan tribal people, the Gonds and the Bhils. Violet could also observe the relics of ancient Buddhist culture at Sanchi, near Bhopal, where the Emperor Ashoka (a major figure at the height of the Mauryan empire in Northern India) built some of the world's most important Buddhist structures in the third century B.C., notably the monument known as the Great Stupa.

Violet's diaries and letters deal mainly with her life in this fascinating region, and with her forays, both by train and on horseback, to its various corners. She visited many of the cities of Central India, not only Indore, the most important centre nearby, but also ancient Ujjain, Bhopal, and Gwalior with its huge and historic fort, and she clearly relished their bustling scenes. But above all she liked the villages and small 'unimportant' places, preferring the ordinary life of India to its showpieces. (She was on her later visit to India much disappointed in the famous Taj Mahal at Agra.) It is interesting to compare her reaction to the little town of Dhar, once a capital of Malwa and for several centuries a centre of Hindu learning, with the remarks of another visitor, E. M. Forster. Violet wrote of Dhar when she revisited it in later years: 'Dhar, sitting in the wild Bhil country, with its weird temples, thirty-four miles from a railway, is a place I always loved.'[7] Forster wrote more curtly: 'Dhar in itself is not interesting and abominably hot.'[8]

Although Violet vividly represents the heat and discomfort of the Central India plains, which brought death to many (there was a famine in the nearby Central Provinces 1896-1897), and, though like most other British people the Jacobs fled to the hills for some weeks of cool relief, Violet never tired of India. It is essentially her delight in India that illuminates her writing. However, she was no mere enthusiast. Other expatriate women kept diaries, but Violet Jacob was not only a woman of unusually broad sympathies and creative energy, she was also a gifted writer.[9]

Her experiences are therefore set down with care; her prose is assured, her 'voice' a distinctive one. A notable feature of her style in her Indian writings, as elsewhere in her fiction, is her tendency to economy and understatement. She frequently presents incidents — often comical, sometimes horrifying — with little or no comment, allowing events to speak for themselves. She retains a sense of humour through thick and thin, and is especially good at comical thumbnail portraits, so that her work abounds in characters briefly but richly evoked.

The letters and diaries thus make entertaining reading; they also afford an insight into a developing writer at the beginning of her career. Apparently a lover of storytelling since childhood, Violet Jacob had already collaborated with William Douglas Campbell on a comic narrative poem in Scots, 'The Baillie MacPhee', for which she provided skilful illustrations, and this was published by William Blackwood in 1888. It was, however, during the time she was keeping her Indian journals that Violet Jacob embarked on her first extended prose narrative. There are allusions throughout the diaries to her work on *The Sheepstealers*, which was to be her first full-length novel, published eventually in 1902. Set in the Anglo-Welsh borders, where the Jacobs later lived for some time, it is an extremely competent first novel, a work of historical fiction with some of the power that characterises her later work, especially that dealing with her home territory in Scotland. Beneath the surface tale of romance and adventure there are darker undercurrents, and the prose is lucid and supple.

Besides being at this time an apprentice novelist, Violet Jacob was also an exceptionally talented amateur artist. She drew and painted many of the places and people she saw in India, often rising early in the morning to make use of the cooler weather, and exploring widely in search of subjects. She especially loved to paint flowers, and studied botany with real determination, learning botanical names and terms in a situation which made such a task difficult. Some of her watercolours of flowers and plants are held today by the Royal Botanical Gardens in Edinburgh, and are considered a fine record

of the flora of Central India. Her work is often surprising for its
boldness of composition: these pictures are exquisitely executed, but
they are not timidly conceived.

Violet Jacob was, indeed, anything but timid. The diaries and
letters convey the extraordinary curiosity and zest of her encounter
with India. 'I'm dying to see something of this country outside the
watertight little world of the cantonment,' she wrote in late 1895,
soon after her arrival in Mhow. 'Nobody seems to know anything
about it and I mean to see it for myself. People say to me "there's
nothing to see", and "you'll soon tire of that", but I know myself
and I think I know them and their sort, and I'm going.' (page 26) And,
a strikingly intrepid woman, she was soon going off on 'jaunts' alone
on horseback, riding for miles in the Indian countryside, and roaming
in deserted places never visited by western people, especially women,
at this time. She made efforts to learn Hindustani in order to talk with
the people she met, and her great interest in the customs of Indian
people, their daily lives and festivals, is always apparent. Undaunted
by mishap, she does not blench at a rat running across her pillow in
a tent at night, or the sight of vultures gathered over a corpse. She
empathises with other spirited women who had gone before her in
India, reading with pleasure the works of, among others, Flora Annie
Steele (like herself, a Scot) and Charlotte Canning. Without offering
much overt reflection on women's roles, Violet Jacob's diaries and
letters present a woman far from conventional, and one who knew
she often broke the rules of 'feminine' behaviour. (It's interesting to
note that she smoked, something rather 'daring' for women of her
time.)

However, for all her personal unconventionality, Violet Jacob was
in India as a direct consequence of the *Raj*, since her husband was an
officer in the British Army. She lived in India as part of an expatriate
community, and her writing gives us some insights into the way of
life of the British in India at this time, serving as a valuable record
of an era.

Until the Indian Mutiny of 1857, British rule over India had
been exercised by the East India Company. From 1858, however,
most of India was administered by the British Government. Large
areas still had their own rulers, the local Indian monarchs, and
the Jacobs, to Violet's delight, were stationed in the heart of these
so-called 'native' states. However, even the Indian princes were now
ultimately answerable to the *Raj*, and the British were in evidence in
Central India as elsewhere.

The British administration of India was complex and hierarchical. Since 1858 the British monarch had ruled through the Viceroy of India; in the Jacobs' time this was at first the Earl of Elgin (Viceroy 1894-99), whom Violet met during a viceregal visit in 1896, and subsequently the famous Lord Curzon, whom she apparently did not. Under the Viceroy the two main forces for maintaining power in India were the Army and the Indian Civil Service (the I.C.S.), and the Jacobs knew many people associated with both.

The army in India was made up of both British and Indian soldiers. Most British soldiers belonged to traditional regiments of the British Army, such as Arthur Jacob's, the 20th Hussars, which would send out battalions to the sub-continent for five-year spells to reinforce and keep an eye on the Indian Army. After the 1857 Mutiny there had been considerable reorganisation of the Army to try and ensure that no such disaster would occur again. Formerly, Indian soldiers had greatly outnumbered the British; now the proportions were made less unequal, with Indians of different tribes and castes being mixed to further prevent the danger of uprising.

The cantonment at Mhow had originally been ceded by a treaty of 1818 between the East India Company and the royal Indian Holkar family as a base for a British force, which was intended to maintain the security of the Holkar dynasty at Indore, and generally to protect this part of India from lawlessness. The garrison normally consisted of at least one regiment of field artillery, with one battalion of British and one of Indian infantry. Thus, besides the 20th Hussars, there were several other regiments in the area, including notably the Royal Fusiliers, who were stationed at Mhow 1896-1897, and, at various times, the 4th and 20th regiments of the Bombay Infantry. The Jacobs made a number of friends among the local military, especially from Arthur's regiment and the Royal Fusiliers. These friends included General Nicolson, the District Officer of the Bombay Command, and his wife, while other locally based army officers are referred to only by their initials. A few army wives are also mentioned by initials.

On the whole, however, the Jacobs' closest friends appear to have been drawn from among the officials and administrators of the Indian Civil Service, the main governing force in India besides the Army, and a massive bureaucratic structure. The Indian Civil Service had three main departments, Political, Judicial and Executive. The Jacobs had several friends in the Political department, which was staffed partly by civil servants and partly by Indian Army officers; their work was mainly diplomatic, and the posts included those of Residents and Agents. The Mhow garrison was not far from the Residency at Indore, the most important centre of British administration in Central India at this time. It became a focus for the Jacobs' social life as from early on they became friendly with Colonel (later Sir) David Barr, the Resident at Indore and Agent to the Governor General in Central India, and therefore a figure of some importance locally. (In 1899 a separate Resident was appointed, but the post was later abolished again.) In fact, although Violet does not mention it, a school was opened at Jaora in 1897 and named the Barr High School after him. Colonel Barr made a good impression on Violet from the first: 'He has a merry wit, a wife and daughter and three sons' (page 30); and he proved a fund of stories about India, some of which Violet recounts. Evelyn Barr, Colonel Barr's wife, often referred to simply as 'E', also became a close friend and frequent companion on Violet's excursions on horseback; as Violet says of her, 'She is a great satisfaction to me for she likes knocking about the country' (page 90).

Other good friends included Captain Pat Bannerman, the First Assistant at the Residency at Indore, and Mr Ernest Barnes, the Second Assistant, who arrived in September 1897. His wife Eugénie, who followed a little later, was half-Italian and tri-lingual, and became another of Violet's companions, especially after the departure of the Barrs on home leave in 1898. Ernest Barnes later became Captain Barnes, and acted as Political Agent in Bhopawar, Southern States of Central India; among his achievements was the establishment of a small archaeological department in Dhar in 1902, as he recognised that this small state, so much loved by Violet, contained important ancient treasures.

The Jacobs' other friends were an assorted crowd. Arthur Napier, guardian to the young Muslim ruler, the Nawab of Jaora, appears often in these pages, usually as 'the Sahib', in affection emulation of his Indian title; and 'young Kingcome', the head of the Indore branch of the Bank of Bombay is also generally referred to, again in Indian style, as 'the Bankwallah'. Dr Caldecott, the Surgeon at the Residency, plays a very active part in local activities, while various other characters come and go, including Marian Doughty, a woman Violet encounters at a social gathering, who turns out to have once been a little girl Violet knew at a dancing class in her childhood days!

Violet clearly derives pleasure from her relationships with these

and other European people she met in India, and she participates
in the usual activities of the community, parties, polo and hunting;
there is talk, too, of her London club (the 'Ladies' Empire'), and of
balls and servants. Like others of her time and place, Violet Jacob
enjoyed the privileges of the British *Raj* in India, and she shows the
self-confidence afforded by her position and aristocratic background.
She is never critical of the British presence as a colonising power;
rather she seems generally to accept the situation and enjoy it. Indeed,
she and her friends toast the birthday of the Queen — Victoria,
Empress of India.

Nevertheless, she sometimes shows a distinctive dryness, an acer-
bity of tone that is a mark of her own strong personality but perhaps
derives obliquely from her Scottishness too. Certainly she displays
a notable sense of detachment when she talks about some of the
British people she meets, and is often scathing about the attitudes
and behaviour of the British 'society' she encounters in India. She
declares a firm preference for the 'native states': 'twice and three
times as interesting as British India' (page 130), and she and Arthur
were 'entirely averse to going to the real, official, dreadfully social
hills' (page 150) in the hot season. Violet tends to find polo matches
dull in comparison with more 'Indian' activities, which invariably
capture her interest.

Furthermore, although it is not directly acknowledged, the uneasi-
ness of the British role in India sometimes comes through in the
narrative. The Residency at Indore, where the Jacobs' friends were
employed, had been attacked by troops of the local Indian prince,
Holkar, in the 1857 Mutiny; the Resident had been forced to flee,
although Holkar himself had personally given protection to the
British people under threat. Memories of the Mutiny evidently died
hard, as can be seen from Violet's account of the death of her friend
Arthur Napier in 1898. He had been too long in India without a
break, says Violet: he dies in a fever babbling deliriously of his fear
of mutiny, and claiming that a Eurasian woman hired to care for
him is actually a German spy. There may be shadowings of other
conflicts here, too.

Violet herself wrote three stories which express both directly and
indirectly the troubled response of the British to life in India. These
tales, 'The Black Man's Hand', 'Other People's Gods' and 'The
Fringe of the Jungle', appeared in a collection called *The Fortune
Hunters and Other Stories*, published in 1910. None of them is her
best work, although one, 'The Fringe of the Jungle', evokes quite

powerfully the fascination and fear felt by Europeans encountering the hot season in India:

> To Europe, the words 'hot weather' stand for very little, conjuring up, maybe, some vision of oppressive skies, langour and white umbrellas; to Asia they mean anything between a time of discomfort and tension, which to be even dimly understood must be endured, and a three months' fight with death. For with the flowering of the *dhak* the shrill pipes of the East play up for tragedy, and the European, riding home in the evening under a low, hot moon, hears the crickets' intrusive and throbbing chorus in the darkness of the wayside trees crying to every British subject that the time is at hand when he must take up his little corner of the Empire's burden and stand up with it. Then the flight of women and children to the hills begins, and the furnace doors close upon those who are left. (*The Fortune Hunters*, page 320).

And indeed Europeans and Indians die regularly in the pages of her journal, from enteric, plague and fever. Violet did voluntary work at the Mhow military hospital, and although she is reticent about the details of her experience, her brief journal entries speak for themselves. Sometimes she notes down grim understatements: 'There has been another death from enteric in the hospital. Plague, fever, war and approaching famine — which is now certain — are not cheering' (page 180).

Thus Violet Jacob provides a personal chronicle of the strains of life during the waning British *Raj*, as well as its pleasures for the more fortunate: for it *was* by now on the wane. The first Indian National Congress had already been established in 1885, some ten years before the Jacobs arrived in India, although this is something never mentioned by Violet.

A further important facet of Indian life at this time is illuminated by these diaries and letters, however; for Violet records most vividly her acquaintance with some of the rulers of the Central Indian states, both Hindu and Muslim, whom she grew to know quite well. At this period the rulers of the so-called 'native' states were in a curious position, their role and status having been altered and undermined by the British *Raj*. The Hindu institution of kingship was an ancient one. The word 'Rajah', or 'King', had a double meaning: 'one who rules', and 'one whose duty is to please', denoting the ruler's relationship with his or her people. The ruler was expected to protect the people, while they in turn were to offer their obedience and a share of their produce and possessions. This tradition survived waves of invaders, and was even adopted by them, so that the Muslim 'Nawab', for example, became a variant of the 'Rajah'.

British imperial rule, established by the East India Company, and then in 1858 assumed by the British Crown, weakened this tradition. Approximately three-fifths of India was directly governed by the British, but while the remaining states still had their own rulers, these were now answerable to the *Raj*. The British divided the huge number of royal states into various categories; the most important were 'First Division States', or 'Salute States' as they were known, for their significance was measured by the number of gun salutes accorded to their rulers on formal occasions. Then there were 'Second Division' or 'Non-Salute States', and, finally, there were hereditary landholdings, whose families ruled estates rather than true states. Queen Victoria in 1858 undertook to 'respect the rights, dignity and honour of the Native Princes'[10] — of whom there were some 565 — but although their kingdoms were perhaps more stable than formerly, the princes had lost their full authority, and Victoria became Empress of All India in 1877. The British never really acknowledged that the Indian rulers had truly been 'kings'.

The Indian princes, like their states, were diverse, varying greatly in style, personality and sense of social responsibility. Some had lavish, self-indulgent lifestyles, while others worked hard to better the lot of their people. Violet met several of those deemed most 'important', but also some who were especially interesting, and even downright eccentric. Her accounts of their meetings are lively, with entertaining descriptions of the princes themselves, their families, court life, and their palaces and gardens.

The first prince Violet met was the young Nawab of Jaora, a small state in Malwa which, despite its size, earned a 13-gun salute. The Nawab was a Muslim of Pathan origin, and still a child in 1896. With his cousin 'Jimmy' (an Indian endowed with a Christian name, as was not uncommon in royal families)[11], he was then living in Indore, while his uncle, Jimmy's father, Yar Mohammad Khan, was acting as regent of Jaora in the young ruler's minority. Violet became fond of the two little boys; on one occasion, she, Arthur and some others accompanied them on a trip to their native Jaora, and they, in turn, came to visit her son Harry.

At the opposite extreme was the elderly Maharajah of Dhar, a small state traditionally ruled by Puar Marathas. In Violet's time the Maharajah was a tiny crippled old man; Violet records their awkward and embarrassing meeting with great humour. She remarks, too, that he was 'loyal' to the British, and was considered a good ruler and loved by his people. He died in the summer of 1898, to be succeeded by his adopted son, a practice which was quite customary, failing a direct heir.[12] Violet met his successor again many years later, when the boy was grown up with children of his own.

Unfailingly interested in the lifestyles of such Indian rulers, Violet nevertheless always presents them as people rather than as monarchs. The Maharajah Holkar, for instance, ruler of the large and important state of Indore, and a Hindu of the fierce Maratha race, belonged to one of the most powerful ruling families of the region, deemed worthy of a 19-gun salute. To Violet's irreverent eye, however, he appears (in January 1896) as 'awfully and fearfully fat, and wearing a garment that looked as if it were made out of a grey eiderdown quilt' (page 29), although she later admits that he was nevertheless rather imposing.

The Holkars had a reputation for hostility towards the British, but official visits by senior representatives of the Imperial Crown could not be ignored, and the Maharajah Shivaji Rao gave a great ball in December 1896 attended by the British Viceroy, the Earl of Elgin. Violet attended, too, and offers a vivid picture of the occasion in all its pomp and absurdity. She herself spent some time talking with Lady Elgin, an old acquaintance who seemed to Violet 'terribly homesick' (page 49). Holkar gave another ball in November 1897, when Violet and her friend Evelyn Barr stayed at the palace to assist with preparations. At this event Holkar appears as a great 'character', as some of his predecessors had reputedly been. Indeed, Shivaji Rao was forced to abdicate in 1903 because of his behaviour towards the British — he beat up the British Resident!

Gwalior, famous for its tigers, was another very important (21-gun salute) state visited by Violet. The Maharajah, Madho Rao Scindia of Gwalior, belonged to a prominent Maratha family that, like the Holkars of Indore, was of humble origins, and was their old rival. Madho Rao Scindia was, in fact, to be a progressive ruler, who introduced a considerable degree of democratic government to his state, and also brought about practical improvements, encouraging modern industrial and farming methods; but on Violet's first meeting with him in 1897, she describes him just as 'very cheery and pleasant; he is a short fat youth of 21, looking quite 35' (page 98). Unlike Holkar, Scindia was to prove sympathetic to the British, and formed quite close bonds with British royalty. Violet offers some interesting observations on the lifestyle and role of his wife; and indeed, some of the most valuable insights she gives are into the lives of female royalty, with glimpses of life in the *zenana*, or women's quarters.

Other royal Indian women she encountered were the two Ranis of the Hindu Dewas state, whose rulers were Puar Marathas like the royal family of Dhar, and had links with Gwalior through marriage. Dewas state, where E. M. Forster lived and worked in 1912, getting material for *A Passage to India* and *The Hill of Devi*, was founded in the early 1700s by two Maratha brothers, and was divided in two parts, known as the 'Junior' and 'Senior' branches. Under British rule from 1818, the state continued to have two Rajahs; Violet, however, was more interested in their wives, Lelita Rani, who was married to the Rajah of the Junior branch (and not, as Violet mistakenly believed, to that of the Senior), and Tara Rani, wife to the Rajah of the Senior branch. E. M. Forster, who was secretary to the subsequent Rajah of Dewas Senior, Tukoji Rao Puar III, says of Tukoji's aunt, the same Tara, in 1921, that she 'had long been known to me as Dewas-Nuisance-Lady No. 1',[13] but Violet liked her. At the time of their meeting Tara was twenty, 'which is considered close on middle age for an Indian woman. But Tara does not seem at all middle aged, also she is clever, and they say has managed to make her husband bored with his mistresses' (page 106). Violet Jacob, always a keen observer, notes the severe restrictions on the lives even of royal women, whose husbands not only frequently took mistresses, but sometimes other wives. At the same time, she conveys the often powerful personalities of women in such positions.

One of the most interesting Indian ruling families she encountered was surely that of the princely Muslim state of Bhopal. Bhopal city, site of the appalling chemical factory disaster in December 1984, is now the capital of Madhya Pradesh. In Violet's time, Bhopal had one of the leading royal families in India, founded by an Afghan in the eighteenth century and now rating a 19-gun salute. It was unusual in having been headed by female rulers for over a century. In 1899, Violet briefly met Shah Jehan, the Begum of Bhopal, who had ruled since 1868, although for many years under the oppressive influence of her husband. Violet was later to meet, and indeed become quite closely acquainted with, Shah Jehan's daughter, Sultan Jehan Begum, who was a very active leader and a fascinating character; Violet's account of her is of considerable historical interest.

On her later, short visit to India Violet was to encounter the families of several of the Indian rulers again; but, as she began to fear in 1899, her present stay was drawing to an end, and she had no way of knowing that return would be possible. Throughout the second half of that year there were rumours of war in South Africa, and the Jacobs lived in continuous uncertainty about their future, as it was thought that troops would be called for from India. Nevertheless, Violet's diaries close on an optimistic note: the sound of the new year, 1900 — and the new century — being rung in. This dramatic ending is a a reminder that we are reading the work of an imaginative writer whose most significant achievements in fiction and poetry still lay ahead. However, in all her long life, despite her active writing career, Violet Jacob would probably never again know the personal happiness she had enjoyed in India; it is as well she did not foresee the sorrows that lay ahead.

Arthur Jacob's regiment did indeed have to leave India to fight in the Boer War. Violet left India too, with deep regret, and returned to Britain. Thereafter the Jacobs lived mainly in various English garrison towns where Arthur was stationed. They had homes in Herefordshire and Shropshire, areas which Violet seems to have liked. She formed a friendship with A. E. Housman, the poet best known for *A Shropshire Lad*, who was at one time a neighbour; and several of Violet's own works have a background of the Welsh Marches.

Apart from two years in Egypt with Arthur's regiment, travel abroad in the years following the departure from India was mostly confined to holidays in Europe. A few pleasant sketches and paintings remain of parts of Italy, Spain and France, as well as England. Some of Violet's lighter tales written for magazine publication also feature foreign settings. Violet, indeed, wrote in a wide variety of genres, and after the publication of *The Sheepstealers* in 1902 she produced, among other things, a number of books for children, with Harry Jacob no doubt an early audience for her tales and poems. Her children's books show the same imaginative delight in the world that can be seen in her Indian writings, and some of them are illustrated by their author.

The outbreak of the First World War in 1914, however, was to bring many changes, including the great grief of Violet Jacob's life. Harry Jacob, scarcely out of boyhood, died in France from wounds received at the Battle of the Somme in the summer of 1916. He had fought in the 4th Battalion of the Royal Fusiliers, the regiment which the Jacobs had come to know well during their time in India, and he is mentioned in their Roll of Honour.

Violet never fully recovered from this loss, and the work she wrote following the war reflects this. Her volume of poems, *Songs of Angus*, had appeared in 1915, to great acclaim (partly because it appealed to national spirit during the war); its successor, *More Songs of Angus and Others* of 1918, is dedicated to 'A.H.J.' — Harry — and is a much more sombre volume. Many of her poems register the impact of war, both on a personal level and within the local community, as in one Scots poem:

> They gaed frae mill and mairt; frae wind-blown places
> And grey toon closes; i' the empty street
> Nae mair the bairns ken their steps, their faces,
> Nor stand tae listen to the trampin' feet.
>
> ('Glory')[14]

For the reader of the Indian diaries and letters who knows what lay ahead, it is poignant to read in these pages of the small boy with his football and his love of Indian legends.

Although Violet and Arthur were able to visit India over twenty years after their first stay there (they spent some months in India in 1922-23), their return was overshadowed by the death of their son. Violet wrote in January 1923 when they revisited Mhow:

> I don't know whether all this is greater pleasure or greater pain. My old love of the place wrings my heart and I see ghosts, though not where others see them. The best of all my life was here; youth, health, spirits, and Harry, who began his life here among soldiers and who ended it, a soldier among the soldiers who knew him here as a little boy, when the great test came.

For all her sadness, Violet Jacob lived on, perhaps gaining support from her quiet Christian faith, and she was throughout most of her life actively engaged in writing. She gained some reputation as a poet, particularly in Scots; some of her lyrics were published in 1920 by C. M. Grieve, better known as the poet Hugh MacDiarmid, in his journal *Northern Numbers*, which he edited from Montrose. A critic difficult to please, Grieve considered Violet Jacob, in 1925, as 'the most considerable of contemporary vernacular poets',[15] and like John Buchan he saw her as following in the tradition of aristocratic Scottish women poets and songwriters that includes Caroline Nairne and Jean Elliott.

Grieve, however, did not fully appreciate her fiction, and to this day the quality of her prose remains under-valued. Several of Violet Jacob's novels are merely well-written romances, but others and some of her short stories are of much greater interest, in particular *Flemington* (1911), a fine novel set in the Jacobite period. This work greatly impressed John Buchan and his wife Susan when it appeared, and their friendship with Violet Jacob dates to this time. Several other volumes, notably *Tales of My Own Country* (1922), and some of her late stories collected in *The Lum Hat and Other Stories* (finally published in 1982) are also extremely poised.

In general, Violet Jacob has not yet been satisfactorily placed in the Scottish literary tradition where she belongs. Although in her Indian diaries and letters she tends to talk about 'England' and 'the English', and only rarely mentions Scotland, in fact she thought of herself emphatically as a Scot. The themes of her historical fiction are related to those of Walter Scott and R. L. Stevenson, whose life was in part contemporaneous with her own. Her fiction resembles Stevenson's also in its craftsmanship: like Stevenson Violet Jacob is a stylist, her prose always elegant and yet richly suggestive. She might be usefully compared, too, with other women writers, especially those of her own region, not only the poets Helen Cruickshank and Marion Angus, but prose writers such as Willa Muir, Nan Shepherd, 'Lorna Moon' and Jessie Kesson.

Her Indian writings are surely of wide general appeal, but they add something in particular to the body of Scottish letters. They may also shed some light on our past, serving to increase awareness of Scottish 'colonial' history. The Scots contributed disproportionately to imperial enterprise in India, as elsewhere, but the distinctive Scottish experience of Empire, subtly different from that of the English because of Scotland's own experience of domination by English culture, has yet to be fully understood.[16] The complexities of Violet Jacob's perspective, as a woman and a Scot of aristocratic background, with broad sympathies and a love of India, are particularly intriguing.

In her own time Violet Jacob's literary achievements — her fiction and poetry — were publicly recognised when she received an Honorary LL.D. from Edinburgh University in 1936. This was also the year in which Arthur Jacob died; he does not seem to have been strong in his later years.

After Arthur's death, Violet retired to Marywell House, Kirriemuir, not so very far from her old childhood haunts. She lived there for ten years, until her death in 1946, and is buried beside her husband at Dun.

It is perhaps interesting to note that in the following year, 1947, her beloved India gained independence. As her life closed, a new chapter in Indian history opened.

NOTES

1. Helen Cruickshank, *Octobiography* (Montrose, 1976), p. 135. The 'Mains of Dun' is the farm at Dun.
2. Violet Jacob's original title for this volume was *Four Good Years*.
3. Page 180 of this volume. Further references are given in brackets after quotations.
4. Mr Garden's account of finding the diaries and letters is included in his article, 'Violet Jacob in India', *Scottish Literary Journal*, 13, no. 2 (November 1986), 48-64.
5. In Violet Jacob's as yet unpublished *Indian Diaries 1922-23*.
6. Joanne E. Cooper, 'Shaping Meaning: Women's Diaries, Journals and Letters — the Old and the New', *Women's Studies International Forum*, 10, no. 1 (1987), 95-99 (p. 96).
7. *Indian Diaries 1922-23*.
8. E. M. Forster, in a letter of October 5th 1921, *The Hill of Devi and Other Indian Writings*, edited by Elizabeth Heine, Abinger Edition (London, 1983), p. 84.
9. A number of accounts of life in nineteenth-century India by expatriate British women have been reissued in recent years. For more about the lives of British women in India, see Margaret MacMillan, *Women of the Raj* (London, 1988).
10. See Charles Allen and Sharada Dwivedi, *Lives of the Indian Princes* (London, 1986), pp. 52-53.
11. See *Lives of the Indian Princes*, p. 13, on the use of Christian names.
12. *Lives of the Indian Princes*, p. 13.
13. Forster, p. 48.
14. The poem 'Glory' appears in *More Songs of Angus and Others* (1918), and in *Scottish Poems of Violet Jacob* (1944).
15. Hugh MacDiarmid, 'Violet Jacob', *Contemporary Scottish Studies*, First Series (London, 1926), p. 45.
16. For some brief remarks on the significance for literature of the Scottish experience of colonialism see Cairns Craig's Introduction to *The History of Scottish Literature*, volume 4, edited by Cairns Craig (Aberdeen, 1987), p. 5. *The History of Scottish Literature*, volume 3, edited by Douglas Gifford (Aberdeen, 1988), pp. 411-427, contains Alan MacGillivray's 'Exile and Empire'. See also Martin Green, *Dreams of Adventure, Deeds of Empire* (London and Henley, 1980), pp. 3-11. There are a number of historical works dealing with Scotland and colonialism.

PREFACE

When I went to India in 1895 I told my mother, who had always longed to see the East, that she should see as much of my bit of it as my pen could show her; and for the six years that I was away I wrote every week with the exception of the many that I finally spent in the Mhow Military Hospital. Some time after my return, when literature had become a serious matter to me, she gave me a packet of such letters as she had kept and I put them away and thought no more about them. But now, after more than thirty years, when motor cars and other things have changed life in India so much, I have gathered them together with bits of a diary spasmodically kept. This book should be called 'Shreds and Patches' but it represents such good days to me that I give it a more sympathetic name.

V.J. 1932

1895
Letters to C.K.E.

*Violet's letters to her mother (Catherine Kennedy Erskine) run
from November 1895, soon after her arrival in India, to the end
of 1896. Her first letters describe their new home in Mhow, its
garden and their servants; subsequent letters recount her impres-
sions of Indian wildlife and of the landscapes around Mhow.*

Mhow, Central India.
Nov. 1895

. . . Here I am in a house at last. We are very lucky to get it, it is
such a good one. Its owner is an elderly Parsee[1] called Kori, spoken
of by the servants as 'Kori-master'. He is rich, stout and bespectacled
and wears a grubby red flannel scarf round his neck.

Imagine yourself in the porch and coming up the steps. You go
up across the verandah and through the front door that opens into
the drawing room; it has a fan-light and is very tall. All the outside
doors and windows have wire shutters like meat safes to keep out
insects. They are a great luxury here. The drawing room is about the
height of Dun kirk[2] and a sort of chancel arch runs laterally across
the middle; it has six doors running down each side of it opening
into other rooms and the effect is rather pretty, as all have fan-lights
over them. There are seven windows and nineteen ventilators so there
ought to be plenty of air. We've got stone floors instead of the mud
ones which most bungalows have and all the whitewash is tinted pale
green. There's a crimson drugget, the wicker chairs are painted white
and the general effect isn't bad at all. One thing I like is that the
two little windows in the wall between drawing room and dining
room let you see from one into the other. A window *inside* a house
always fascinates me and you can look through these into the back
verandah that is used by the servants as a serving room and see the
little brazier fanned up and the crows being chased violently away
during meal time with dusters and abuse. Opening off the drawing
room is Harry's nursery where his woolly cockatoo hangs over his
cot. Six thousand miles has done it no more damage than the loss of
its tail feathers. Rachel, the *ayah*,[3] keeps her bedding on the floor in

a roll that she unwinds at night and she snores so that you can hear her all over the house. I can't help thinking this is because of the stud she wears in her nose. . . . Now I hope you can see something of what this place looks like when you come into it, and I'll tell you about the garden next mail if I can, but I've a lot to do, settling in as you may suppose. . . .

Mhow.
27 Nov. 1895

. . . You would like the garden, I think. Its two gates that open on the road from the railway station have each an arch covered with a thick bower of bougainvillea, not the pale sort but dark, gorgeous red-purple. Low whitewashed walls go round it with poinsettia bushes and white oleander and there's a big plot of grass in the middle which has been wonderfully kept, for grass out here. There is a large basin in the centre full of maidenhair with a fountain playing into it and pots of carnations all round. Outside that again are many rosebushes, mostly 'Marie van Houtte', and in this country they are pale cream-colour with all the shades of a sunset on the outer petals, yellow, crimson and rose with mauve turning into purple. When one sits in the porch one can see all this between the pillars and it looks mighty pretty, like the garden in 'Beauty and the Beast'. Perhaps you can remember a picture book I had as a child that contained its very counterpart. Nearly every evening the sky turns gold, no clouds but a fine golden yellow and the cypresses, of which there are a good many, stand up against it. We have a spacious compound with much waste ground and scrub of all sorts and bushes which look as if they would flower and be of much interest to me. A road runs outside one wall of it across which are tall trees, tamarind and *peepul*, and a mauve *convolvulus* with cut leaves called here, the 'railway creeper', climbs nearly to the tree tops and hangs in thick masses of blossom all the way down. No one seems to admire it, I suppose, because it is so common, but that doesn't prevent it from being perfectly lovely.

It's a pity you can't see Gaya Din, the gardener; I am told his name means 'Gift of a Cow'. He looks more like a gift of the devil. He is a small, impish, very high-shouldered gnome, much blacker than most of the others, who despises the whole world and every living creature in it, including myself and A. though I believe he rather likes us. My particular vagaries he looks upon as those of a crazy child, but on the whole he is anxious to condescend, and frequently humours them. He holds up his turned-up nose — which is an inverted semicircle — so high that the back of his head seems to lie flat on his shoulders. When he walks, he never goes quicker than a funeral; when he runs, which he often does, he goes like greased lightning, a flash of white clothes and black heels. It has been given to me to see him chase a bullock out of the compound; he had it by the tail and when, in terror, it leapt the compound wall, he did not let go and was whirled into the air like a child's jumping jack at the end of a piece of elastic. Some of the other servants were in the garden and we all shrieked with laughter and I think he was rather offended. Natives adore children of all sizes but Gaya Din despises Harry and looks at him as if he wasn't there. Being neither a 'panjeji' nor a 'kahteen', he thinks he can be of small profit to the world. (Pansies and cuttings are his hobbies.) With Rachel to interpret, I showed him the seeds you gave me and I think he was rather interested. He arranges flowers very well for an Indian and makes buttonholes that look as if they had come from a shop.

The only time I ever saw him moved to mirth was when an importunate *tonga* driver came to the door to be paid. Soloman, the butler, interpreting, said that he wanted his money at once. A. produced it, saying that the man needn't fear that he would run away with it, as he expected to be in Mhow for five years and on this Gaya Din broke into a falsetto scream from behind a bush. The thing he perhaps despises most are wild flowers. When I first came I admired a bush — as I do still — in the waste part of our compound, which has large leaves like a glorified ash and clusters of blossom like large buttercups. When it was conveyed to him that I wanted some in the drawing room his face was a study and Dugaroo, A.'s dressing-boy, who was officiating at the interview, observed, 'He say this very bad', and I perceived that I had lowered myself. But I got some in the end. Rachel shares my interest in plants and when she was in England with somebody, learned all she could about them. A bungalow here which was occupied by a former employer of hers, is full of nasturtium from seeds she brought back with her. The other day when I went off for a prowl about the outskirts of the place (nobody out here ever prowls but me) I came on a native house covered with a sheet of brilliant blue *convolvulus* so I ran home for her to see them and tell Gaya Din that a garden without them was a Sahara and that I must have some and after the rains he must plant them. He wasn't much offended at the thought, I suppose a thing that grows on a house has acquired merit for him. Anyhow, if he fails me, I'll give his bones to the vultures.

There are two other gardeners whom I know nothing of except

that one is lazy and wears an old uniform coat and the other is, A. says, the best looking man he knows. Then there is the *bheesti*, who is a very remarkable person, more like an animal than anything else but not at all unpleasantly so, because not like an ignoble one. I have never seen anyone at all resembling him. Perhaps statues of Pan are more of his type than anything. I don't think he ever smiles. He is very tall and solemn and stoops from generations of water carrying. He strides along with his goat beard sticking out in front, wearing a large flat *pagari* which he sometimes unwinds and swathes the lower part of his face in; a faded cherry-coloured cloth is bound tightly about his middle. If you saw him sitting alone on the edge of the compound wall plunging his goatskin bag in the water below, you would think him a wonderful sight. Practise has made him such an adept at knowing how to fill things to a nicety that he never wastes a drop though he throws it about more violently than anyone else would. The mouth of the goatskin — which bag is the whole skin, minus legs and head — is tied with a leather thong and with one hand he can loosen this and let out exactly the right amount of water and then stop the flow instantaneously while, with the other, he is doing something else. He is the most un-modern looking being possible to imagine and I feel sure he has lived since the foundation of the world and will never die. His dignity is immense, his voice very deep and far-carrying, all the more impressive because, unlike all the rest, he speaks so seldom. He is our only Mohammedan servant. I wonder if all these details bore you — I hope they don't. Every afternoon the garden streams with water, for they water here before the sun is down. I like seeing the process; the *bheesti* stalking about drenching the place with his goatskin, the fountain playing and the lazy and the un-lazy gardener filling and re-filling their water cans from it; the rosetrees dripping in the heat whilst Gaya Din flits about, pouncing from behind bushes and then pacing slowly with such arrogance that it's little short of an insult to everybody. One peculiarity of his walk is that his great toes stick quite straight up while the rest of his foot lies flat.

I wish you could see the Punjabi Mohammedans belonging to the native infantry regiment[4] here as they go walking about, sometimes hand in hand, and often accompanied by their tame partridges which they take out walking, as if they were dogs. They keep them for fighting, as Englishmen used to keep gamecocks, and the birds run after them like little well-brought-up terriers; when one has had enough exercise his master, who is carrying the cage dangling from a ring on his finger, picks him up and puts him back in it as a nurserymaid in Kensington Gardens returns her charge to the perambulator when it has played enough on the grass. These Punjabis are grand looking men, generally tall and brawny, with high cheekbones and gold rings in their ears. They are more of a walnut than a mahogany brown and many of them not much darker than a dark Englishman; they are the most masculine looking creatures I have ever seen and, oddly enough, their earrings and the straight petticoat they wear reaching the ankles make them look more masculine still, as they accentuate their bold faces and their stride. For looks they beat any race of men I have ever seen, especially when they are clean-shaved. I really must stop this rigmarole now. . . .

Mhow.
Xmas Eve, 1895

. . . The birds are interesting here. One sees a lot of the crows, bold, thieving things, rather smaller than ours. Twenty of them live in a tree opposite the dining-room verandah, from which they can observe the food being carried in and out; they are handy for the well which is just outside too. When the dirty plates come out with anything on them they come down and having looked carefully round to see whether anyone is noticing, they hop up the steps and steal. The most numerous of all the birds here is the kingcrow who is jet black and about the size of a blackbird with a long tail which has a divided end; he scolds loudly and is, I am told, a terrible fighter. Then there is a beautiful kingfisher who lives quietly near the fountain and looks, when he appears on the wing, like a piece of a painted window; emeralds and sapphires are nothing to him. There's a blue jay too (called the Roller here), he spends much time sitting on the telegraph wires that run through this garden, making periodical dives at insects, and he is so tame that if you are in the front verandah he'll fly so close that his wings brush up the fine dust from the path as he swoops down. Hoopoes come about too and walk about, letting their lovely crests up and down as if they were pulled by strings, and out in the country one sees flights of green long-tailed paroqueets. But the most important birds are the kites, without which nobody, I suppose, could live, as they are the scavengers of this otherwise unscavenged country. They are about all day and even in a clear sky which the eye may think empty, if you throw a dead mouse or a piece of meat into the air the firmament will produce them in numbers and the tit-bit be caught before it has time to come down. At least, so I am told, and the next time the mousetrap has anything in it I mean to try the experiment and see if this is a lie or not. Kites make a long, shuddering whistle which you hear all day. Personally I like it, though some people don't. Now this is a creepy thing. I was on the polo ground the other day watching a game and I noticed a commotion in mid air among the kites and remarked on it to a man sitting by me. He said he shouldn't wonder if there was a funeral going on somewhere, and in about two minutes a little procession emerged from the trees that border the polo ground carrying a corpse under a white sheet to the Mohammedan burial ground. To go back to the birds; every evening the same programme takes place; just as the very short dusk sets in, thousands of 'flying-foxes', which look like large, slow-going birds and are really bats, pass over the garden on their way from trees and buildings where they have hung up all day like so many legs of mutton in a larder and come with their heavy flight across the gold of the sky, just going out to work, so to speak, when others are going home. They are revolting creatures infested with vermin, but so like kites that it takes a little practice to tell them apart.

We are still negotiating for the chestnut country-bred pony, Trilby; I want her very much for she is up to my weight and I'm dying to see something of this country outside the watertight little world of the cantonment. Nobody seems to care or know anything about it and I mean to see it for myself. People say to me 'there's nothing to see,' and 'you'll soon be tired of that,' but I know myself and I think I know them and their sort, and I'm going.

There has been an awful row among the gardeners. Gaya Din was running round the fountain like a flash of lightning, scolding and raging and A. had to be fetched, but he was so much overcome by the absurd sight of Gaya Din that he was not of much use. Anyhow, it all settled down and the tumult fizzled out soon. . . .

1896
Letters to C.K.E.

Mhow.
30 Jan. 1896

. . . I've got Trilby. She's a chestnut, very strong, with rather a bad mouth and not too good a temper, but she's perfectly wonderful on her feet and I think she'll just suit me. I went out on her today and in a hedge of prickly pear behind the railway station saw a white flower with the growth of a *convolvulus* except that the petals were pointed, which made the rim of the blossom more star-shaped. Prickly pear thorns are like darning needles and Trilby was too cunning to go near them. So I dismounted and plunged after the flower and came out — literally — with blood dropping off me in two or three places, for they pierce clothes as if they were paper. I pulled out the thorns as well as I could and a worthy old man journeying towards the town with a staff raised hands and eyes to heaven and seemed to be saying that it was a dreadful business, and I clambered up the side of Trilby and made for home, lacerated but content. Another flower I have seen has a double leaf and grows on a small tree; it is like a pinkish mauve orchid with crimson markings and it's not unlike an azalea too. It smells delicious, as nearly all flowers do here.

I send you a sketch of a man I sometimes see on my rides: from what Rachel says he is some sort of agricultural character. There are two holy men who live in a *nullah* not far off and I am sorry I don't know enough Hindustani to have a word with them as I ride by. They are quite filthy and live in a straw hut like a haycock on the top of a mound. Going by that *nullah* with A. the other day we saw a hundred or so of vultures — real ones, none of your common kites — tearing the caracass of a bullock to pieces. To make it worse, a *pariah* dog was disputing it with them, growling and quarrelling as much as he dared over the good bits. The horses were frightened but we got them up to it as horrible as it was, we could not help wanting to see exactly what they did. It is easy to understand why they are called 'the Obscene Bird'.

Mhow is in a great plain of about a hundred miles and the Western Ghauts⁵ stand on a part of the horizon. There are one

27

or two great main roads, unfenced, and when you get off them
there are just tracks leading into the *ewigkeit*[1] and to the remote
villages. There is little real green now and the whole country is burnt
straw colour. The horizon is immense and desert-like and it appeals
to me more and more as time goes on; one comes upon varied things
in one's rides; wells under clumps of magnificent trees with bushes
and creepers; little Mohammedan tombs, dead white, with small
domes and minarets, none over about five feet high, and Hindu
shrines smeared with red. Natives are always lighting fires and, just
before sunset, the whole country is dotted with tiny flames and one
wonders why this tinder-dry expanse does not go up in one roaring
bonfire. One sees dark figures crouching under trees with twisted
roots, suddenly illuminated by some unexpected glare; how anyone
but a dolt can call such a weird country dull, I don't know. And
yet there are people who see nothing interesting in it. One comfort
is that they all congregate together and so can be easily avoided.

The villages are like haycocks to look at; low mud walls and
thatch — all mud colour. One rides straight through them though
they have no street and one winds in and out of the nest of dwellings.
The inhabitants generally say '*salaam*' and one replies in the same
way. I know too little as yet to have any talk with them but, later
on, I hope it will be different. The other day we were riding along
a great stretch without a tree and saw some way off a cloud of dust
and some gigantic shapes journeying over the tracks towards the hills,
elephants journeying slowly with their loads. We galloped up and
followed them a little way and when we struck off over the burnt
grass we still saw them for a long time in the sunset, far away near
the Ghauts with their little clouds of dust rising about them. They
are very little used about here so one sees them with some interest.
Wildness and civilization are very close together in this country.
Even round this civilized house we live in the jackals yell at night
and have often been up into the verandah and about a couple of
miles from here a man has been known to meet a panther, which
seems an odd thing in conjunction with a church and a club-house
and a place where you can buy ice. . . .

*In January 1896 Violet meets a number of the people who are
to figure large in her life in India.*

Mhow.
Jan. 1896
. . . We have been over to Indore[2] to stay at Gwalior House, the

house which the little Nawab of Jaora[3] has taken; it really belongs to
Scindia,[4] but has been hired for him as a residence while he is at the
Daly College. This has been founded at Indore for the education of
Rajahs' and noblemen's sons. Arthur Napier, a man I used to meet
at balls in London, is in charge of the Nawab; when we landed at
Bombay last November he was almost the first person I met on the
hotel verandah and he came over to see us the other day. We did not
put up at Gwalior House, though we were there all day but slept in
the traveller's bungalow, for Mr Napier has not been in charge long
and does not yet know whether he will have permission to put up
ladies in the Nawab's establishment. The boy is an attractive little
fellow of thirteen with excellent manners, but he looks younger as
he is so light and slim. In Europe you would never take him for an
Indian but more likely for a French boy, he is so fair-skinned. He
has a cousin,[5] the son of the Jaora prime minister, who is being
educated with him and he is a nice lad too, but more eastern looking
and bigger; they dress like English boys except for the red *taboosh*
(what English people call *fez*) on their heads. Mr Napier is very
fond of them both. When they heard they were to have an English
guardian they asked immediately if he would beat them! He teaches
them to ride and shoot and to behave truthfully and honourably,
but I think what they really like best is that he makes catapults for
them. We spent some time in the lovely gardens there at Indore.
A slow river runs through them near the Residency and there are
islands with clumps of palms and rich vegetation trailing into the
water. All sorts of mysterious looking backwaters go in and out and
great leaves hang in festoons from above. A mauve *convolvulus*, the
'Elephant' creeper, as it's called, winds about among the palm stems
and bamboos. I don't care for bamboos as a rule, but here they are
just right. It was about six o'clock when we were there and the usual
golden sky was at its best.

   At dinner the Nawab sat by me and translated the Hindustani menu
for my benefit. Then A. and I and Mr Napier went off to a dance at
the Residency. It was good fun though pretty hot. The Maharajah
Holkar[6] was there, awfully and fearfully fat and wearing a garment
that looked as if it were made out of a grey eiderdown quilt. It made
one almost suffocate to look at it. He was dignified and unwieldy.
He has several palaces and one, the Lal Bagh, has a beautiful garden,
but Mr Napier can't take us there as he has been very uncivil to the
Nawab. At the same time he wishes the Nawab to call upon him
which Mr Napier says he shall not do till he has Holkar's word that

he will return the visit; but this has not yet been given, so relations are strained between the Palace and Gwalior House. Colonel Barr, the Agent to the Governor in Central India, is charming.[7] He has a merry wit, a wife and daughter and three sons.

At three in the morning A. and I returned to the bungalow and found our butler, Soloman, a fat dull lump of a man, snoring in the verandah with his *pagari* off, a sight I had never seen before. His head was like a yellow mammoth football. The accommodation was bare but not bad and we slept well and went over to Gwalior House for a late breakfast. There were races in the afternoon and the Nawab was much excited because Mr Napier won two. It is pleasant seeing new things and living out in verandahs and driving to balls in the starlight in open carriages. You would be amused by the Nawab's carriage, which is a huge landau[8] ornamented with a gold crest representing a camel, a crocodile, an elephant and the Nawab's initials. A footman stands behind hanging on to a strap. He and the coachman wear tight white trousers and blue tunics, the front of the latter embroidered on white cloth in gold initials as big as teacups and both are large, bearded men from the north. The carriage is fearfully shabby and the horses are pink-nosed fleabitten greys that look as if they had come out of a circus. . . .

Mhow.
Feb. 1896

. . . The reason you got my letter on Friday was that the *Caledonia* brought the mails. She does the journey quicker than the other ships. . . . We have been at Indore again. Dr Caldecott, the Residency surgeon,[9] is very good to soldier-people here and has a charming house with a great *stephanotis* plant over the porch at the back. And such a cook! He knows everyone worth knowing in Central India. We had a pleasant dinner, the Residency people, Mr Napier and several others, and next day we went to the Lal Bagh palace just outside the city. Here the heir apparent of Indore[10] lives, the *Bala Sahib*, as he is called, aged about five. Gardens being utterly different out here to those in England, they are difficult to describe. The main feature of this one is rambling disorder and beautiful turf — and no one knows how glorious emerald green turf like that can seem out here in the burnt-looking world. In the middle of it there are white marble tanks of water, oblong in shape and on their margin stand pots of petunias, single ones, larger and more diaphanous than any in England. These are mostly white, or very pale mauve and pink.

They trail over the marble copings into the water and are reflected below; their scent is silky, sweet, bitter and ethereal all at once. One sort, the loveliest of all, is white velvet, with a primrose-coloured flush in the throat and black markings like fine network. Round these lawns the trees are dark and thick and the boughs hanging downwards, so that there is not much headroom. Then there are masses of unpruned roses, white, chiefly, but also pink, lemon, red and yellow in thick sprays; a certain amount of orange blossom too, and jasmine like stars. The scent was enough to stifle some people but I am thankful to say I can stand a lot of that sort of thing. The palace, not particularly Indian in architecture, is in the middle, and not very imposing.

The *Bala Sahib*, Holkar's heir, was in the garden, a light brown child and I should think a horrid brat, resplendent in a pink silk coat with gold buttons, scarlet socks with white spots and yellow shoes. This was crowned by a small black cap like a pill-box. Troops of very common-looking servants were round him and an *ayah*, who beside Rachel, would look like a beggar and twice as dirty as many. Behind the *Bala Sahib* walked a youth carrying a long filthy looking sword which, I suppose, no one in the whole retinue could have drawn, not if they were attacked by assassins. Dr Caldecott, who likes children, began to play with the little boy, who was shy at first but eventually they ran after each other round the bushes. At this *all* the servants ran too, sword-bearer and all. First ran the *Bala Sahib*, then Dr Caldecott, then the *ayah* and the rest of the crew, then myself and A. holding our sides with laughter at the appearance of the procession, for all were perfectly solemn and sped along from a pure sense of duty. In the middle of it we were told that the Maharajah was in the garden. We found him sitting under the trees in his down quilt arrangement, enormously fat and wearing a pill-box cap. We were presented to him and he was very polite. He and I sat side by side on a yellow garden seat. He speaks English perfectly well. He said to me, 'I am much pleased to see you. You are a most aristocratic person; I have seen people like you in Buckingham Palace.' It was a difficult speech to reply to and I don't know what I said. Then he asked A. much about the regiment and enquired of me whether I bought my hats in Paris. He also said he had designed the garden himself and to that I was able to reply truthfully that it was beautiful. When we left, his carriage was outside, high and like the chariot of the last century, on very heavy springs with the addition of a good deal of gilding. A small guard of his cavalry was with it. We are going back to stay with Dr Caldecott for the *Mohurrum*, which is rather good at Indore although it is a Hindu state. Holkar has a great tall palace in the city painted blue and green which I admire much. He is really a man of low descent[11] though I am bound to say that he does look like a prince, grey eiderdown, fat and all. But the *Bala Sahib* might be a *bazaar*-child from his appearance.

Now I must tell you the true story of the two *banana-wallahs*. A *banana-wallah* is not a dealer in plantains, as you might suppose, but a man whose trade it is to make something, an artisan, in fact. We wanted a long bamboo sofa made for one of the rooms and told Soloman to get someone to do it. Two men who said they were brothers came together. One was a very Adonis, tall, slender, with an elegant and languishing air and a voice like silk; so handsome a person I have not often seen. He might have stood for the hero of *Lalla Rhookh*,[12] or a prince in *The Arabian Nights*. The other was older, short, square, with a plebeian and ill-favoured countenance. As they measured the place I looked at them with great interest, observing to A. that the smaller one might well be a near relation of Satan, and that the beautiful one had a dark scar under his left eye. Their task done, they departed. Next day, on coming in in the evening, we found the sofa ready and in its place and gave Soloman six *rupees*, the price settled, to pay the brothers. A few days after as we sat in the verandah, out of the dusk there arose two *salaaming* figures. Soloman was called in to interpret. The two men looked like the *banana-wallahs* but were dressed quite differently and clean shaved; the neat moustaches which the original men wore were absent. The tall one remarked that the sofa was ready and that he had brought it and wished to be paid. 'But,' said we, 'the sofa you made is in the house and you have had six rupees for it.' 'No,' was the reply, 'we have never brought a sofa. Some other man has brought one and has deceived you and taken our money.' At this we were flabbergasted and all the more so because the two were so like the pair we knew and yet seemed different. Then one of us remembered the scar and insisted on their stepping into the light of the wall lamp. There was the scar and there was the evil countenance of its owner's brother, unmistakable. We told Soloman to tell them that when people had scars under their eyes it was undesirable to personate others. Whether Soloman, who we have for some time suspected of being very little better than a robber himself, translated this truthfully, I do not know, but in any case Adonis joined his hands in prayer and said he was a very poor man. We replied that he was also a very wicked one, a remark which made the ugly one grin. After much haranguing we were persuaded to look at the other sofa that had been brought, for it so happened that we really wanted one for another place. So we bought it for four *rupees*, which was a weakness, though it looked a very nice one. But we were well punished. It was set in its place and paid for and the brothers left.

Next day A. tossed something down on it and lo! the back collapsed and a large piece — nearly half — fell to the ground for the cane was rotten all through. The *banana-wallahs* were sent for and Adonis came and confessed with shame and contrition that his brother was a very bad man; that he had bought the sofa at a lumber sale; that he had fraudulently cooked it up and sold it to us; that he had unjustly seized all the price of it for himself and that the whole affair had been his doing. He then proposed to mend it for us. 'And how much will you charge if we do?' we asked, it being our turn to be deceitful. 'Twelve *annas*,' said he. This we knew to be rather more than six times what the rotten thing was worth and A. gave one roar and fell upon the *banana-wallah* thrusting him violently down the verandah steps. He was purple in the face and the *banana-wallah* fled like a deer into the shadows and was seen no more. Not long after, when Moolchund, the *bazaar* tailor's man, called, we showed him the better sofa of the two and asked him how much it ought to cost. 'About two *rupees*, *sahib*,' said he, rubbing his chin and looking rather sly. And that was the last of the affair. But who was who, or who sold what, we know not to this day. All we know is that *we* were sold. The earth is full of wickedness out here, but sometimes it is very funny.

Today I rode through a lovely mango *tope*. Mangoes look like sycamores, only without their hard outlines, and the small greenish flowers that compose their trusses of blossom smell like hothouse plants. From under this I came out into a field of opium poppies, mainly rose pink with fringed petals, and growing among what looked like young barley; intersecting this, ran little irrigating channels that caught the evening light. I got home long after dark and coming across country rode along the top of a deep *nullah*. Far down below, remnants of the light touched the water though all the rest was dark and one could just see an encampment of *dhobies*, or washermen, who were driven far out into the country by the drought and were washing, with fires lit all along the bank, while their bullocks, which carry the loads of linen as donkeys might in Europe, lay in groups hard by. I have just finished painting the *karunda* flower. Its Latin name is *Carissa carandas*. I hope to have a collection of flowers to show you some day. I rode some miles along a dusty road to a place where I had seen an attractive mango grove, knowing there are generally wells in them and sometimes flowers. A *karunda* bush was scenting the air and looking something like a white daphne, in full bloom and about eight feet high. From behind it appeared a young woman in the usual red garment with silver bracelets. She offered to cut me a spray and made me a bunch after which we parted with many *salaams*. Now good-bye. Next week I will enclose a blossom of some sort. . . .

Mhow
25 Feb. 1896

. . . Thank you so much for *The Second Jungle Book*.[13] I'm delighted with 'The Undertakers', the story about the crocodile. The drought here this cold weather is so great (for the Xmas rains never came) that the *muggers** in the tanks can be seen moving about, the water in them is so low; they say these brutes come out at night and travel from tank to tank when there are great droughts but I don't know if this is true. It would be an awful thing to meet them. . . .

The pony Trilby is a pig; a black-hearted thing and very vicious, but she is a good useful animal who never puts a foot wrong over any kind of ground, which is just what I want. There is nothing she can't get down or up or through. I don't go near her except to get on her back, and when there I am careful to stay where I am, for if she were to put me off she would kick out my brains. Lots of these countrybreds are vicious but there is really nothing like them for getting over bad ground. A. has a very good charger that we call Talisman, a chestnut arab with perfect manners.

I have just finished painting an opium poppy of the pink sort. I had many vicissitudes in getting it. My first idea was simply to go out and steal one, but A. insisted that I must not do that, so a friend obligingly did it instead, but on the way home, morality triumphed, for it dropped to pieces and I was no further on than before. I then armed myself with four *annas*, learnt from Rachel how to ask for a poppy, and mounting Trilby, rode off to the poppy fields, where I found a group of natives collected round a well by a mango *tope*, watering the crop. The water was running from it into the irrigating

* crocodiles (Violet Jacob's own note)

channels and they had filled the main channel so full that it had become a ditch, so in order to approach I had to jump it and the vile Trilby spoilt it all for she refused to face it and when I smote her she made one bound into the air and landed in the very middle of the poppies, spoiling nearly half a dozen. There arose a yell of wrath and reproach and I hadn't the face to ask for anything and started home discomfited and with no language at my command to explain that I had come to trade, not to destroy. Rachel was very sympathetic and found she had a friend in the *bazaar* who worked in the opium fields and was a relation of the *dhobi*'s. So a couple of poppies finally reached me through all these hands and I painted them with great care. Flowers flag here so quickly that it is often almost impossible to paint them, but I am doing a lot. I send you a rough sketch of a dog-boy. Dogs of good birth and respectable, family dogs, have boys to attend on them just as horses have grooms. . . .

Mhow, Central India.
18 March 1896

. . . Yesterday we had an interesting ride towards the Ghauts. We were crossing some very arid ground when a little way on before us there suddenly opened a chasm with bluish mist floating about in it. We redoubled our pace, as it was getting towards sundown, and reached it to find that a *nullah* flowed into it and plunged far down over a deep fall. There was green water below, rocks, trailing foliage and stones that looked like dried lava; the *nullah*'s side was just rideable and we crept down. Trilby and the old troophorse that A. was riding are countrybreds and as wise as goats and they never made a mistake. It was wonderful looking about two hundred feet below into the depth of the chasm and we did not care to venture very near. Turning up the *nullah*'s bed we passed an oleander bush of the most delicate pink with its feet in the water, the colour of an apple tree in spring and standing with the wild rocks for a background in the fading light. We had to push on to get back to the tracks before dark and leave the exquisite, surprising thing. Can't you come out and see it? I would find you a pony that would walk with the discretion of a dowager and not so much as move its ears and I would run beside you, leading it! We passed some other oleanders on our way out of the gorge, red ones, but there was no time to stop to look at them. Trilby almost won my regard, she stepped and waded about in the water so sensibly, letting me have a good look at everything. I brought some buds home and as I kept

them in a cool, dark place, they revived and opened. As soon as I
have finished this letter I am going to paint them. It has been borne
in upon me that an oleander is a glorified hairy willow herb, just as
a hollyhock is a mallow. It shows how ignorant one is not to have
guessed it before. It's a dreadful thing to know no botany and to be
in a country where no living creature can tell you anything. . . .

From March onwards the hot weather brings disease in its
wake.

Mhow.
24 March 1896

. . . I have got a botany book, the only thing I could hear of,
Roxburgh's *Flora Indica*,[14] but it is so learned that I can't understand
it. But it's better than nothing, for I can just puzzle out a very little
and I am immersed in it over my head. It gives Latin names of plants
and Hindustani ones, but no English; and as natives neither know
nor care one farthing for such things and pronounce any name they
happen to know, anyhow, it is awfully difficult to discover anything
if you are devoid of Latin. Gaya Din is no good, because of his
contempt for nearly everything in the world. Show him something
you have brought home and he knows just enough English to say
'This Jungle-flower — bad,' and that's the end of it.

The heat is considerable now, 80° all night long; nothing to what
it is up country, all the same. The mosquitoes are awful and Mhow
is a hotbed of them. It is nothing to have thirty bites on your two
arms. Creatures of all sorts are coming into the house, especially the
mason-fly, which looks like a wasp with long hind legs and lives in
little holes in wood or masonry. His eggs, or rather, her eggs, are
laid there. Then a live spider is caught and *partially* killed, so that
he will keep, for a little, and put in; then the hole is covered up
with mud whilst the egg hatches and the little mason-fly lives on the
spider until he is strong enough to make his way out. A very large
flesh-coloured lizard has come to live in my dressing room and as he
eats flies he is a very desirable companion. He won't make friends but
his bland stare makes me think he is well disposed. When I dress for
dinner he is usually flattened motionless against the bathroom door
and sometimes I hear a soft thud and know that he has jumped down
on the floor; very often he will spread-eagle himself near the wall-lamp
over the dressing table waiting for the flies which gather on the wall
round it and making lightning inroads on them. Sometimes he and I

have a hunt together, I beating for him; I take the buttonhook and guide some portly insect towards him while he stays as still as if he were dead. Then his tongue suddenly shoots out and the fly is gone and only the gulps in his semi-transparent throat show what has happened. . . .

We have had a smallpox epidemic and a cholera scare; everybody had to be vaccinated and we attended the hospital in batches. It was a funny sight; rows and rows of horses and ponies being held outside while the doctor plied his little knife in the hospital verandah, while officers, civilians, women and children all went up in turn. I was done among the rest and perhaps it was as well, for I 'took' for the first time in my recollection. Then a draft of infantry from Doolali brought cholera with them and some men died. They were quietly buried in the night, so I had not the benefit of their funerals. This house is on the road to the cemetery and it is just outside that the band strikes up, and one hears quite enough of it. A great part of the regiment was isolated under canvas and are out still, but it is a fortnight now and not one other case has occurred. The sick are in a little cholera camp a few miles out, with signals up to warn people not to come too near. I've seen it in the distance when riding and it looked rather weird after dark with a fire burning in front.

Tomorrow we are going to ride off with a map and compass to look for a waterfall that we want to see in the Ghauts. I have nine flower paintings now and I wish I could run over to you for an hour to show them. F.B's[15] French maid is in hospital with enteric; she can't speak much English, so it's rather dreadful for her, but F. goes to see her and talk a little and I do sometimes but the last time I went she was too bad to see anyone. There's a good deal of illness and this letter seems to be all illnesses and insects. They're rather the principal topics just now. . . .

Mhow.
8 April 1896

. . . A more severe hot weather is on us than has been known here for long, for the want of the winter rains seems to have upset the country and the climate. Instead of a clear sky we have leaden clouds and the air is full of thunder that will not burst. The result with me is sleeplessness, as the thermometer registers over 90° already and only drops a little at night. I have splitting headaches and the night is often a nightmare. One's hands and neck and face all feel like one's feet after wearing goloshes that 'draw' them. Mosquitoes are in full swing too and the *koel* bird makes night dismal with its shrieking in a succession of yells, each a little higher up the scale than the last, till you think he can get no higher. It goes on for ages and if you are trying to sleep it is hateful. Last night I only got about half an hour and one night last week I went to bed at ten thirty and lay awake till long after five streaming with perspiration and listening to the maniac screeching of that bird; then I could bear it no more and sent for Trilby and went out for a ride. It is the leaden but electric atmosphere that is so unendurable. If it would only thunder! I'm much better than last week, all the same. The beginning of the hot weather in the plains tries everyone, natives and all, but A. and I have not had fever, and I think we owe this to our active life, for he has a lot of work and I ride and walk as much as I can and we are never for a moment in the sun without our sun-helmets. We are not properly into the hot weather yet and we shall get more used to it as time goes on. Someone said to me lately that it's like a long black stifling tunnel stretching across the path that has to be got through somehow, and he knew what he was talking about, for he had been many years in the Indian political service. But one can get out and do things a certain amount still.

The *dâk* tree is out in the jungle, lifting great scarlet claws to the sky. It's a sinister looking thing and its triple leaf is sacred to Shiva, the Destroyer,[16] which is very appropriate, considering the time of year at which it comes out. It is later than the scarlet blossom. It has many names; 'Flame of the jungle, Glory of the forest, Coral tree', are a few of them. There are not many flowers to be had and there will be fewer as the heat increases but I have painted a few and my collection grows though rather slowly. When the rains come I shall be rather busy as everything will come out with a burst and there will be new things to see and get hold of. Here, they tell me, you get a good proportion of fine days and only occasionally a real soaker of many hours. However, we're not there yet and we shall have to pant and stifle for a good few weeks to come. . . .

Mhow.
15 April 1896
. . . Yesterday morning I arose before six and went off on Trilby to a queer place I know to look for *Bombax malabaricum*. Doesn't that sound grand? But it only means the common 'silk cotton tree,' of which there are plenty to be seen in the country, though not just about here. I found out its name in Roxburgh, which I am beginning

to understand a little better, and thought I had seen it, so I went off to make sure and found I was right. It is covered with scarlet flowers like open tulips and has no leaves at the time of blossoming. The place I went to is a nest of small hills that rise like pointed ant heaps suddenly out of the plain with a village hiding among them. It is very solitary and there are images under a great tree on the track and the burnt grass is high; it's a weird neighbourhood, very still, and the images and the surrounding hills add to it. I like it very much but I always feel Trilby's presence a comfort to me when I am there. It's like no other spot I know. Not far away there is a single stone figure standing straight up in a *karunda* bush; it's about five feet high, cut out of a boulder. You can see it a long way off because the ground is so flat round it. Behind it is a plain and then the village I speak of among its pointed hills. I am fascinated by it, for the weirdness of this whole country appeals to me like nothing ever has yet; it is impossible for anyone who cannot see it to have an idea of it, and there are enough and to spare of those who can who have none either. I keep thanking God, like the Pharisee in the parable, that I am not as other men, and certainly not as other women, in this matter. There are vast stretches, intense silences, sudden, odd-shaped hills, a night that swoops down with no twilight, heavy, hot, sweet smells; after dark, stifling air and little fires lit all over the country; and, one may add, the knowledge of the presence of these idols and Hindu shrines and Mohammedan graves lurking in the waste places. Above all, there are no footfalls in a land where man and beast go unshod. I have grown to love it passionately. That Indian life that one reads of in books, made up of clubs and what passes for society, the only India that most people know anything about, never touches one, or one would die of boredom; and if, as in my case, one's brothers and sisters-in-arms are a very good lot, one is not lonely. . . .

A report has been going about that the water supply will hold out for forty days *and no more* and that horses and regiment will have to go out into camp a long way off for two months. What is to happen to us women doesn't transpire, for we shall have to be washed and water supplied as much as anyone else. However I don't believe it's anything but *bazaar* talk.

I have painted some white *oleander* and *Lantana indica*. It is very interesting reading Hare's *Two Noble Lives*[17] and finding from Lady Canning's diary[18] that she saw the same flowers as I do and found the same difficulty in naming them or discovering anyone who could give her any information. She also sent specimens to her people and thought the *karunda* must be a *daphne*. I am making notes in my Roxburgh, underlining every plant I identify and writing against it where it was found and when painted. It's awfully hard to paint in this heat, but I do. . . . A cobra was killed in the riding-school the other day. It was just disappearing into a hole when a sergeant killed it with his sword. Harry is in that stage when he must seize everything near him and he has tried to get hold of this letter all the time, which makes writing precarious work.

We were at Indore again a few days ago and at the Lal Bagh. The Maharajah was not to be seen but saw the *Bala Sahib*, also his little eight year old wife,[19] very pretty, who smiled all the time. It made one regret that she is married to that little toad. She had a pale blue silk coat and little cap with gold buttons and tight white trousers and her hair was in a pigtail. A nose ring loaded with pearls too. He is such an unmannerly goblin with his sly, common face, but no doubt he is spoilt by hosts of dishonest sycophants and every fault he has carefully developed by them for their own ends; that is the fate of nearly all highly placed Indian children and it is to counteract this that boys like the Nawab have English guardians like Arthur Napier. We always call him 'the *Sahib*,' because he was the first man who came much to see us and the servants always spoke of him in that way. The last time we were at Indore we were afloat on the river with him and another man in canoes and we passed, hanging over the water, a red *Lantana* bush that was alive with clouds of butterflies with wings like black crêpe, transparent, with red underneath them and long tails. Insects love *Lantana*. I wonder if you know it, for I've seen it in some hothouses in England. If you don't, I may tell you that it looks like an orange heliotrope, and has a rough leaf like sage. The butterflies made me think of ladies in long, Paris dresses, they were so elegant. Some *Cannas* were growing at the water's edge but we couldn't get near them, for a swarm of bees came out from among them and we had to paddle off as quick as we could. I saw a kingfisher too and a horned owl glowering out of a palm tree. . . .

In June 1896 Violet describes a Muslim festival, the Mohurrum; *and the monsoon starts.*

Mhow.
21 June 1896
. . . These days before the breaking of the rains have been dreadful. I can't describe to you what one's state was. I've done no riding,

no walking and very little painting, neglected the hospital and been sometimes utterly floored. I was to have gone to Indore to see the *Mohurrum* and alas! wasn't fit for it. But the Monsoon is here at last and there is a great coolness and I shall soon be riding again. You can't imagine what the world is like, waiting for a delayed Monsoon. You see the clouds come rolling up and hope fills everybody and nothing happens except that the heat grows worse and the people who have been through the hot weather feel they can bear no more; and when the rain comes at last with a roar, a wave of relief runs over the world. I am grieved to have missed the *Mohurrum*. The other evening Rachel rushed into my room crying, 'I have seen the new moon!' and sure enough, as she spoke the *Mohurrum* drums struck up in the bazaar. At four in the following morning the shouts of 'Hassan! Houssein!' began in the same quarter. The *Mohurrum* takes place at the end of the Mohammedan fast of *Ramadan*, during which the sons of the Prophet drink nothing till sundown. How they manage it in the hot weather I can't imagine, but some of them, at any rate, do. The *Mohurrum* commemorates the deaths of Hassan and Houssein, nephews of the Prophet. Great pasteboard images of their tombs are carried in procession and their names are shouted by the Faithful the whole of the day. Green banners surmounted by little flat hands cut out of tin are carried too, but what these mean, I do not know. The Hindus, in derision, dress themselves up in painted stripes to look like tigers and rush about thumping the members of the procession. In some states this ends in free fights; but here I think the Indian is more concerned with the day's entertainment than with any principle it suggests, and as we are Hindus here, perhaps the son of Islam thinks it safer to look on the tigers as a joke. Mohammed's steed is carried in the procession, a monstrous pasteboard effigy like a rocking horse whose proportions are so grotesque that no child of six would accept it as a hobbyhorse. It is extremely funny to see it swaying about above the heads of a crowd. . . . Almost the most lovely flower here is *Petrea stapelia*, which grows on a tall bush and is a mixture of periwinkle blue and French grey in colour. . . .

Mhow.
20 July 1896

. . . I am enjoying the rains very much. There are many days when it is dry enough to be out a lot and though there are some swampy bits that restrict one's steps the country is quite rideable in the main. I'm beginning to get on with botany and in the hot

weather, when one could only go out before eight or after six,
I ploughed into Roxburgh's pages and began to get the hang of
things. It's extraordinarily interesting though one sometimes runs
into a blank wall for want of a little help. There is a great tall
plant growing all over the rough ground a few miles off that has
puzzled me but at last I've got it. *Clerodendron serratum*. It's as
high as a bush, has rusty red stems and large rough leaves and
the flowers, that grow in a pyramid upwards, are two shades of
mauve-blue with long curved stamens, most beautiful.

I heard the other day that the great pink lotus was to be seen in
flower at a place called Sherepore tank a few miles from Indore. I
was mad to go there and appealed to a friend we have, a pleasant
young man who is head of the Indore branch of the Bank of
Bombay. His name is Kingcome but the natives irreverently call
him 'the *Bankwallah*' and so do we, for we know him pretty well
now and see him very often at the Residency. He is very sympathetic
about plants, for he likes them himself and he said he'd see I got
to Sherepore; I said I would go in anything or on anything that
could be produced. He suggested, though he did not recommend,
a *shigram* and I jumped at it. This is a native conveyance like a
small Black Maria, in that nobody can see out of it, and nobody can
see in, and for that reason, women of the *purdah* sort can drive
in it. In fact it's the only way a decent woman whose husband is not
rich enough to own a closed landau can get about behind a horse.
It's hung low and has two wheels and plies for hire in the *bazaar*.
So I took the train to Indore early one morning of last week and
found the *Bankwallah* in his verandah with a *shigram* moored up
in the garden. He had got a respectable driver and told him where I
wanted to go; very necessary, as I can't speak much Hindustani yet.
He was just off to his office, but stopped to see me off, throwing up
his hands and saying he didn't envy me. When I'd introduced myself
with some difficulty into the thing and we had set off I discovered that
I didn't know how to get out of it, for it was too dark to see where the
door handle was, as the only light came from a tiny window stained
a violent blue and yellow that ran round the top of the vehicle. It was
not much wider than a ribbon and did not open. I can only suppose
that there was some ventilation from the fact that I reached Sherepore
alive. The roof was too low for anyone of my length to sit upright
and the seats too narrow for anyone of my breadth to sit at all for
more than a minute; they ran along the walls like wagonette seats
and so one went forward sideways. I never realised before how very

small native women are compared to Europeans. As a matter of fact they probably, for preference, sit on the floor, and there I was with them, though I had more sense than to do it myself, not being able to see its condition and knowing the requirement of betel-chewing. All the way to Sherepore I don't know what I did; I neither sat, stood, knelt or lay, but a mixture of all, as occasion served. And I clung a good deal, for we went over country tracks full of ruts and stones that must have been more like small rocks and in and out of deep hollows. What the landscape looked like I had no idea of for I saw neither it nor anything else, though I felt bits of it from time to time. At last we stopped and I wriggled out with difficulty because of the odd angle we were at. We had drawn up beside a creek on the outskirts of the tank, which had shrunk much in the heat and was a mere patch of water surrounded by baked mud. But the creek was full of lovely rose-coloured flowers standing with their heads raised above the thick masses of leaves about four foot high. It was most wonderful to me who have only seen it in pictures. I got some to paint, scrambled back into my box and arrived at Indore. I had spent my way out trying to preserve my own body intact and I spent my way back trying to preserve the lotus'. But it survived too and I had luncheon with the *Bankwallah* and went home to Mhow in the evening with my treasures. I sealed up the stems with wax to keep them fresh and now have the portrait of one of them. It's a great delight to be able to get out at all hours of the day again. . . .

Violet describes the pleasures of plant-hunting and reports that Arthur has been promoted to adjutant.

Mhow.
31 August 1896

. . . Yesterday we walked many miles over awful ground, sometimes up to our waists in grass. It's very thirsty work, but we leave a couple of soda water bottles and a flask of whiskey in the buggy, so that when we finish our wanderings and get back to the road where we've left it we refresh before setting off home. It was a glorious day. We waded through scrub and up and down hillsides where we emerged from the undergrowth and came out on an open place upon the hill whence we looked down on a wide bit of country, new to us, with a long blue tank lying in it, and the hills beyond. We thought it looked like the promised land, it was so still and the colours so lovely. I don't think I have ever, except perhaps hunting, enjoyed anything so much as these days out, whether we get any game or not. I have had untold fun out of this country since we came to it. If you are hunting plants you go along never knowing what strange thing you may come on at the next step. I don't suppose I shall ever find anything rare, but that doesn't matter to me though I should dearly love to do it. The delight of a new wide country is enough for me and plants that I have never seen are the crowning part of it. . . .

The place is now carpeted with small pink balsam of which I confess I am rather tired for it strikes the eye so much that it overpowers everything else, but I see there is a certain amount of a lilac convolvulus that I make out to be *Lettsomia setosa* and mean to paint. *Convolvuli* interest me and there are a great many out here; Roxburgh gives over sixty different kinds for India, generally. We saw some small land crabs yesterday in wet places. The bastard teak grows profusely, never growing much higher than a large bush; its leaves are enormous, some are about twenty four inches by sixteen, for I measured one, and the heads of blossom remind one of white *spirea*; when the leaves fall and get dry they crackle underfoot with a noise like rattling tin, so that if you are pursuing anything you have to avoid stepping on them or they would advertise your presence handsomely. Rocks and stones are everywhere and the going is very bad. I got a lot of *Gloriosa superba* yesterday, and as we stood on the road divesting ourselves of our burdens before getting under way for home an old countryman passed. He eyed these flowers and asked the *syce*, 'What does the lady want with such things?'. They had a long talk, for everybody here wants to know everybody else's business just as they do in Italy. The *syce* knows a little English so I asked what they had said, 'He say: what *memsahib* can do with this? I say, *memsahib* she read it on paper. He say, that flower like poison. If touch it too much they dr'ec'ly dead'. That is their idea about many flowers and *Gloriosa* is a poison if eaten.

A. is now adjutant.[20] His predecessor was a fine fellow, very handsome, who had beaten the champion lightweight boxer for Scotland when he was only twenty two. Last Christmas he went off shooting big game and wounded a bear which sprang on him and knocked him down, and as he lay he caught her — it was a she-bear — by the throat and held her off at arm's length till his men came up. His arms were frightfully torn by her teeth and claws and he was in hospital for weeks. Then he went off to Matabele[21] and now we hear he has been murdered there. It is dreadfully sad.

He was a Scot and such a good sort. . . . We are having awful rows with Soloman, the butler. He meddles with bills, lays hands on all he can in the way of provisions, opens the parcels and tells acres of lies. Last week I found he was giving us inferior meat and charging at the higher rate. Butlers are all-powerful here and there's nothing in the way of wickedness that many of them won't do, and they can compel the other servants to do almost anything. I have heard of an old Mohammedan called Sayid Khan, who I am told is decent. Soloman happily does not know I am in touch with him, and I am going to have the old devil out, quite suddenly, so that he hasn't time to do any mischief. . . .

Violet goes to see a Hindu festival, the Dusera, *at Indore.*

Mhow.
Oct. 1896

. . . We've been over at Indore to see the *Dusera* procession, which is a Hindu affair. At the end of the day a bull is killed with a sword but I did not want to see that part of it, for the bull is tied up and it is sickening; Arthur saw it and loathed it. The *Bala Sahib* was of course prominent in a fine yellow Maratha *pagari* and a necklace of emeralds and diamonds. His attendants sat round him and a man held an orange umbrella with fringe over him; clinging to either side of his *howdah* were men who waved white horse-tails to keep the flies off the person of the illustrious child. The elephant's face was painted crimson, trunk and all, and a large bell hung on a silver chain at his side and rang as he walked. On the other side there was a green velvet ladder for the *Bala Sahib* to mount by and parts of the harness were studded with silver dome-shaped bosses. The little boy waved his hand languidly and looked very stupid when he saw anyone he knew. Dr Caldecott, who took us to the show, was like a dog at a fair, seeming to know every soul, whether black or white, and bawling — he has a very cracked voice, which is a squall and nothing else — and keeping up a running comment to those below. I say 'below', because we were on an elephant too. 'Ha! ha! *Bala Sahib! salaam! salaam!* — Gulab Houssein, how are you? Is your father well? Ho! ho! what a *pagari* you've got on!' (to those below) 'Now then, you animals, get out of the way — do you want me to be mending your bones? Here you silly fellow, move, can't you? I'll tell the Maharajah about you! Hah, there's Gopal Dass — *Ram, Ram,* Gopal Dass, et cet.'

Soon after the Bala's elephant came a closed landau and pair, driven by a gorgeous being and containing the Bala's fat old nurse, perfectly entranced with her position. We and Dr Caldecott all waved to her and she *salaamed* and grinned out of her window, looking as dirty as ever. Then came more elephants and then a coach and four on the *back* seat of which was an apparition which made lively signals of amenity to us. It sat in a heap like a great toad with blue goggles and an old yellow handkerchief round its neck. We returned the *salaams* mildly, wondering who it could possibly be who thought he knew us. But it was Holkar, who, having lost a relation, had shaved his moustache and come *incognito*. The native bands played the most remarkable musical instruments; some were trumpetish-looking things painted green and with mouths like the heads of serpents, which twined round the bodies of those who played them. The Nawab and Jimmy[22] were there on a painted elephant but being Muslims, were only lookers-on like ourselves and, I think, a little scornful of the general naïveté of the show. The *Sahib* pranced among the crowd on a grey arab. On the way to the procession I saw a *fakir* lying flat on his back with his mouth open and a stone about the size and weight of a large cannon-ball on his chest. That sort of gentry flock to festivals where pious innocents are ready to reward their sanctity.

In December 1896 Violet tells her mother of the visit of the Viceroy, the Earl of Elgin, and of the great ball given by Maharajah Holkar of Indore at his palace, the Lal Bagh.

Mhow.
8 Dec. 1896

. . . There is so much to tell this mail that I hardly know where to start. The Viceregal[23] visit is over. A. and I went to Indore on Wednesday morning and lunched with the Nawab at Gwalior House, spending most of the afternoon dawdling about the polo ground looking at the various Rajahs' equipages and movements; the place was alive with their big tents, lavishly beflagged and decorated and surrounded by retainers in every colour and half-colour invented by man. Native cavalry on browns, greys, duns, piebalds and chestnuts, to say nothing of droves of whites, pranced about and discordant bands clashed and banged and blew. The Nawab, who was much admired, making the *Sahib*'s heart glow with almost paternal pride, went off in state to receive the Viceroy in the Jaora tent. He looked so slim in his tight fitting coat, rose-coloured silk, nearly reaching his heels, tight white trousers and a necklace of flawed emeralds about the size of thrushes' eggs hanging all the way down his chest. Jimmy, whose official position is that of one of the Nawab's *Sirdars*, or Generals, was in red velvet and gold lace and looked really handsome, with his heavier cast of countenance. It was funny to see the two boys with whom one had been shouting and playing hockey on the verandah of Gwalior House, transformed into two gaudy and very solemn young nobles, one taking entire precedence of the other and departing in a carriage surrounded by bedizened people, followed by a squadron of Jaora cavalry and heralded by a flight of running footmen with long sticks.

In the evening we started for the Lal Bagh Palace, four miles off, A. and some others in a Jaora carriage and I and the *Sahib* in a mail phaeton.²⁴ It is difficult to give you an idea of that drive, as you have never seen an Indian city. There were three miles of lights. We drove through a blazing road, so bright that surrounding objects were as distinct as in the day. On right and left, at a height of a man's head, was a double row of lights on parallel wires about eight inches apart. Behind this in many places small trees were hung with paper lanterns with another row of lights under the boughs; this sent up a great glare into the blue-black sky and made the whole skyful of stars look like steel. In the smoke that hung round the houses, many of which were carved about the windows, some buildings stood out dark and some light. The entire female population stood, sat and leant out from roofs and verandahs in a confused tangle of wood-smoke, glare, teeth and brown arms, and dressed in every colour of the rainbow. This made a seething background on which the gold and silver of bracelets and nose rings shot out like flashes of moonlight on water. Some of the houses had plants growing on the housetops and at the carved wooden window ledges, so dirty and so picturesque. Below, in the light, the male population swarmed in its holiday clothes, kept back from the road by Holkar's cavalry whose lances made dark points in the crowd and whose half-broken horses stamped and squealed. All this continued for three miles and disappeared into a distance so long and giddy that it seemed like a geometrical pattern receding in a nightmare of one's childhood. Over it all was the undulating hum of a whole city talking, and to me, that was almost the most impressive part of the business. There is a square in Indore about the size of the Campo dei Fiori in Rome and here there are two palaces, one on either side, one stone built, the other stucco and

painted a raging blue. Both can be seen far out into the country
as they are much higher than the other buildings. Most people hate
the blue palace but I like it very much though I've no desire to see it
in Piccadilly or Grosvenor Square. But here, in a country where the
light covers and justifies everything, I think it is fine. Every angle and
projection of these palaces was outlined in lamps and an arch raised
between them; and the streets jutting away from them looked like
endless black tunnels. I sat on the high phaeton and looked down
on a world of *pagaris*.

When we got to the Lal Bagh gardens elephants were looming
like castles in the shadows under the trees but the spectacle was,
to my mind, inferior to that of the city. When we drew up at the
palace steps the *Sahib* got down to help me out, the phaeton being
high and I encumbered by the tail of my white satin dress, and
the moment I touched the ground the silly *syces* let go the horses'
heads and away they went in among the crowd but were soon
surrounded and caught by the servants swarming like bees about
the palace and no harm was done. As one looked at it, ablaze, like
everything else, the gardens were on the right, full of high trees and
strong-scented jasmine, and on the left, the river. At the top of the
steps the Maharajah Holkar stood, receiving his guests in a white
silk coat and rose-coloured *pagari* and behind him a mass of Indian
bigwigs, Englishmen in political uniform, artillery officers and our
own 20th Hussars, whose full dress is, as you know, splendid.[25]
During my few words with Holkar I had just time to see that his
only ornament was three rows of pearls as big as peas.

To cut a long story short, the banquet was not long, though
very bad as to food, and I had a dull, semi-important being on
my right and happily a nice man, whom I knew, on my left. At
dessert, Holkar came in and he and Lord Elgin made the usual
complimentary speeches and polite protestations and when it was
over, the Viceregal party went out to seats on the terrace overlooking
the river, on the opposite bank of which the fireworks were in full
fling. Very soon an aide-de-camp came after me to say that Lady
Elgin wanted me, so I went out too. She was awfully pleased to see
me, I think, and I sat with them both and the Maharajah most of
the evening and saw the fireworks well. They were very good, much
the same as the Crystal Palace ones, but looked better by reason of
the running water in which every star and wheel was doubled. I
can't say I saw it very carefully because I felt that nothing could
be compared to the spectacle of the lighted city and because Lady

Elgin talked so much and told me such lots of things of the four years since we had met. We drove home through the city but the people had gone to bed and the lamps were waning. Next morning I went to see her again and spent an hour with her. She looked very worn and delicate and I really pitied her when she told me how hard she has to work, whether well or ill. Her eyes were full of tears when we said goodbye. I think she is terribly homesick. . . .

Violet and Arthur enjoy camp at Ujjain, and Christmas at the Residency.

Mhow.
11 Dec. 1896

. . . If by chance you don't hear from me next mail don't be alarmed. We are going for three days into a camp with Col. Barr to Ujjain,[26] a very ancient and holy city and I don't know that we shall have a *dâk,* or road post, unless he had laid a special one for himself. We look forward to it very much, as you may suppose; I don't know which day we shall start but we shall be out for Xmas. It's sure to be fun for they are such a good lot; and Capt. Bannerman, the First Assistant, is going too. You shall hear about it when we get back. Last week I took out the arab charger, Talisman, who is young and just out of school, and A. rode the old troophorse. He went very well and is much more agreeable than that she-cat, Trilby; coming home in the dusk a cart met us making an awful rattling and filled with tall branches of trees that wagged against the sky. Both horses were frightened and whipped round and Talisman ran against a dust heap, crossed his feet and came down on the hard road and lay on my legs. I writhed out and fled on my hands and knees for he was so surprised that he lay quite still and I was rather afraid his leg was broken, but we persuaded him to get up, which he did, unhurt. The crutch of the saddle was bent and my habit cut and he, poor beast, was gored by my spur when he rolled on it, but that was all the damage. My left side is black and blue. I was afraid he might object to me after this incident but I have had another very good ride on him since. . . .

Yes, I know you would keep my flower drawings most carefully if I sent them home but the truth is I can't part with them! Whenever I feel down on my luck — which isn't often, certainly — I take them out and gloat over them and they comfort me. I never thought I could do them and haven't got over the pleasant surprise yet.

The other day I was lunching at Indore at Jaora House and a

girl who was globe-trotting sat opposite me. Beyond thinking her
rather nice I paid no particular attention to her but before the end
of the meal I looked across at her and suddenly saw in her face
something familiar and knew I had seen her as a child. Do you
remember Marian Doughty, a pale, fat little girl who used to be
at the dancing class we went to in the days when we wintered at
St Leonards? She remembered me too. She has grown into quite a
different personality and is not at all lumpish. We had a long talk
and she is coming over to Mhow to see me.

I've been painting a lot lately. One day I went to examine a stone
idol which lives in a grove of mangoes abutting on the Bombay
road and on the way I passed a *sadhu,* or Hindu holy man. They
are amazing people to look upon. His hair was piled up in a high
chignon on the top of his head, his face smeared with grey ashes, he
had a scanty yellow cloth round his middle and small iron tongs in
his hand. When I had settled down in the grove and begun to paint,
in comes the *sadhu,* sits down under a tree and begins, like a witch,
to make a fire on the ground. I was hidden behind the wheels of the
buggy, for I had moored up there, so I left my other drawing and
began to paint him. Whether he saw me or not I don't know but he
took no notice and I worked hard and managed to get him finished.
Since then, I have returned twice to paint in the landscape that was
behind him and now I have done it. It *was* a chance! That grove
is a choice spot. It seems that all who travel the road halt there to
rest and drink at the well and some say prayers in front of the idol.
Last time I was there there were about twenty others besides myself.
Bullock drivers, beggars, women and children et cet. One old man
who I afterwards learnt was a baker from Palassi village, lay flat
on his back and sang to the company for the hour and a half I was
there. They took little notice of him, but I liked it very much; his
twirls and quavers and half tones were wonderful.

It seems almost impossible to find out anything about these idols.
No English person that I have yet met has the slightest interest in
them and Hindu mythology is so complicated to an unassisted
beginner that I despair of ever knowing anything about them. It
seems that different characters have many different names and turn
into other people at every stage of their existence and there isn't a
loose end hanging out anywhere from which you can pick up a clue.
The common people are most un-religious, as far as I can see, and
each caste seems to have a different kind of worship. They know,
I should imagine, as much about the real meaning of their religion

as a street child in England does of church history. But Providence has come to my help at last, and I have lit on something about this idol. One has to piece all sorts of things together, and never neglect a turning from fear it should lead to a blind alley. One observes a little, thinks, puzzles, and sometimes a chance word, or inspired shot and the thing begins to work out. A woman I know was telling me what a sharp fellow her *syce* was and I pointed out the grove to her and made her ask him who was the image inside; the man, who speaks a little English, said, 'the King of Ceylon', and added that people who prayed to him made him laugh. This made me no wiser but not long after I caught sight of a native picture of a host of monkeys led by a being called Hanuman to conquer the island of Ceylon. So back I went to the grove to see if the idol was anything like a monkey. But there were people there and I did not like to go near for fear of annoying them and waited in the background, hoping that they would go and I should get my chance. All at once another holy man dressed in a rag and a piece of string came in and fell on his face, praying aloud before the image. In the middle of his devotions he cried out 'Hanuman! Hanuman!' and I could have cried out 'Hanuman' too, I was so delighted.[27] Now, I have found many other Hanumans all over the country; he always has one foot raised above the other and that is really how one identifies him best, as he has a man's body and little resemblance to a monkey in the face. I must stop this rigmarole. What an endless letter. . . .

Dr Caldecott's house
Indore. 31 Dec. 1896

. . . We came in here from camp yesterday and have been spending the night here for a farewell feast and go back to Mhow this afternoon. It has been a splendid holiday and has done A. a world of good, absolutely putting work out of his head for eight days. Now we can buckle to again and go on for months. Our new butler, Yessoo, a considerable improvement on Soloman, wrote to us about Harry and with Rachel we knew he was absolutely all right. As soon as we reached Indore last Wednesday week the Christmas rain began blowing up on all sides so Col. Barr postponed our departure and we all stayed in the residency for Christmas. We had the most enormous cake you ever saw, as big round as the seat of a chair and a foot high. We consisted of Dr Caldecott, without whom nothing goes on, Col., Mrs and Miss Barr and two sons, one in the army and one in the police, Capt. Bannerman[28] and an elderly relation of the family called 'Uncle Percy', who is, I think, globe-trotting. We were very jolly, and the eldest boy and his father kept us in shouts of laughter. The father, especially, has one of the prettiest wits I ever heard.

On Boxing Day we departed into camp to Ujjain. We had thirty tents, all told, seven horses, a couple of elephants and a squadron of Scindia's irregular cavalry to guard the sacred person of the Agent to the Governor General in Central India. A. and I were in a large double-pole tent the size of a marquee and were in clover. We were about a hundred souls, including servants and sentries. The camp was on open ground outside the city walls. One of Captain Bannerman's horses was brought out for me but as my saddle did not fit him Col. Barr lent me an enormous mare like a carthorse, which he rides himself, when he does ride, which is not often, for he is a very heavy man. She rolled like a ship at sea but carried me well. The two elephants were big ones and I was amused to find that one of them's name was *Anarkalli*,[27] which is, being interpreted, Pomegranate-Bud.

Ujjain is a wonderful place, much of it dating B.C., but the river running through it has swallowed a great lot of it and the present city, though very old, is built on an older one; they dig up bits of this still. Holy men come to it from all over Asia and it is so full of temples that one suffers from indigestion of the mind in thinking about them. Even the most awfully dirty old houses are built of ancient stone and shrines and graves are in masses in every street; the filth of native India is beyond description and Ujjain is, I should imagine, about the dirtiest bit. But of course I have not seen Benares which is supposed to beggar everything else in that way. Humanity, rubbish, dust, old rags and decayed vegetables are thick together in Ujjain and the streets are so narrow that, as we rode through one part of it on Pomegranate-Bud's broad back I had to tuck in my legs tight to the *howdah* not to touch the eaves of the houses with my feet and Miss Barr, on the other side, had to do the same. In the principal street nearly every house was carved; it is a little wider than the rest and a mass of colour; one old temple fronting on it was built of white plaster weathered into all kinds of shades and one looked up and saw its tower against the deep blue with its white domed and pillared balcony high above, with a man sitting in it in a coat with a pattern of large red roses.

If I were to write for ages I could never make you understand what it looks like out here in a place like this one. The impression of heat, crowd, dirt, violent colour and endless detail is extraordinary. Then there is the great bathing place, paved, at the edge of the river; thick with temples and tombs, walls with turrets and ruined stone-carved windows, full of people, many of them wild-looking *sadhus* and pilgrims. The stones built into it are so much covered with carving that each might be a study in itself. Some of the buildings were cut out in the rock and had pillars that looked almost like Corinthian ones. In front of them *sadhus* and others were making their little fires and cooking their food. On the opposite shore the river runs under a high bank with trees and temples and flights of steps where cows and goats wander about. The smells are frightful but, personally, I don't care. There was no use in trying to draw though my sketch book was in my pocket, the scene was so complicated, but I made a few rough scrawls from the stability of Pomegranate-Bud's mountainous back. The only thing I got satisfactorily was a strange and very beautiful figure of a cobra cut in a stone that leaned against a temple wall. I went into the city every day I was there, being never tired of it. Once I rode the mare so as to get a different level from that of the elephant. A. spent most of his time shooting at various tanks with the young Barrs but he had one day in the city which he enjoyed very much.

There is a palace up the river, standing on a rock, and the water has been diverted into it and runs into all sorts of channels round it and through ancient bathing tanks and carved stone arcades; it is nearly intact though Akbar[30] built it three hundred years ago as a summer palace for his wives. It was beautiful but I felt it was almost tame after the city. One shouldn't see such things one after the other. It is Scindia's property, as Ujjain is; it was he who lent Anarkalli and the escort. I rode the big mare to the water-palace and we went most of the way at a hand-canter, as one does over any kind of ground in this country; it was like riding the dome of St Paul's in an earthquake as she lolloped along and I looked down to earth and saw Captain Bannerman and Miss Barr flying beside me on their little horses, whilst a native cavalryman raced in front with his *pagari* streaming, on a pink nosed arab to clear the way.

I did hardly any painting in camp. There was too much to look at and too many people about to do anything that took time. We had the Christmas cake with us but it was so big that a quarter of it remained uneaten on our return though nine healthy people ate it for five days. The last morning we went off to breakfast with the only Europeans

near, a Dutch-French family called Onreit. He is in Scindia's employ.
They live in a whitewashed house with a courtyard full of roses,
very plain and clean; they smacked of this country though all spoke
English very well and seemed nice, collectively, and individually dull.
That house made me think of the sort of house you read about in Bret
Harte[31] with its courtyard in the middle. Mrs Onreit gave us French
coffee of a sort I had not tasted for years. It was a real delight and we
drank it in a long, cool, whitewashed room with roses on the table.
Her French-Dutch-English mixed with a native accent was rather
fascinating, though she was middle-aged and plain, but there are
several ways of being plain and hers had the advantage of being a
French one.

There were a multitude of *borahs* at Ujjain station when we got
there. If I wrote for a year I could never give you a sufficient
idea of what a *borah*'s appearance is like. One may call them the
rag-and-bottle men of Central India; they deal in every kind of
secondhand thing from old tins upwards and downwards, becoming
rich in the process, and their wives are often beautifully dressed and
covered with jewels, but they themselves are so frightful to look
at and so pantomimic and farcical that it's difficult to believe one
isn't dreaming when one sees them, as I did, come running in a
stream across the platform and over the line. There are fat ones
and lean ones, but all have shiny bald heads, those of the thin
ones set on the necks of vultures in which the Adam's apple is
the main feature; goat beards like the fag-ends of 'carpet switches'
wag from their chins. They are crowned with very small hats like
narrow-brimmed billicocks. Dignity is unknown to the *borah* and
the lack of it is the more blatant in a country where so many are
dignified, at least, outwardly. To see a *borah* fly gesticulating down
a railway platform is an unforgettable sight, especially as he wears a
garment fitting his shoulders tightly and spreading under the armpits
into folds that reach his ankles; he is like a gander pursued across a
farmyard. The final touch to him is the obese black cotton umbrella
which he is never parted from and which is never rolled but tied
securely with a string round its waist. There was one *borah* I saw
whose place in the train had been usurped, bawling open-mouthed
for a policeman to assist him. He had only one tooth and that in
front. We changed trains at Fahtiabad where we met a holy man in a
saffron garment. 'O *Sadhuji*,' said Col. Barr, 'have you always been
like this?' 'No,' he replied, 'but when I had settled all my children
in life I had nothing to do, so I became holy.' He then took Col.

Barr for the station-master and asked him to put him in the right train for Gwalior. . . .

I have nearly forgotten to tell you of the absurd looking vehicle that plies along the road to Ujjain, an omnibus drawn by a pair of camels; it is two storeyed and the natives who patronise it look exactly like fowls in crates as they go by.

1897
Diaries and Letters

From January 1897 Violet keeps a diary. In this year she is working on her novel The Sheepstealers. *She also enjoys trips early in the year to, among other places, Jaora (with the Nawab and Jimmy), Dhar and Mandu.*

21st January

Rode in the evening to the opium fields, now in their glory, a carpet stretching for acres and acres in a mass of colour, crimson, purple, rose-pink and white mixed with the greyish green of the leaves, and paddy birds, dead white, wandering about among them. Central India is the land of poppies. There is the *Argemone mexicana* too, long established as a weed, and in appearance the nearest approach to the English horned poppy that is thick on the shores of the south coast in summer; it is a lovely roadside thing springing from the dust and lifting its gold crowned head and grey, thistle-like leaves over rubbish and stones. It doesn't seem to be admired, as a rule, or even noticed; I suppose, because it was only the Almighty who put it there and not a gardener. It is as common as the nettle is in England, and exquisite; the dry seed pods burst open and look like elegant brackets with handles standing upright; bend them down and a small black shot-like seed pours from them; if it all fertilized it would surely swamp Central India and make agriculture impossible. Mrs Barr has gone to Gwalior and taken some of my flower drawings with her for Scindia's Scottish head gardener to see and name. But out of the twelve I sent he could only name four, two of which I had already found out. I am getting on much better with Roxburgh and can identify, to a certain extent, for myself, and I hope soon not to need anyone to help me except in specially difficult cases.

23rd January

Gwalior House, Indore. Marian Doughty is still here and I have come over for a small race meeting. She, I and the *Sahib* went for a drive in the starlight tonight. The two dogs, Patch and Billy, come over with my saddle tomorrow as we are going to hunt with the scratch pack next day.

24th January

An idle day playing about with the boys and went to a fair in the city at which I bought two clay parrots painted grass-green.

25th January

With the scratch pack after jackal. A stupid hunt, and A J-B's dog,[1] Lady, a long-dog who arrived here yesterday, has been my bane. She was lent for today's hunt and I took her to sleep in my room but had the folly to tie her up on a black buck-skin rug. This, I afterwards found, tickled her ears, and she shook her head, flapping them, all night long so I got no sleep at all. A *nuit blanche*, with a vengeance. I rose at an unearthly hour, being wearied out for want of rest and thankful the hateful night was over, dressed and got on Sterling, the pony the *Sahib* was lending me; and when the sweeper was told to let the dogs loose, Lady, who perhaps had not forgotten the night to which I had condemned her, made a bee-line for the horizon and was seen no more. Fear of A.J-B's wrath, should he never see his precious long-dog again, was on me and I sent out emissaries of all sorts — even the town crier — to the *bazaar*, but to no purpose. I then went to the telegraph office and wired to A.J-B. to look out for the animal, and my wire ran thus: 'Watch Indore road for Lady escaped from Indore'. It chanced that the message was delayed and he received it in the Mess during luncheon and read it aloud in his amazement to the accompaniment of shouts of laughter and many innuendoes about his private life. Lady was brought back in the evening to my intense relief, having been found in the city. I sent her home with a servant and was thankful to see the end of her.

Met the Maharajah during the day and had some talk with him; he really knows English wonderfully well. He remarked that I had grown very thin and presented me with a tightly tied bunch of mignonette that he was carrying. I was not able to return the compliment, for I think he gets fatter every time I see him. After dark I went over to the *Bankwallah*'s to paint the moon-creeper that grows on his verandah; it is like a great white *convulvulus*, clove scented and only opens at night.

26th January

Hunting, this time without Lady, whom I hope never to see again as

long as I live. A short run over bad ground. A globe-trotter was out.
One doesn't see many here and I don't know who mounted him. In
the cool of the evening the *Bankwallah* took us to see a silk merchant
in the city and we sat on a divan in his shop. There were gorgeous
stuffs and he was rather gorgeous himself for he wore rose-coloured
silk, white cotton stockings, much darned, gold earrings and a pen
behind his ear like an English counter jumper. A crowd came to look
on which threatened to be overpowering and the *Bankwallah*, who
conducted the conversation, said 'You must not come too near unless
you pay two *annas* a head to help the bargaining.' This found great
favour as a jest and one old man with no teeth who was hovering on
the outskirts of the press was beyond measure delighted. There was a
young man in an embroidered waistcoat sitting in the shop who knew
a few words of English. The *Bankwallah* asked the merchant who
wore the kind of stuffs — very rich ones — what we were examining,
but the merchant, like many Indians when asked a question, made a
long reply about something quite different. This happened several
times and the *Bankwallah* began to get rather impatient. At this the
young man in the waistcoat was suddenly struck with the knowledge
of what the question meant and, from the further end of the shop
roared 'King-mans!' at the top of his voice, meaning, of course,
the families of Rajahs. There was a squalid little shrine at a street
corner; a low square cave in the wall. It was dark and inside was a
shapeless stone painted red with two glaring eyes. This is a shrine
of Bhiru,[2] one of the twin sons of Kali,[3] the great goddess of all
terrors. Returned to Mhow with Marian Doughty, who is coming
to stay with us, and the two dogs.

27th January
Nothing special. Saddles, horses and guns have gone on to camp
in Jaora where Yar Mohammed, Jimmy's father and uncle to the
Nawab, is on the banks of the Chambal.[4] I have been lent a saddle
for tomorrow evening. Did hospital and some odd jobs.

29th January
A. I and Marian left in the evening, picked up the *Sahib* and the
two boys at Indore and departed for Jaora. All slept in the train.

30th January
Chambal river, Jaora. Woke in the early morning to find our carriage
shunted to a side line just outside Malhargarh railway station, in

Jaora state. A long plain, palpitating with heat and only broken by the tiny station house. Soldiers were doing sentry outside. The Nawab is in his own country and ceremony is observed, so a brilliantly coloured crowd of his subjects were there to make their *salaams* to him. We breakfasted on such provisions as we had with us, in the station, and then got into two very unsophisticated *tongas* with a pair of ponies to each. Marian, the *Sahib* and the Nawab were in one and Jimmy, A. and I in the other. We started on our twenty-four miles straight into the open country. Two Jaora cavalrymen were in attendance, barbarous but rather smart; the roads were no roads and we went as hard as we could. Marian, who is thin, says she is black and blue. Often we had to get out and help to push the *tongas* out of ruts and over, not stones, but boulders. We passed through about twenty villages, mud-walled, most of them and buried in a world of poppies brilliant in the sun, with high mango *topes* like clumps of plumes standing in their midst. Great banyans put down their aerial roots making arches and pillars of twisted fibres and wood, many with stone shrines hidden in their sinister darkness. Village people, according to the custom, ran to meet the Nawab, presenting him with small coins which he touched and gave to his *tonga* man, who must have made a good thing of his day's work; the women came separately, some beating tom-toms. Peacocks flew about, trees loomed, grey and heavy, in the hot morning air, poppies blazed and native cavalrymen galloped and pranced and on we went again. In many villages pillared tombs and cenotaphs were huddled up among temples, rough thatch and mud walls in the dark mystery of the banyans, and at one place high stone stakes, rudely shaped at the top, stuck out of groves and cactus hedges; once there was one jutting up right in our road and we had to manoeuvre our *tongas* carefully round it among the ruts. Tourists have never come along these lost places and would not trouble to notice their surroundings if they did; here was nothing obvious, nothing labelled to look at, but the suggestiveness of old rural India with its dim beliefs and dark gods. Most of the time I was driving. There are no traces to a *tonga*, only a pole with a yoke and you do a lot of the steering with a stick, pushing the ponies' quarters either in towards the pole or outwards. It is a very good plan, for across country, you can guide them among big stones when going at a smart pace and in and out of ruts which are often anything from six inches to a foot deep.

After five hours of heat and dust and being flung like shuttlecocks from one side of the *tonga* to another we reached the camp on the

banks of the Chambal near a village called Pesawar. Yar Mohammed
is regent of Jaora during his nephew's minority and now he is on tour
through the state, looking into agriculture, administering justice and
settling leases and other things. He stops about four days in each
place till his tour is done. He is a good-looking man, lean and
hatchet-faced, more like a Spaniard than an Indian, a little grey
and wearing gold spectacles. He wears an 'Imperial' too, which is
uncommon here and makes him look French as well as Spanish. He
has been a great deal in Europe and at various spas for his health,
so he knows English very fluently, but I suppose underneath he is
as Oriental as anybody else. The mixture was well illustrated by
his clothes when we arrived and found him wearing a suit of very
British flannels and the pillbox cap, common to Hindu and Muslim,
on his head.

   We are high above the river which runs eventually into the Nerbada[5]
and the stream here is about four hundred feet wide, curving under
wooded banks; it has small islands in it and reminds me of a picture
I am very fond of in the National Gallery, by Patinir,[6] which is in the
Dutch room. In it you look down on the water just as you are doing
here and see a long, serpentine raft floating down stream. But here
there are no craft of any kind to be seen. The camp is pleasant with
its fire lit, camels picketed and a cheerful noise going on. We have
had tubs, sorely needed, and a good meal of which we were equally
glad and after which I went to my tent and slept till evening. A. and
I then went to prowl about and see what we could see; peacocks
or alligators, or anything, but we came back for dinner without
any surprises. Yar Mohammed and a relation were at dinner but
the relation didn't seem interesting and I think we were all rather
shy. The Nawab's dog Judy and five other terriers played riotously
under the table. We went to bed early. When the stars came out it
was lovely to see them reflected in the river and during the night
flights of the great Sarus cranes passed trumpeting over the camp.

31st January

A. and the *Sahib* went out in a boat hidden away somewhere below
us and A. shot a crocodile. Afterwards we went junglewards on an
elephant but had no luck of any kind, for though the jungle was
beaten for panther and pig both beats were blank. As we sat in our
posts listening to the beat drawing nearer and nearer with shouts
and tom-toms and banging of kerosene oil tins, all it produced was
a hyena exactly like a Noah's ark beast, ignobly loping away in the

distance. As sport it was nil but I liked it. In the afternoon Yar Mohammed lent us his *tonga* and A. and I went off to see the country: on our way back we fell in with the *Sahib* and Marian on a baggage camel. They said they'd had enough of it and we offered to change conveyances, a thing they jumped at, so up we climbed, astride, one behind the other, and rode home through the dusk. We made the camel trot as hard as we could and though we had no kind of idea how to guide it we got home all right. There is only one bit of rope as a rein which is tied to the ring in his nose and if you try to pull him up you seem to meet with no resistance and get his head wound back against the hump, for he has a neck like an ostrich. The others stood shouting with laughter as we streaked away from them, for they said we looked so like twins in our *topēs* and khaki clothes and leather leggings. We had a delightful evening sitting under the stars round the camp fire and listening to Yar Mohammed, who is a born *raconteur*, as he told us a blood-curdling murder story that he had had to deal with on one of his tours. I only wish I could remember it, it was so picturesque and so complicated, but I think nobody could who did not write it down at the time.

1st February
Today we had no sport either, though we spent the morning on the Elephant 'Hara Raj'. It was hot and we lunched in his mighty shadow. A. brought home a heavy bag of sandgrouse and pigeon in the afternoon and we had another delightful camp fire and stories. As we sat round it a splendid falling star crossed the heavens in the middle of the afterglow.

2nd February
Up early and went off by myself up the river to paint a little temple I had seen from the camp, an odd white place with two domes, squatting in the undergrowth on arid ground with some people round it. It was such a fiery hot little picture and the figures wore brilliant colours. In the morning we started for home, for Yar Mohammed is moving on; I was sorry to leave the Chambal. I could wander for ever about this Indian country. With all its drawbacks it is the most congenial environment to me that I have ever been in. On this occasion we had the Nawab in our *tonga* and a fine time we had with him. He had got his gun beside him in front so that he might bag anything he fancied. What he did fancy was peacocks; and bits of Holkar's territory through which we had to pass cropped out into

Jaora state and are inhabited by Hindus, to whom the peacock is sacred. All the way along he let drive at anything that had so much as the shadow of a moon on its tail, and when we got near the Indore bits, Satan entered into him. Though we besought him to stop nothing would make him listen. To the *tongawallah* he was a reigning sovereign so he stopped whenever the young imp told him to. The *Sahib* was some way in front and out of sight and we knew how particular he would be that nothing irregular should be done by his charge. A climax was reached when he sprang out of the *tonga*, gun in hand, and began to stalk a peacock just under a village wall. He missed it and the bird made for the houses with him after it; both vanished followed by Judy. A moment after there began a perfect fusillade from among the mud walls, so we leapt out and rushed after him into the village where we laid hands on him and dragged him out of the place, fearing that he might be in difficulties with the Hindus. He was anything but pleased but we got him fast and never let him out of our sight again till, after two breakdowns of harness, we drove into Malhargarh. Dined, very hilariously, in a tent just big enough to hold us all, outside the station and then retired to bed in the train.

2nd February

Arrived at Indore in the early hours, breakfasted and spent the day at Gwalior House. Marian came back with us and the *Sahib* went off to Bagli to buy horses.

6th February

I rode to Akolia to paint the poppy fields. The *dâk* tree is coming out, a sign of the times. The cold weather is fast ending and in a few weeks the gruesome days of sickness and death and heat will be coming on.

8th February

Went to paint the idol in a grove near Bercha and was home before noon. Later I went to meet B. and F.B. and Bobby R.[7] and talk over a projected camp we have in mind.

15th February

I hear we start for our camp on Saturday. A. says he can't come but the other two men have got their leave.

16th February

F.B. Bobby and I rode out to Holkar's deserted shooting bungalow at Nandlia. We spent the day there. The place has always attracted me ever since I first rode past it last year. You take a track from Bercha across country near Killod village and round the foot of the hill of Nandlia, that solitary hill that juts like an ant-heap out of the plain. There is a rocky track between it and a high mound covered with scrub and bastard teak, that is stiller than any place I know. I hear there are stone images up the hillside in the brushwood. I must go one day and see what I can see. After passing the hill you come to Nandlia village where there is a red god crouching under a banyan by the path side. The roof of Holkar's bungalow only just appears from a thicket with one or two cypresses set about it; it is all very silent with scarcely any track and high grass, high enough to submerge one, all round. One day not long ago when I was painting near, I went into the trees to look for plants and suddenly realised that I did not know my way out, for I had turned about several times. But it was one of those days when the moon is visible in daylight and I chanced to remember that it had been on my right hand when I went in so I got out easily; but that gives one an idea of the height of the lemon grass there. We found a village man to look after the horses and made our way into the garden, a deserted, tangled place with a dilapidated wooden erection, something between a pergola[8] and a cage, smothered in a creeper I had never seen before with long, twining whips of shoots and a blossom very like a horse chestnut in shape and colour, but not so stiff; cream-white touched with pink and a scent like the scent of all the east, with its heaviness and strangeness. The bungalow was locked but we got in at a window. It had evidently been deserted for a long time. It is two storeys high, or it never would have showed above the grass, and the rooms are small and the walls colour-washed a violent Reckitts' blue[9] with terrible, antiquated framed photographs hanging on them. From the upper verandah we looked down on the overgrown, soundless garden, drowned and forgotten in the monstrous, crowding grass. We could see the further hills beyond Jamli. We rode home in a hot sunset that seemed to press down on the earth.

20th February

Dhar. — B., myself, F.B. and Bobby were off early for Dhar in a dilapidated state carriage belonging to the Maharajah of Dhar,[10], changing horses every seven miles. Unluckily B. developed fever on the way and retired to bed as soon as we got to the guest-house here. We were hot and dusty. It is an old white bungalow on a circular plinth, the rooms high and carpeted. (I haven't seen a carpet for nearly two years, and had no desire to, and it strikes me as incongruous and tiresome.) The gravel round the house merges into the jungle of an old native garden and there are tall oleanders by the well and large tubs near the door with the finest bushes of the mauve-blue *Petrea stapelia* that I have ever seen. These make a background to two stone Buddhas. There is much *mogra*, double and scented. We shall not pay our respects to the Maharajah, who is ill now. He is an old man, a good ruler but crippled and paralysed.

When the sun was down we went to the fort that stands on a high rock with the town clustered round it; it has a great breach in its side, blown by the English in the Mutiny, which is not allowed to be filled up but is left gaping as a perpetual witness to the people. I find that the creeper with the horse-chestnut-like flower is *Hiptage madhablota*.

21st February

Mandu.[11] — I was up early this morning and went to paint the fortress. B. rested most of the day but insisted on going on in spite of his fever. In the streets of Dhar we saw two women of the shop-keeping class standing crying aloud; first one cast herself into her companion's arms, then the other; their voices were hoarse with wailing and they raised their arms to heaven. Many watched them. On enquiry we found that one of them was going away for a couple of days. It is the custom, if absence includes as much as a single night, to make this public hullabaloo, and true politeness demands an exhibition of agony. We had been full of compassion, thinking some awful catastrophe had happened. Reassured, we listened with great interest. It is so seldom one gets the opportunity of hearing howling dispassionately; you have to be concerned in a measure, one way or another; but here it could be heard without bias, as a phenomenon. We started for Mandu when it was comparatively cool and arrived just before dark.

The last part of the journey was done on an elephant. Approaching the deep ravine, blue with mist, which cuts Mandu from the rest of the country, you see beyond it the domes and mosques of the ruined town rearing up through the thick jungle in the evening light. Twenty-eight miles was the girth of this city on a crest of the Vindhyan range, over one thousand two hundred feet above the Nerbada and now deserted for more than three hundred years; voracious nature has engulfed the once famous capital of Malwa and the massive walls, broken down in many places, which still surround it; a small Hindu village in the midst of it is all that remains of human life in the place, now a tract of jungle and brushwood with large beautiful tanks and clearings here and there. The grey apes go rushing through the trees and the Bhil people do a little desultory cultivation of opium where they can. As you cross the ravine to enter it by one of the city gates you can see an inscription of the time of the Mughal emperor Aurangzeb telling that he had repaired the gateway in 1668. We went along the rough road bisecting the area within the walls; carved stones lay about in the undergrowth and all round were arches and tombs, the latter with their stone domes rising from the tangle on every hand.

Our camp is pitched by a long tank in a grove of mangoes stretching for about a hundred yards; there are about eighteen acres of still water west of us and on the eastern side a mosque with three domes, the dead wall of which shelters our tents. This lovely building is used by the Bhils for storing wood and there is a broken stone window in its southern face near the ground choked with cut branches to keep their cattle from getting in. As soon as I had put my traps into my tent I went out to look about me and crawled in at it to find myself in a sort of cloister running all round supported by carved pillars, most wonderful to behold. The large centre dome has elaborate carvings inside and is inlaid with peacock blue Multhan tiling[12] and there is an entrance at the further end with more pillars supporting a row of circles like the setting of rose windows. It would be truer to say that they supported them once for they are so much broken that it is just possible to imagine what they must have been. All round are undulations of wooded ground. Mosques and ancient walls moulder on the flat sweeps of shore by the tank with strange piles of building overrun by creepers. The grey stone of this place has touches of pink and golden discolorations. It all seems a fit setting for some fantastic Eastern drama; for travelling merchants and wandering princes and disguised ladies. They ought to be coming out from the heavy trees across the water. I have a good tent and shall sleep soundly in it I am sure, for I am too happy for anything.

22nd February
Out before the others stirred in a yellow sunrise that flamed behind the mosque and a little transitory breeze that made shivers in the mango over my tent. I took my botany book in my haversack. Poor

old Roxburgh — he is a terrible weight to carry about but he always goes with me. I explored mosques and came on scattered graves, sat under ilex trees and in crumbling courtyards, and never a snake did I see in this place which must be a nursery of them; but much as I abhor them I don't fear them. And no one need who wears the leather leggings and stout khaki that I do and who is never parted from a stick. The tracks cut and wound in and out and I gathered seeds of creepers I did not know and pried into thickets and read Roxburgh and sat thinking about nothing and gaping like a yokel at a fair on the different trees. The only living things I met were five roaming *sadhus* and certainly they were blood-curdling to look at and I had to pass them at a very narrow place. I could not help wondering what English villagers would think if one of these creatures were to appear suddenly in an English lane. They would certainly believe that they had seen the devil and I should not blame them. Their bodies, almost bare, were covered with ash-smears which, on their very dark skins, had a livid effect, and their matted hair was twisted in high piles on their heads and stained with red dye; this, with the usual rolling eye of their class, gave them a far from reassuring aspect. I made a slight detour, keeping a tree trunk between me and them as I passed and one of them stopped to stare at me with great curiosity. He was probably as peaceably inclined as I was but you never can tell with these semi-savages and the jungle is one place and the high road another, so I was glad when he had passed on with his brethren. The creepers enwinding the buildings I went into were thick and to reach one of the most beautiful tombs I had to cut my way with my Norwegian knife; the arched portal was filled by a stone door, or rather, a half door, immovable and firmly built into the jamb, thickly carved in intricate patterns, and through the empty side of the arch you could see a stone sarcophagus. I would give much to know the names and histories of all these great people who lie hidden away in the vegetation of this lonely place. I made a careful black and white drawing of the entrance. Another tomb I went into had an open arch looking far over the stretching jungle and blue distance and here I did a little watercolour and got a scrap of the green-blue tiling that you may find lying among the brushwood. It was a perfect morning's prowl. B. has had his tent shifted to a cooler place and is better. Last night I dragged my bed outside and slept under a high mango tree. Before getting to sleep I lay looking at the stars that seemed entangled in the boughs above my head and thinking of the good fortune of my life that had brought me into places the like of which many people have never even dreamed of, places that would convey nothing to so many I have met; but I did not forget to remember those who would give anything to see what I was seeing and would never get the chance.

23rd February

After breakfast Bobby, F. and I mounted the elephant and took a path leading to one of the city gates which looks over the plain to the sacred river Nerbada. We passed a gorge two or three hundred feet deep running down to a misty distance of trees; it opened at the wayside at our feet and we could see, looking down, a flat white roof built against the rock, far below. We dismounted and started down a flight of steps that looked as if it would never end, but at last they stopped in front of a white Hindu temple. It was built in three sides of a square on a high platform with a few steps going up to the entrance. From its open arch a rushing, clear stream of water ran down an inclined stone slab into a pool, polishing it till it had grown like a piece of marble. Here lives a *sadhu*, or holy man, such as I met yesterday, protected by the Maharajah of Dhar, and a little more prepossessing in looks than some of his kind. The water flowed on down far deeper than we could see and he had made on the brink over which it disappeared a little garden of a few marigold plants set in the ubiquitous kerosene oil tin, for these men always plant a flower or two by the shrines they tend, to be used as offerings. I longed to stop and paint the strange place and as the others meant to ride on to the city gate I suggested staying where I was and letting them pick me up on the way home. The lonely spot and the queer company made me think a little but I could not resist it and made Bobby, who speaks better than I do, ask the *sadhu* whether he would object. He was quite willing and I suggested that I should consider myself under his immediate protection, for strange visitors come to places like that one and I thought it likely that the five *sadhus* of yesterday might be about. He agreed and I sat down to my picture.

I worked for two hours. There was a splendid mango tree in full bloom but unluckily I couldn't get it into the drawing. While I was there my host cleaned the temple out with a brush, rang bells, beat drums and prayed aloud. Though I have no doubt he may have been a very zealous man, I fancy a good deal of it was done to impress the stranger and that if he had been alone he would have spent the morning in sleep. Two men came to visit him and I could understand just enough of what they said to gather they had come for advice. They were ordinary village men in *dhotis* and they addressed him with respect; before they went he took out a book and read aloud to them. When the others came back my sketch was done and we asked him if he would like to see it. I handed it up to the plinth and he considered it carefully. 'As it is, so it is painted,' he said. He also said that if we would take off our shoes we might come up into the temple. I had laced boots on but was very willing to do so, so up we went. The place was like a white, open hall with its back to the rock and it was hung with withered garlands; the temple drum, in shape like a hard boiled egg cut, laterally, through the middle, hung at one side. Far back in the arch, hollowed in the stone, was another pool of water where the stream came from the rock behind through a stone lattice, trickling into the pool round the lingam, the symbol of Shiva and of generative power. A bunch of red flowers was placed where the water could pass over it. The *sadhu* continued to read aloud to the two men, who regarded us with curiosity, but he stopped occasionally to talk with us, for he was very polite. We bade him goodbye with thanks and he gave us each a *tulsi* bead from his necklace; this looked like a string of empty cotton reels, but the *tulsi* is a sacred plant so it was not so prosaic as it seemed.

It was pretty hot going home so we stayed in camp till sundown when the elephant had a bath in the tank which he appeared to enjoy; the *mahout* went in with him and encouraged his satisfaction with suitable words. Later we went on to the palace of Rup Mati, the heroine of the love story that hangs over this dead city. From what I can gather, it runs thus: Baz Bahadur, the last King of Malwa, was hunting on the banks of the Nerbada which lies southward, far below in the plain. As he went he heard singing and saw a beautiful Hindu woman sitting in the shade. This was Rup Mati, daughter of a neighbouring *Thakur* of high family. The King fell in love without further ado, after the fashion of people in romances, and went to the *Thakur* to ask for her hand, only to be refused. No child of his should ever marry a Mohammedan, he said. The lover besought Rup Mati to elope with him but she told him that though she liked him she could not do that because in going with him to Mandu she would be leaving the holy river. So he went back, repulsed, to his city on the height and such was his constancy that he began engineering works that were to divert the course of the Nerbada through his country and up to Mandu. Whilst he was watching the work one day the

Spirit of the holy river stood before him in a vision. 'Why do you torment my stream?' it said, and Baz Bahadur told it the truth. It then pointed out a place within the walls where there was a spring that flowed into the river and, being a tributary, held a part of its sacredness. 'Dig deep,' he was told, 'and you will find it.' He obeyed and found that the Spirit's words were right; then he went off to Rup Mati, who demurred no more but left her father's house and fled with him. They were pursued by the *Thakur* but reached Mandu in safety and the lover built a palace on the southern edge of the hill where she might sit looking out to the Nerbada that could be seen like a tiny thread in the far distance. To please her, the building was of Hindu architecture with two pillared pavilions and cupolas. With the exception of one Hindu temple of much later date than the city, Rup Mati's palace is the only one that is not Mohammedan within the walls. The twin pavilions, high in air, are a landmark for miles over the plain. Baz Bahadur's palace is quite near, but at a lower altitude and much of it remains to this day.

The story ends in tragedy for Mandu was invaded by Akbar, Baz Bahadur was taken prisoner and the Delhi general, Adham Khan, entered the city, a conqueror. Having heard of the beautiful Queen of Mandu, he sent to tell her that he was coming and meant to see her. According to one tradition she replied that no man should ever look on her face but Baz Bahadur. The general sent to say that Baz Bahadur was killed and she replied that this time she would receive him; but when he entered her presence it was to find her dead. She had taken poison. It is disappointing to hear that Baz Bahadur became one of Akbar's captains. According to the 'Ain-i-Akbari',[13] the King and Queen of Mandu are buried together and their tomb is in the middle of a tank at Ujjain.

24th February

Dhar. — B. is better and we came back to Dhar this afternoon. We are in the guest house again and he felt well enough to be at dinner. I am dropping with sleep; I should like to write much more about Mandu but shall have to try to remember many things without putting them down. I am looking to this diary to keep me from forgetting things I shall always want to call up in the years to come. At the moment my wits are addled with fatigue and we have thirty miles to drive back tomorrow. It's really far more tiring to joggle along in these ramshackle state carriages than to get across country in the saddle.

25th February

The Maharajah sent his photographer and wished us all to be photographed. This was done and then we were taken out in a most extraordinary old paddle-boat on the lake, a craft that has a kind of deck-house like a bathing machine which takes up a great deal of room and is extremely uncomfortable to be in, either sitting or standing. We could see wonderful temples and *ghats* on the shore. Even after Mandu, Dhar is fascinating and I must try to get back here some day to see so much that there is no time for now. Happily it is nearly always possible to get permission to come. It was awfully hot when we left and it was a long dusty road back, but A. came out and met me with the buggy near Gopalpura.

27th February

Mhow. — Marian came back to stay. The *Sahib* sent us four teal by her which did not come amiss.

28th February

Marian and I took horse and went to Pitumpura village, being anxious to see the temple there that is a landmark in the scrubby country, and hoping to cajole our way in. We started late and got there late. We rode into the village and having marked from the outside of it exactly where the temple stood, plunged into its mazes and finally found ourselves at a square of dead wall. If we rode round it once we rode round it twenty times in the dusk. The light faded quickly, as it does in this country and we could never come on any sign of an entrance, and yet it was there, solid, before us. How do people get in? And why was it like that? The more we thought of it the less we could imagine. We got home pretty late and A. was fuming about, rather anxious. Marian is much bitten by the study of Indian plants.

1st March

Mhow. — A. left for manoeuvres. Marian and I departed for Indore where the *Sahib* and the Nawab received us into Gwalior House that we might go to Deva Garya (or Degararia, as the country people call it) Fair. The Nawab did not come himself but he lent me a white Waler, one of the most delightful horses to ride that I ever had the luck to be mounted on. How different from the piggish Trilby! Perfect paces, perfect mouth; I longed for that horse. As we hand-cantered along the track to Degararia, just under the hill of Rala Mandl, there was a thorn hedge at the side and the *Sahib* said 'Put him over it.' He took it without changing his pace, as if it were a stick in the way and if one's eyes had been shut one might not have known what had happened.

Degararia Temple is at the end of a space enclosed by a high wall and the middle part has a sort of two-storeyed *loggia* whitewashed and tinted a violent blue. We left the horses and went up into it to look down on the pool which was the centre of the enclosure. Men and women were wading in from all sides and the space round the brink was a swarming mass of itinerant *sadhus,* beggars, musicians, country folk, wearing much the same expression as country folk do in England — their lips drawn back from open mouths as they looked at things — and riff-raff of all kinds. A *gular* tree and a few others shaded this spectacle which was, from where we stood, like a coloured Turkey carpet. The Maharajah Holkar was to have been present but he did not come. When we were tired of it we went down into the crowd and there I saw what I have never forgotten. Passing under the wall, I looked up and saw a young *sadhu* sitting cross-legged upon the coping, bronze-coloured, practically naked and with a short, thin beard, so absolutely motionless that it was difficult to realise that he was not a part of the temple decoration. But the arresting thing was his expression. His eyes, very long and half closed, seemed to be focussed on something invisible and yet one could not tell whether he saw anything under his heavy lids. His features were almost Greek and he had a faint, supercilious shade of a smile that never changed. That and the eyes together gave him a look that it is impossible to convey in words; among the, so-called, holy men of this country I have seen a suggestion of it but never any thing to compare with this. The nearest approach to it might perhaps be described as the knowledge of everlasting evil, not violent but deadly. There is a faint reflection of it in the blank stillness of snakes' faces. I am always afraid of seeing more than there is in a country where every second person tells you there is nothing to see and I drew Marian and the *Sahib* to look at him and both saw the extraordinary personal atmosphere of the man and his appalling attraction. I am sure of one thing and that is that, though he never stirred or turned all the time we were there, he was as well, perhaps better, aware of everything round him as anyone else. No doubt he had built up that personality as an asset. There were wandering men playing those stringed instruments which appeal to me as Indian music always does and I listened as long as the others would let me and then we mounted and went on through a string of booths. We rode right into one big tent and sat there on horseback looking at a performance hardly to be called a *nautch*, though it consisted of three girls dressed — all that one could see of them — as *nautch* girls, who were set, each in a sort of recess of looking-glass wall. Nothing was visible but the upper half of them as they postured with head and hands; it was as if they had been cut in two and the top half set upright on a glass counter. One wore a magenta flannel coat covered with tinsel ornaments, which must have been pretty hot. We rode home across country and I parted with regret from Rocket, the white Waler, at Gwalior House.

2nd March

Returned to Mhow late and drove all the way in a curricle.[14] Marian drove the first stage; I second. A very dark night and she nearly put us into the tank at Rao village. If she had, not all the waters of Jordan could have purified us.

6th March

A. came back from manoeuvres.

7th March

Painted *Petrea stapelia* and happily made rather a good business of it. I was most anxious to, for it is the most beautiful of all the flowering shrubs with its fresh green leaves and trusses of lavender-blue blossoms, each of which has a dark purple, star-shaped centre.

11th March

Painted *Asclepias gigantea*. It is an extremely tall, leathery-leaved plant that abounds in the fields and has a juice that blisters horses if they knock up against a broken piece. It has livid mauve blossoms in clusters and I admire it in spite of its sins. Marian left and I went out with A. for pigeon behind the hill of Gopalpura where we met a native soldier home on furlough, a pleasant fellow who told us of duck not far off. I made black and white drawings of some *suttee* stones in the long grass. One of the tracks was so bad that we nearly lost a tyre.

20th March

Indore. — Have come to stay with Dr Caldecott over the weekend.

This afternoon, at Gwalior House I met the wife of the best hated Briton (I should think) in Central India, a terrible, ill-conditioned, dirty fellow, unfortunately in a position in which a decent man could be of infinite use. It is an authentic truth that his own *dhobi* sprang out on him from behind a wall and beat him with a stick. The man, naturally, had to be punished but most people only wished to present him with a piece of plate and a suitable address on vellum. The wife is a harmless, down-trodden soul who cannot pronounce her s-es properly. I was having a peaceful, after-luncheon cigarette when she suddenly asked me if I liked smoking. Consideration for a woman of so many troubles forbade the obvious reply that I should hardly be smoking if I didn't, and I merely said yes. 'But isn't it very — very — *awkward?*' she continued, mysteriously. I said no, and asked why? She drew her chair closer and said with bated breath, 'But don't you have to — SHSHPIT — a great deal?' When I told this to Evelyn Barr her brother said 'if that doesn't show you what ——'s home habits are, nothing will.'

21st March

To the Chatri Bagh, where the cenotaphs of the Holkar family are, surrounded by a battlemented wall on the big *nullah* in the heart of the city. There were lights burning in many of the monuments and as the sun went down the tom-toms and conches and pipes set up that wild music, shrill and measured, that is like none other; the musicians were perched high up in the gallery of a very tall gateway. There was a tree of *Nyctanthes arbor tristis* close by, a thing I never happened to have seen before and the scent pervaded the place. Its white flowers are rather like jasmine but with orange tubes inside the blossom. Painted *Dendrobium pierardi* in the Residency orchid house.

24th March

Mhow. — I had rather a surprise this evening as I was painting the red *Bombax malabaricum* when General Nicolson was ushered in.[15] He seldom goes anywhere and is oftenest seen driving with his wife in the dusk. She is a tiny, fair, very strange woman, vilely and impossibly clothed in a short skirt like a schoolgirl and a little round cape; her hair hangs down just touching her shoulders and is cut square on her forehead. I always find her rather interesting, though of course everyone mocks at her and I can't help doing it myself sometimes at the really absurd figure she makes. The General entered and announced plainly that he had heard I like books and as hardly anybody in the place did, or ever spoke of them, he had come to see if it was true. I was a little taken aback and rather pleased. We set to and talked steadily for an hour and I must say I enjoyed it and liked him. He is a tall fine-looking old man, I should think quite thirty years older than his wife and not unlike a hawk to look at. He wears most awful clothes made in the most extraordinary way.

27th March
Sister Lloyd, of the Indian Nursing Service, dined with us. A nice woman and a good whip. In fact she is the only woman in the place who knows how to handle reins from a box.

As usual, the hot weather is difficult, but Violet and Arthur enjoy another visit to Dhar.

4th April
Talked with an old countryman today who gave me the native name of what is here called the 'Drumstick tree' and thanks to him I have found it to be *Moringa pterygosperma*.

5th April
Painted *Argemone mexicana* and nearly put out my eyes and broke my back doing the spikes and prickles of the complicated foliage. It is very hot. I met the civil engineer's wife being carried to hospital.

10th April
A. and I set out for Dhar before the heat got too bad for we have had permission to stay for a couple of days in the guest house. The Maharajah lent us a carriage and we had the most awful jibber in the traces on the first *dâk*; the harness broke in many places, starting him, but we got there by 11.30. An official called bringing the Maharajah's compliments. We went about looking at the things of interest and into the fortress but it was too hot to take in much and one's brain was tired.

11th April
Dhar. — Heat very great here. Instead of trying to go out we lay on a bed all the morning, half dead, and read *On the Face of the Waters*, a book by Mrs Steel,[16] which we have heard a lot of. It

is enormously interesting. At twelve we got up and breakfasted and I painted *Taberneamontana coronaria,* and a weary, burning business it was. In the very late afternoon we went to the temple of Kalka Devi, high on a conical hill above the big lake; it stood straight up against the sky into the hot sunset and has the largest and most beautiful frangipani tree growing out of its walls in the crevice of a platform in mid air. I tried to paint the hill and temple against the sky but made a bad business of it. Even at sunset, the heat dried the colour on the paper between one brush-stroke and the next. Back to the guest house to dinner, and it was a good one too. It is a most sympathetic little place with a curious attraction, being both comfortable and, in a way, god-forsaken, and behind it there is a low, stifling, jasmine-filled pergola filled with the sound of trickling water when, beyond it, the unsuspected well is working.

12th April
Back to Mhow when the heat gave a little promise of abating. Before we left we were photographed, by order of His Highness, in the back verandah, by a most ridiculous-looking fat Hindu whom he had sent for the purpose, for he is interested in collecting the portraits of all his English guests. Such a pair of guys we looked too, as we sat for it, half melted. An easy journey through the dusk till we got to Akolia, where the last *dâk* began; there, our old friend, the jibber, came on again. By this time it was moonlight, very brilliant; the hard, hot moonlight in which you can see colour. The arid grass seemed to stretch for miles, for it is very open country at Akolia. First that horse jibbed then flung himself about like a wild beast and plunged off. Crack! went some of the harness and we found ourself flying sideways off the road and over the rough grass, or what remains of it at this time of year, to the fields. We bumped annd swerved and heeled this way and that and there seemed nothing but the horizon that would stop our rush and I thought my last hour was come, but the coachman stuck to it like a man and at last pulled the horses up and induced them to get back to the road. I wonder the ramshackle old landau held together.

13th April
Heat pretty bad. Slept outside.

14th April
Awfully hot night; it has begun with a vengeance.

15th April
Hot, hot, hot. Sleep difficult.

16th April
Did hospital.

18th April
Easter Sunday. Church. Lay up most of the day, clothes being a burden.

19th April
A little cooler. Two funerals.

20th April
Another funeral early. Dust, storm and wind. A trifle cooler in consequence.

21st April
Marian left for good and sails in a few days.

24th April
Summoned up energy to go to Indore for the weekend. It was rash, as Indore is hotter than Mhow. Canoed on what remains of the river late in the evening.

25th April
Painted *Alpinia nutans*. Went to the Chatri Bagh, the *Sahib* driving tandem through the *bazaar,* a feat which often brought my heart into my mouth, for I was sitting by him and he drives very fast. In the silver *bazaar* a tightrope walker was performing on a cord stretched from house to house across the street. The *Bankwallah* drove me out to see that white temple I have looked at with such curiosity ever since I first saw it from the train between Mhow and Indore. It sticks up out of a high clump of trees near Rao and has a gilded ball on the top. Two lovely *Bauhinia* trees stand by it, pale rose, pink, like azaleas when in flower. Dined at Dr Caldecott's.

26th April
Up at 5.15 to avoid the heat and returned to Mhow. Hot night and little sleep.

29th April
Went to see F.B. off to England. Ourselves, General Nicolson and some others. Painted *Ruellia hirta*.

2nd May
Drove out in what is called by courtesy the 'cool of the evening'.

3rd May
Very hot. No sleep.

4th May
Headache and every other ache under heaven.

5th May
Cooler night.

6th May
Very hot. Painted *Cassia fistula* and very badly. I paint almost in a state of nature. Cotton dressing gown and nothing else.

7th May
A better night and ever so much better. About four weeks more of this will see it out, I hope.

9th May
Up at 5.30 to dodge the heat. Rode to the funny little shrine I found a few days ago. I took out my paintbox but could not get at the place in a good light and by the time I got at a possible aspect of it, it was too late and stoking up so much that I had to leave off. Annoyed but comforted by making out *Clerodendron phlomoides*: I wonder what the identification of a plant you don't know would not solace? Saw a large bush of *Jasminium arborescens* and got home to find the Nawab and Jimmy in the verandah being entertained by Harry. They are so nice to him.

10th May
Painted *Jasminium arborescens* and dined with the Nicolsons. The General has fever. I sat with him a little.

12th May
Everyone seems going off to England. Two from the regiment today. I

am very glad, heat and all, that I am not going. I haven't seen enough of this country yet.

13th May
Coolish morning and went to see the departure off. Rode to the level crossing and saw the last of them as they passed. I rode in the late evening to see a strange deserted little shrine I've marked down to paint near the Neemuch road, it is swallowed in *karunda* bushes; the sort of place one discovers by accident. There is an effigy there of a small stone cobra sitting up on his tail.

14th May
Painted that horrid thing, the prickly pear. It is not really indigenous, and the man who imported it incurred a great responsibility.

15th May
To Indore, Saturday to Monday, to the Residency. They really are the kindest people in the world, the Barrs. We are more than lucky to have such friends.

16th May
Evelyn and I rode very early and last night slept on the roof, the house being unendurable. To cool ourselves we sat up in our night things under the flagstaff in a bright moonlight with the hill of Rala Mundl and the surrounding country lying in sharp black and white and the voices of the *bazaar,* that are never quiet, especially in hot weather nights, rising from the city. In the middle of the night the wind rose all in a moment and blew a hurricane and we had a fight to keep our beds and bedclothes from disappearing into space. But it settled down and we got some sleep before morning. The Sikh orderly, Mana Singh, posed for me and I got a drawing of him, a fine figure of a man on his cow-hocked old charger. I rode the elephantine mare Diana when it got cooler. She is cruelly misnamed, but Col. Barr, who bought her, called her Diana of the Crosthwaites[17] because he got her from a man of that name.

17th May
Came back to Mhow, after finishing Mana Singh.

21st May
Out riding in the cool of the morning to Shaida village, having seen

Adansonia digitata in blossom. One would never guess, from the grotesque ungainliness of the tree, that it could produce such a lovely flower. It is said to be an importation from Africa and it is not much seen in any other part of India but in Malwa. The first sight of it makes one laugh for it looks as if it had got elephantiasis, the stem being swollen to a huge girth and the branches comparatively slender. Most of the year it stands naked in its shameless ugliness and when the leaves have dropped and the fruit ripened it has nothing on it but a moderate amount of things that look like elongated gong-sticks or the clubs of savages. The leaves when they appear are fresh, light green and the flowers a revelation, almost as large as water lilies and of the same waxen cream-white as magnolias. They have a thick white protuberance in the centre which bears a golden brown bottlebrush of stamens. I'd heard of this flower and had been waiting for it and now here it was. Rode home as hard as I could, the two dogs panting behind, and carried it to the coolest place I could find in the house to paint it before it should turn brown, as so many blossoms of full habit do. But handsome is as handsome does and it began to stink in an unbelievable way; I shut the door and worked away with all my might, not waiting to change my dusty clothes and hoping for speedy release from its neighbourhood. A. burst in in the middle, horrified by the odour that met him as he dismounted outside, and loaded me with reproaches for having brought it in; I was almost afraid he would lay violent hands on the *Adansonia* but I got rid of him, finished the drawing and cast it on the muck heap. It really was beyond a joke, but I have got its portrait and all is well. . . .

23rd May
To Indore for the Queen's birthday parade at the Residency tomorrow.

24th May
The heat is very bad and I had to paint *Quisqualis indicus* in one of the cellar-like lower rooms of the Residency. There was a dance, which was out of doors but the heat was such that I left it and made for bed on the roof before it was a quarter over. Evelyn of course could not get away and came up, half dead, after the guests had gone.

26th May
Back to Mhow. Very Hot.

28th May

Col. L. arrived to see my drawings. That dog of his is a character, a rough, short-legged mongrel of the Dandie Dinmont persuasion.[18] He came uninvited to live with his present master, who did not care for him and turned him out several times. But it was no use. They quarrelled often but the dog did not mind. One day he thought to terrify him so he tied a string to a tiger-skin that had a stuffed head and drew it to meet him as he came in one evening in the dusk. The dog fled, horrified, but returned again. He is awfully disobedient but when Col. L. threatens him or cracks his whip, he only thinks he is mad. I have never seen a pair like them, but I believe they like each other, really. Some money has been stolen and we have discovered that A.'s dressing boy, Duggaroo, is the culprit, so, he is gone and another one is coming.

31st May

A really cool morning and I rode towards the Towers of Silence.[19] Trilby shied as we passed the fort, apparently for no reason, as I was coming home; I was sitting loosely and half turned round when she whipped across the road like a rabbit. Out of the saddle I went and hung over the off side like a wet towel but scrambled back assisted by the knowledge that, if I fell, she'd kick my brains out. Looked round to see if anyone was near and saw Mr Hill of the Royal Fusiliers and wondered sneakingly, if he'd tell anyone.

4th June

There is a new horse come who is by way of being mine, a young Waler mare; dark brown and with her head set on badly; she is just out of riding school and is a tractable creature, rather obstinate, but she'll be a pleasant change from the pony and at any rate we'll get on well, I hope, and not hate each other as Trilby and I do. We are rather like Col. L. and his dog but our hatred is more real. I believe the mare likes me and it is a relief to have a horse that is pleasant in the stall. I went out at five this morning hoping it would be cool enough to paint but it was no use and I nearly rode into a huge hole left by a removed telegraph post near Gopalpura hill. The mare just missed putting her foot in. We were going along a good pace and it would have been all up with us both if she had done it. We've christened her Trefoil, as both the other horses' names begin with a T.

8th June

Out at 5 a.m. Heat greater than ever. I came home by Ganghelkheri village and riding cheerfully out of the mango *tope* the mare swerved aside from an obstacle, which was a dead man wound up tight in a sheet. I suppose his people put him near the edge of the *tope* till they could take him to the burning *ghat*.

9th June

An early ride along by Tom the Barber's *jawari*-fields. He is a rich man and has a certain amount of property about the place. Heard, when I came home, that part of the world is out of bounds for the troops. Cholera or more probably smallpox, I suppose. It's a bad time of year and many people are ill in various ways.

10th June

Tremendous rain. The *Chota Barsat*, I do hope.

11th June

A bad night of heat but woke at 5.30 to find a blazing golden sunrise and the row of young *goldmohur* trees outside, emerald green. I never saw such colour. Oh, the freshness of that dripping green, after the night! A shower had come. Got up and rode to Harsola where the hedges are full of green *Hoya viridiflora*, which I want to paint. Its long winding shoots were so tough that I was almost dragged out of my saddle in pulling a spray out, for the mare mistrusted it and insisted on backing. I kicked her furiously and hung on but the thing was like an india rubber rope and I could get no purchase on it. But a piece broke at last, just as a bullock cart was coming along to get in my way, and I had time to whip round with my treasure and make for home before the sun should wilt the blossom. When I got there it had closed up and was hanging in a miserable rag but as a last resource I threw it into a *chatti* of water in the bathroom and put on the lid, and when I came back after breakfast and lifted the thing off, there the *Hoya* lay, perfectly fresh and beautiful, the exquisite clusters of sea-green blossom lying spread on the water. Spent the rest of the morning on its portrait.

12th June

Went to Indore, this time to Pat Bannerman's, and the *Bankwallah* drove me out to the Ranibagh near Rao. That temple there with its gilt top is very quaint (to use a dreadful word) and I mean to paint it if the Almighty spares me long enough but it is so ornate that I feel it will probably take me the rest of our foreign service to finish; it has the incongruity of being both rather modern and absolutely deserted and the result is a curious atmosphere. The place was once a country house for the ladies of the palace. We went home late to Mhow. The sky is clouding up for the monsoon. Let us pray it comes quickly.

17th June
Clouds gathered at evening and hung all night. The monsoon must be close on us.

19th June
Tremendous wind. Recommenced *The Sheepstealers*[20] which I haven't touched since I left England. I have a faint hope it may be worth while.

20th June
MONSOON!! Wet day and pouring night. The Queen's Diamond Jubilee. Early commemoration service.

21st June
It's a pouring day and I feel a terrible worm.

22nd June
A. had to go alone to help at the Diamond Jubilee tea for the women and children of the regiment, as I wasn't up to it.

23rd June
Am better. Sent one of my best black and whites to my mother. In bed most of the day.

24th June
Wrote more *Sheepstealers* and went out in the evening. The world is getting most wonderfully green and it is like new life to see it. B. to dinner and a long talk about cavalry.

25th June
Sheepstealers.

26th June
To Harsola, for *Asclepias suberosa*.

27th June
Painting *Asclepias*. Col. L.—— came in today. He looked at the cracks in our walls and ceiling, which are enormous, and advised us to report them to the engineers.

29th June
To Indore. Went with Dr Caldecott and Evelyn to that queer place, the Pilia Kall, where the *Mahunt*, or Hindu priest of Indore, lives, also the Maharajah's wrestlers. Found the place full of *sadhus*, one of whom, naked and smeared with ash, his long hair hanging over his shoulders, addressed Dr Caldecott in perfect English. These things are extraordinary.

30th June
Got one of Holkar's cavalrymen to pose for me, mounted. The *Sahib* came to dinner. Very hot and no rain and Col. Barr is ill. I hear we shall have to turn out of our house as the engineers say it is not safe. Certainly I have looked up at the crack in the roof while at dinner and seen the stars twinkling merrily through it, so I daresay they are right and we'd better be off.

1st July
The cavalryman did not turn up. Rode.

2nd July
Cavalryman.

3rd July
Finished him.

4th July
Went again with the *Bankwallah* to the Ranibagh and began a fair-sized drawing of the temple there, which I shall have to finish as occasion serves. Transferred ourselves to Pat Bannerman's. The *Sahib* to dinner.

5th July
In the cool of the day we went again to the Pilia Kall, where Pat

had business with the *Mahunt*. The *Mahunt* was absent and we left the carriage and walked. The Pilia Kall is a forest of temples on both sides of a steep, narrow *nullah* and the road from Indore runs down to the bridge spanning this and rises sharply from its further side. The temples are set thick, huddled together on the banks with the dirty water in chains of stagnant pools below them. The sky was beginning to colour for sunset as we walked across the bridge; Pat meant to enquire further for the *Mahunt*, for he was not quite sure if he was really not there. On the top of the hill about a hundred yards in front we saw a solitary stone cenotaph, or *chatri*, close to the road with the usual four pillars supporting the dome. Steps ran up to its high plinth; it stood out very sharp against the sky and I was surprised to see that there was a sitting figure under the canopy against the light. There never are large images in these *chatris*, which contain generally only Nandia, the holy bull,[21] and the usual phallic emblems, so I was rather interested. We went up towards it and as we drew nearer the figure slowly reared itself up and came down the steps. It is startling enough to see what you have taken for stone begin to move but, added to that, its appearance might have raised anyone's hair. It was a gigantic man, naked but for a loin cloth, who must have been nearer seven than six foot high. His hair and eyebrows were shaved close and his impassive face had an expression that was simply appalling — narrow eyes, seemingly lidless, and a half smile dreadful to look at. He came along like some malignant sleepwalker, then he turned and disappeared among the buildings. After a short time of wandering about and hearing nothing of the *mahunt* we went along the bank among the maze of temples and soon found ourselves in an open passage so very narrow that two could not comfortably walk abreast in it, a cramped place between high walls with all these buildings huddled round amid dirt and squalor. Some way down it my heart stood still, for the figure we had seen was coming to meet us and his bulk and stature choked the narrow way. He still had that malignant, half-conscious, narrow-eyed smile; Pat was in front, I next, then Evelyn and A. I was taken with cold panic and wondered what the others behind me thought of it, for the moment was so dreadful to me that I almost expected to see Pat turn back. But I told myself I was a fool and determined that as long as he went forward I would go too. We approached the man, met him and passed him. The alley was so narrow that we were almost pushed against each other and could only just get by. But it almost unnerved me and I could not help remembering that we were only four and that the place, of which none of us knew the geography, was a nest of *sadhus* on the outskirts of Indore, in which city some people say one should never go on foot. But I suppose all was well, for the *Raj* is great and it was the supernatural touch and the look of the man that was too much for me. I was thankful when we got back to the road. He was one of Holkar's wrestlers, who live in the Pilia Kall as well as the priests, but that did not explain what he was doing under the dome of the *chatri* and possibly he was a sort of *sadhu* as well as a wrestler. Any predominant characteristic seems to suggest an occult sanctity to this intensely self-conscious race. Perhaps the man sat there like an image for pure effect. Pat could not tell but thought it possible. I asked A. when we got home what he thought of it. Being apt to be affected by these half-seen things I wanted another opinion, wondering how far my imagination had taken me. I asked him if, by chance, he had felt afraid. He said 'not exactly afraid, but that man was one of the most awful things I have ever seen'. So I felt less guilty of folly. I said little to the other two; Pat, with all his official *Raj* behind him, may go where he pleases safely, I suppose, and its *aegis* covers all. But for no bribe would I go alone through Pilia Kall and that is saying something, for 'I am', as the Hindu says in excuse for every conceivable thing, 'but a poor man'.

9th July
Painted one of Holkar's *carabiniers*, who stood for me. Back to Mhow. Harry, who has been with us, sat up in the carriage as we went to the station like a grown up person, *salaaming* to everybody as we left.

10th July
Rode out in the afternoon to look for a house. Chowri, the *syce*, was drunk.

11th July
Rode towards Indore and were caught in a heavy rainstorm and home drenched; A.'s boots contained over a half tumblerful of water and had to be emptied out like jugs. The country is looking beautiful.

14th July
Much cooler. Worked hard at *The Sheepstealers*. Heard of a possible

house and went over it; a large, rambling place, two houses in one connected by a passage that slopes downhill. It is the very last bungalow on the Indore side of Mhow and has been a native infantry mess. There is a huge, overgrown compound, a large fine well under a *peepul* tree and a verandah that has been a billiard room and is consequently large enough for any purpose — or even five or six purposes — to which we might want to put it. I rather like the idea of the house because of its wild compound and general oddity, though I suppose these are unusual reasons for taking it. Anyhow there doesn't seem to be any other one available, so that ought to settle the point.

31st July
A pouring day which cleared late. Rode Indore way and came upon Sergt. Major Pearce catching butterflies on a *Lantana* bush.

> *August brings disease and many deaths among the British locally.*
> *The Jacobs move to a new house.*

1st August
Painted *Asclepias volubilis* which I got yesterday. Corpl. Vyner died of enteric.

2nd August
Vyner and a Royal Fusilier buried this evening. I have heard enough of the Dead March lately, for they always strike up as they pass this house, the cemetery being not far off.

5th August
To Gopalpura Hill where I roamed about the *nullah* and found a good many plants. Captain Burton of the Royal Fusiliers is dead. Enteric, as usual.

6th August
Rained all day. Painted the *asclepias* I got yesterday. Captain Burton was buried.

7th August
Dined at the Nicolsons' to meet a man who is an authority on orchids and an old liar; he told me a hamadryad[22] had once run over his toe.

12th August
Cricket match between Mhow and the Indore Mohammedans. Was nearly felled to the earth by one of them who wore orange breeches and pursued a ball with such impetus that he could not stop at the boundary. A. made a good score.

15th August
Rode to Jamli with A. and got a good many plants, among them, *Martynia diandria,* which the natives call '*vinchu*', or scorpion, because of the horny, hard seed vessels, armed with the most terrible hooked points. They are so tough that a hammer would scarcely break them. It has large, coarse, bright green leaves and a lovely rose-coloured flower not unlike a *gloxinia,* which many people don't know is there. If you turn over the foliage you see them; not otherwise. I got some *datura* and the mooncreeper in a bit of jungly ground, also various *momordicas.*

18th August
Went over to the new house. We move in on Friday. Two funerals today; thank heaven I shall not see and hear them in the new place. This season of the year is dreadful in that way.

20th August
Gut into the new house. We started work at eight o'clock. A. got a day's leave and went to the arrival end while I stayed at the departure end. We got in by quarter past seven at night, dead beat, having worked all day.

21st August
Very busy. It rained profusely and I was very worn out by bed time. The servants have worked splendidly.

26th August
Painted the pink *mimosa* that I find grows wild in the tremendous jungle of stuff in this compound which is full of flowers that Gaya Din won't approve of. It's a wilderness of small trees and pink and white balsams, and peacocks come into it from the country. Wild yellow cucumbers twine about with star-shaped blossoms; I suppose they have no business there, but that's a detail. We went out after pigeon and quail and were very successful round Batkheri tank. Got some *Jasminum auriculatum.* A nice day.

27th August
Poured. Did the women's hospital. Sergt. Cordray is very bad with enteric.

29th August
Rained most of the day. I see we've got *Martynia diandria* in this compound too. Cordray is terribly ill, I hear.

31st August
To Indore with Mrs Nicolson to the Nawab's. The *Sahib* has fever. After dinner she and I went to a party at Kyber, the native banker's house in the *bazaar*, for today is the feast of Ganesh,[23] the elephant god, protector of business and prosperity; his house was illuminated outside and in and had a glittering grotto at the end of the room where he received his guests. In the back of the grotto was a very large mural representation of Ganesh enthroned. Everything was glass, tinsel, silver and gold paper and red and blue colours, tawdry in the extreme, but in the brilliant light, quite pretty. We sat in rows on chairs and were presented with *betel*, burnt sugar and cardamom served on green and pink leaves and after this Mrs Nicolson and I went to see the ladies of the house. We and they sat in awful solemnity opposite each other and they were too shy to speak one single word, though we tried to make ourselves agreeable through the husband of one of them, and Mrs Nicolson speaks Urdu perfectly. One lady had a nose-ring so much loaded with pearls that it almost hid the lower half of her face and the effect was hideous; besides which, she was enormously fat but her eyes were fine. I can only hope that the ladies were gratified by our attempted politenesses, but there was no sign of it. The only event was that we were taken through their living rooms which were clean, but very hot, low and stuffy and seemed filled with divans and beds through which one could hardly thread one's way. Then we went behind the *purdah* dividing their part of the house from the place in which we had been received and I was surprised to find myself behind the image of Ganesh, which I had looked at from the other side without noticing that it was perforated. Ganesh himself was the *purdah* and I was now peering at the festivities from the inner side.

1st September
My birthday and champagne for dinner in consequence; an awful extravagance.

The Lal Bag – Mandu (date unknown): a temple in the ancient deserted capital of Malwa:
'it all seems a fit setting for some fantastic Eastern drama.' *See Diary 21 Feb 1897*

Papaver Somniferum: The Opium poppy.

The door of the Hindu Temple at the Ranibagh (1898): 'Shiva sits surrounded by Parbati, his spouse, Ganesh the elephant-headed and others. Every available bit of space is smothered in patterns and floral arabesques.' *See Diary 30 Jan 1898*

A Sadhu (1896): '. . . in comes the *sadhu*, sits down under a tree and begins, like a witch, to make a fire on the ground.' *See letter 11 Dec 1896*

A Mucham (Sept 1897): 'I painted a bird-scarer's hut on tall legs in a field. It was wreathed around with yellow cucumber flower.'

'A cross-legged Buddha looking fixedly out over the country' at Sanchi. *See Diary 25 Sept 1898*

Plumeraria Acuminata

Alpinia Nutans

Oxalis Martiana

Canna Warascsawizi: or 'Indian Shot'.

Hibiscus Rosa-Sinensis: 'Often called "Shoe Flower".'

4th September
Painted *Trichosanthes lobata* and went to Long John's in the *bazaar* to see a Chinese curtain made of brown satin the exact colour of a liver-chestnut horse. The design was a bronze and gold dragon which sprawled all over it, flying downward through a net filled with red roses. The border deep, all bronze and gold. We longed for it most cruelly but had to resist it though it was very cheap at the money he was asking. On to the station to see some horses boxed.

6th September
Poor Cordray died at four this morning, quite young and leaving a young wife. He will be missed at all the tournaments and mounted events. Enteric is the scourge of this country and there's no doubt that Mhow is a fevery place and the rains, on the top of the hot weather when everyone is feeling cheap, do not mend matters. Went for a walk with A. both rather downhearted thinking of the poor fellow. Things are not very cheerful in the hospital but the unhealthy season ought to be over soon now. Mrs Thompson, who has been very bad in the women's hospital, is getting well.

7th September
Began painting the 'elephant creeper'. One can now sit in the passage where I paint and have one's early tea by the open door above some steps into the compound, for it is cool and delicious. It's pleasant there for the bungalow runs so much downhill that, in the back part of it, you are looking down on all the vegetation. Great rain today.

16th September
To Akolia to paint the Hanuman that stands by the well. A. shot.

18th September
To Indore to the Nawab's.

19th September
Rode the white Waler, Rocket. The going was bad and Rocket fresh. Afterwards we set off for the ford of the Sipra river that is the boundary between Indore and the small native state of Dewas. It is an interesting place, the ford, for you see every kind of person and vehicle going across and the river is shallow there with white Jain temples on the further shore. A. and the *Bankwallah* shot and I sat painting with the *Sahib* beside me for he was too weak from

fever to do anything else. He looks very bad. A Mr Ernest Barnes, just come out as second assistant at the Residency, called at Gwalior House;[24] his wife is half Italian and is arriving soon. He seemed a pleasant man and evidently very well-read. He has asked us all to dinner tomorrow.

20th September
Dined at Mr Barnes' and enjoyed it. He has made his little house very nice for his wife and seems anxious to acquire some congenial company for her; and he has some desirable books, which he is inclined to use as bait. I swallowed it. A man out here with books has to be reckoned with.

27th September
Evelyn Barr arrived to stay. She is a great satisfaction to me for she likes knocking about the country. She brought that beastly, stumbling arab of hers, Gabriel. It's the only horse she owns, herself.

29th September
Rode early and on the border of a *jawari* field Trilby almost put her foot on a cobra lying up on the track. I did not see it but E., riding behind, did. There was another snake on our way, a small, rather thick one, chocolate colour with greyish turquoise spots. E. did not see that one, and when I described it, did not know what it could be.

30th September
E. and I went out to Jamli in the cart and A. rode. I painted a bird-scarer's hut on tall legs in a field. It was wreathed round with yellow cucumber flower. Found a good specimen of *Lettsomia setosa* to paint.

3rd October
We all three rode in the afternoon to Ti village, beyond Batkheri. We started home late and were a long way out in the high grass when dusk fell and had a tremendous business to reach the road, feeling our way cautiously among *nullahs* and marshes.

5th October
Went over to Indore for the Dusera procession, staying at Pat Bannerman's.

7th October

Painted *Bauhinia purpurea*, also a Ganges-water seller who is going about. I went to the city today with Pat Bannerman to see the old Blue Palace, that extraordinary edifice of strange colours that is in the heart of the town. The *Gadi*, or throne of the dynasty, is there in a bare upper room and every evening the ghost of a *nautch* is gone through before it; to look at, it is not much more than an old shabby mattress on a wooden frame. A smooth, quiet young man, a palace official, took us to see it and in the dusk a dancing girl came in, not at all gorgeous, slim, sly and olive-coloured, who went through some evolutions and twirled with uplifted hands in front of it. In a few minutes she stopped and stood silent before the official. Pat asked him in English if she was a professional dancing-girl and the young man explained in the same tongue that there were several in the palace who danced before the *Gadi*. 'Zey combine it wiz *ze ozzer profession*,' said he.

8th October

Back to Mhow for a night and Pat came with us for there was a dance at the club. A. would not go and retired to bed and Pat and I returned at two and found a nice little spread that he had set out for us.

9th October

We all three went back to Indore, A. and I for three days at the Residency. Mr Barnes brought his wife to call; she is very fascinating and talks perfect English with a slight, very pretty accent. That evening Evelyn and I got into a couple of canoes and went up the river as far as we could and then thrust our way up a narrow stream that joins it; there was barely room for the canoes and at last we were pulling ourselves along by grasping the long grass at either side. We got far out of the Residency borders and sneaked home after dark, dripping and dirty. A great rush to get clean for dinner.

11th October

E. and I got a *tonga* and departed at cockcrow to the Ranibagh to get on with my drawing. After working as long as I could for the sun we wandered out of the place through open spaces and a mango grove into a field of standing grain. In the middle of this we came on a large, two-storeyed building, quite empty, the doors wide, the windows broken and all open to the elements; its deserted look was increased by its gaudy colouring and walls with stains that ran one into the other. This was evidently the former pleasure house of the royal ladies and their suites. The corn was breast high and we pushed through it and went in. We wondered whether anyone ever came to reap this weed-bound harvest or how long it was since anybody had entered the gaping doorways. We went up to the top storey and saw the glass-fronted cupboards full of nothing that was the only furniture left. The grainstalks pressed up close to the verandah and I found a new *convolvulus* — new to me, that is — twining round them; *Convolvulus spoehorocephalus*, almost as ugly as its name, its tiny, mean-looking flowers strangling the stems. Took some home to paint. That house was creepy in spite of all the sunshine, and like everything else in this country, suggestive of God knows what. I never can make out what it is. Sacrifice, fate, perhaps death itself; something that is always close, everywhere. I suppose it is death, of which there is so much. But there is an exhilaration in it, I don't know why.

18th October
Painted the *convolvulus* and went back to Mhow. Evelyn came with us for the night.

LETTER TO C.K.E.

In late 1897 Violet's diary entries are punctuated by several letters to her mother.

Mhow.
19 Oct. (1897)

. . . A thing happened the other day so out of the commonly funny that I must tell you of it though I despair of doing it any kind of justice. I expect I told you that there are two small walled courtyards that divide one side of this house from the other. The storeroom is in one of them and I go to it in the morning to give out the day's stores to Karoo, the cook. After doing this, as I went back to my own haunts and he to his kitchen, I saw a *borah* hanging about who had come on some errand of buying disused tins. The minute I reached my room I missed my handkerchief which had been in my hand and went back to look for it knowing it must have been dropped in the courtyard. The *borah* was gone and I called Karoo back to ask him if he had seen it, and, as he hadn't, I felt sure the

bald-headed old vulture of a *borah* had got it. So I told Yessoo the
butler and the matter went out of my mind. Today as Evelyn, A. and
I sat at luncheon Yessoo appeared and, standing in the middle of the
room like a wooden man, one hand laid along his *cummerbund* in
the traditional butler attitude, with immovable face and eyes fixed
on space above our heads, spoke as follows, with neither stops nor
commas: 'I - was - go - to - the - borah's - house - and - I - was - say - to
- the - borah - what - for - you - do - this - thing - and - he - was - say - to
- me - I - no - do - this - thing - and - I - was - say - to - him - this - is - lie
- and - he - was - say - this - no - lie - and - I - was - give - him - one - eeslap
- and - I - tell - to - him - give - me - that - handkerchief - and - he - was - say
- I - no - got - that - handkerchief - then - I was - give - him -two - eeslaps
- and - he - was - say - this - not - true - then - he - was - cry - and - pray - me
- awfully - and - I - was - take - him - by - the - head - and - give - him - two
- more - eeslaps - then - he - was - give - me - the - handkerchief' — and,
as he spoke, Yessoo suddenly produced it like a conjurer and held
up the dreadful thing covered with stains of *betel* juice and I had
just enough self-control to tell him to take it away and burn it before
we collapsed in paroxysms of laughter that we thought would never
stop. It is a curious thing that no uneducated native can pronounce
a consonant without putting a double e first. . . .

(Diary)

21st October
Hospital. I fear Corpl. Thornton's wife is dying.

22nd October
Mrs T. dead.

26th October
Went to enquire for someone who is down with fever and as I
approached her compound saw the servants much excited. They
said a huge snake had just gone into a culvert near the house. As
I had to cross it to get up to the floor I was not quite pleased. The
butler fetched a bamboo about six feet long with a knife fixed at the
top which some wiseacre had contrived as a weapon against these
reptiles, a most unhandy thing and about as easy to wield as a barge
pole. He advanced on the culvert and, standing as far from it as he
could, held the pole upright in the air with both hands raised above
his head, waiting with glaring eyes of terror, for some development.

It was comic. Suddenly a great loop of snake as thick as my arm, surged up from the culvert and he struck. But I stopped laughing and looked the other way, for he made a good shot, wonderful to relate, and the blood — I had never realised how much blood, and how red, a snake can have — went up like a fountain. I got away for it was more than I could stand. It was the biggest snake I ever saw. I think it was what is called a *dhaman* and not poisonous; it is the smaller ones, mostly, that are that, but to the Mohammedan Indian, and to me too, they are all devils together and too horrible for one's common sense to survive the sight of them. I heard afterwards that this one measured over seven feet.

27th October
Third anniversary of our wedding day and the first we have spent together. The first one I was at sea and the second A. was on manoeuvres. To celebrate it we dined in the verandah and had champagne, but having been out in the sun prowling about Jamli and walking a lot, we fell asleep in our chairs when we had finished and woke in the middle of the night, terrified, for we couldn't think where we were.

28th October
Hospital and married quarters. No one dying, mercifully.

LETTER TO C. K. E.

17 Nov. 1897
. . . Holkar has been giving a great ball at his modern palace of Barwai some way down the Nerbada river. A. could not go as he is laid up with a bad foot; he has run a thorn two inches long into his tendon Achilles and cannot get on a boot; uniform being *de rigueur*, he had to stay at home. Evelyn Barr and I were by way of helping in the preparations and we trained down to Barwai on the morning of the affair and were put up in the palace. It is on the Nerbada bank and hangs over it as Heidelberg hangs over the Neckar, a long edifice, painted salmon pink, crowning the height and more than a third of a mile long; a terrace runs below it and the river below that. The palace consists of five high blocks of buildings threaded together by a chain of lower ones and the whole effect is that of a railway train with a guard's van put in between every half dozen carriages. It is frightfully and supernaturally ugly. In the first big building was the

Maharajah and his suite, in the second, the English men guests, in the third myself, Evelyn and Mrs Barnes. We looked out on the river and the terrace, decorated with palms and bamboos most hideously, and on the crowd of tents. The *coup d'oeil* was not attractive but it was helped out by some pink, red and gold draperies; we lunched and rested and then turned up our sleeves and fell to. We did all the seating of the guests with due regard to ceremony and as the table was laid for two hundred and twenty it was hard work; we decorated it with yellow silk and white flowers. The main body of the guests arrived in a special train at five and there was a reception at that hour to which we didn't go because we were wallowing in baths and lying stretched on our beds. At dusk the whole of the palace sprang into light and the palms and bamboos were hung with lamps of every colour and we began to think better of the spectacle. Certainly from our balcony it looked well. At seven we were dressed and went down to the feast. A dull old devil should have been my fate but providence prevented him from coming and the good *Bankwallah* sat down in his place. The dinner was not good, in fact it was poisonously bad, but I can't say that mattered much to me, as I'd expected it. When it was over the Maharajah came in huddled in a wadded brown silk coat and looking quite enormous. He made a long speech. Indian potentates are sometimes dangerous speakers and I could see Pat Bannerman's slightly anxious eye on him. However it all went right and he was biblical in his expressions. He wound up 'It has been r-r-reproached to me zat I haf not love London so much and have gone so much to Pa-r-ris' (he is very fond of going to Paris and generally manages to bring that fact in) 'but to zat I say zees. It is not so. A man does not forsake his revered grandmozzer for a beautiful actress!' I should have said it was exactly what a man does do, but no matter; everyone roared and was delighted, the Maharajah most of all; I know the speech was full of irony, of which he is a master. It is told of one of his predecessors, the late Maharajah Tukerji Rao, that at the beginning of a banquet he finished his speech with 'And I hop ze ladies will fill bellees—'. He was interrupted by some English official with 'yes, yes, Maharajah *Sahib*, we know you hope they will enjoy the banquet you have so hospitably—' But here he was overpowered by the Maharajah — 'No, *no* I do not mean zat. I mean *I hope ze ladies will fill bellees.*' After dinner Holkar preceded us to the balconies from which we saw a first rate firework display and after that we went to the dancing tent. He had spent a hundred pounds on the floor and had it made in Bombay. A better one I never danced on and it was open all round with the curtains drawn back so it was deliciously cool. Evelyn and I enjoyed ourselves and went back by train next day and had a good morning's rest before going. We heard the guests making for the special in the small hours. . . .

(Diary)

In November, Violet goes to Gwalior, visits Gwalior Fort and meets the Maharajah Scindia.

20th November

The dog Patch is missing and we are very much afraid he has been stolen.

21st November

To Akolia with A. He got a little for the pot and met an alligator on the bank of a small *nullah* which slid into the water before he had time to breathe; I was much disappointed not to have seen it too, but I was some way off buried in the high lemon grass which is in its glory now, filling the country with its wonderful scent and almost obliterating the smaller landmarks. No sign of Patch, which is dreadful. The Barrs are going up to Gwalior on their way to other places and have asked me to join them there, which is great luck for me, and I shall return here when they continue their journey; Scindia will put them up; also, incidentally, me.

22nd November

Harry informed Rachel today that he is 'a sweet little boy'. I expect he got that from some gusher he may have met on one of their walks.

26th November

Started for Gwalior at ten last night. That is, I got into the train at that hour, went to sleep and was whirled off up country at three this morning. Changed at Fahtiabad in the early hours and later at Ujjain and Bhopal then on through the Bhilsa jungle across which one could see the Sanchi *Tope* rising in the distance and Bhilsa Fort. Got a most filthy dinner at Bhilsa station. It was a long journey of heat and I did not arrive till one in the morning when I was extracted from the train by the Nazir and glad I was to see his scarlet livery and respectable Mohammedan beard. He conveyed me to the guest house where I found Evelyn up and waiting for me. We share a huge room in the upper storey.

27th November

Woke from a long sleep. The verandah looks out towards the blue ridge of the Fort[25] crowned with its ancient buildings; we spent much of the morning looking out at it and down at the people moving on the wide space below. We saw a stout figure approaching on a trolley pushed along a funny little railway line; it was dressed in semi-European clothes and waved energetically to Evelyn. This was the Maharajah Scindia coming to see Col. Barr. He disappeared into the house beneath us. Later I was introduced to him; he seems a most friendly and kind fellow and he and the Barrs have known each other for many years. We had to go to a garden party in the afternoon where I saw the *personnel* of Gwalior, everyone in their best, and I thought how much I preferred our junglified old Mhow where such things are unknown; but it was quite amusing to see what happens in a new place.

28th November

Mr and Mrs Barnes are here, Mr Waterfield[26] and the *Sahibzada* Wahid-ud-din[27], all up from Indore in Col. Barr's train. We went up to the Fort on elephants; the rock it stands on is a mile long and a few hundred yards broad, the top encircled by the old fortress wall in which you can still see the gaps made in the Mutiny, but the city that was there has disappeared now and nothing remains but temples and bits of its buildings, arches and fragments that were once palaces. A perpetual haze seems to hang over it through which protrude high windows where ladies looked out behind their grilles of carved teak-wood or stone; and walls with crumbling patches of blue and yellow Multhan tiling lean over the depth. Loopholes, enclosed courts, underground passages are all jumbled up in the masonry. You look from the walls down on ruins on one flank of the rock and the present native town on the other, with fine public buildings and Scindia's palaces and gardens spread, as though on a map. He was anxious we should all go out with him later to a miniature villa out of the town and we started in an absurd miniature train on miniature rails to it. The train was a toy upholstered in red leather and carrying every conceivable luxury; from the villa we rowed in boats to have tea in an equally absurd but amusing little pagoda.

The Maharajah was very cheery and pleasant; he is a short, fat

youth of twenty one, looking quite thirty five, darker than most
Indians and rather horsey-looking in breeches and leggings, which
sounds very European and no doubt, did he not sport a cap like
the 'smoking cap' of our fathers embroidered in gold flowers and
wear his shirt outside his breeches, he would not suggest the east.
He has only one wife, a girl of sixteen, and he only leaves her in
purdah because he is afraid of offending public opinion in Gwalior
state were he to bring her out. But she has a good deal of liberty for
an Indian lady as he has built her a villa fourteen miles out where
she can go and play at keeping house with her women friends and
order her garden and arrange her furniture and feel like people in
Europe. Besides this he has walled in three miles of garden with trees
and fountains and paths whereon she may ride about to her heart's
content; at a signal all the gates are locked and she gallops forth on
her pony with a train of dogs. Evelyn has sometimes ridden there
with her and says she is not at all a bad rider but she is amused at
her little top-boots that look very odd under her muslins.

29th November
Spent the morning with Mr Maries, the keeper of the state garden.
He is a Scot and by way of being a botanist and he is the first living
creature I have met from whom I can seek knowledge of these things.
A rather boring gymkhana later at which the Maharajah, very fat and
mounted on a snorting arab, displayed his prowess. A small dinner
at the guest house.

30th November
Four of us went to a fair held just outside the town. I liked this
very much. There were many horses and rows of squealing stallions
with monstrous crests and dyed legs and tails ranged in a row on
either side of the ground in charge of ruffians from all parts of the
country. It was a sight for the gods, fantastic, raw and barbarous;
the neighing, snorting and tom-tomming, the chattering of natives,
the thick dust, the burning blue sky above the clatter and movement.
Though it was stifling and very heavy going in the sand and one's
shoes got full, it was a blessed relief after the dinners and garden
parties and gymkhanas. We got some nice bits of brass too. There
was a semi-official banquet in the evening, terrifically dull except
for a stranger, a Captain Stewart, who sat next to me and with
whom I made friends. He goes tomorrow to Sirdarpur, via Mhow,
so I suppose we shall be travelling companions.

After dinner was over I went with the female half of the party to the Maharani's establishment. She came in to receive us, a tiny creature with a largish face, too large to allow her to be good-looking, a pointed chin and a very gentle, childish voice; she was a bundle of silver-spangled muslin and pearls and a huge Danish boarhound followed her to which she spoke in broken English. An English lady lives with her to teach her English, embroidery and sewing and to ride with her when she wants a companion. The little lady professed herself much astonished at me because I was 'so very big'. She scarcely came up to my shoulder, so I must have seemed really colossal to her. What astonished me was to see a great lady in jewels and fine raiment with her lower drapery drawn up between her legs in front in a way which suggested shrimping. This custom gives a short woman a kind of waddle that, to a European eye, is dreadful. She had pretty manners too, which went badly with it.

1st December

We all left Gwalior escorted by various gold-laced persons and a great *salaaming* went on as Col. Barr and his suite left the station. Crowds of people, swords in velvet scabbards, *pagaris*, colours, policemen, chattering, sunshine, officials — at last we moved off. When we got to Dhatia I parted from the great ones and we started on our journey to Mhow, Indore and Sirdarpur respectively; myself, the *Sahibzada* Wahid-ud-din and Captain Stewart.[28] At Jhansi I got out to stretch my legs and saw an acquaintance on the platform who gave me the joyful news that Mr Williams, in the 20th, had won the Army Cup with Tarquin. There is joy among the elect in Mhow, I fancy. We got to Bhopal after dark and Captain Stewart and I dined there; the *Sahibzada* and Mr Waterfield were too perturbed to dine anywhere because the latter had a touch of fever and was in hourly dread of being snatched away by the plague inspector, who overhauled the train from time to time. It was unnaturally hot and the train into which we had to change was choke full; I knew a hideous night was before us. At last the exertions of all three procured me a place and I got into a compartment that beggared description for horror for it contained three half-caste children and a negress who were devouring jack-fruit which smelt as nothing has yet smelt since the foundation of the world. However it was my only chance and in I got and lay down as best could. Above me, the child in the top berth had the remains of the jack-fruit in beside her. The negress roamed ceaselessly to and fro and I gave myself up for lost and remembered Shadrach, Meshach and Abednego in the burning fiery furnace.[29]

2nd December

After an awful night I got out of my prison into the morning air at Ujjain station. It was six o'clock instead of half past four and in consequence our connection was missed and the prospect of more than half a dozen hours without food or occupation stared us in the face. I met the three men on the platform. Mr Waterfield was so thankful at having eluded the plague-officer that he cared for nothing; the *Sahibzada*, being an Indian, cared for nothing either; Captain Stewart manfully retained oaths. The engine had broken down in the night though we had known nothing about it. We had a council of war and I remembered that not far off there lived the good Dutchman, Onreit, at whose house the Barrs and I had been entertained. So we raised a pencil and a half sheet of paper and I wrote an appeal to him and told him that we were four souls, homeless and hungry, with six and a half hours before us and the prospect of native sweetmeats or nothing at all. We caught a man and sent him off with it, and in an incredibly short time a strange vehicle drawn by an aged white horse was seen afar off approaching over the dusty tracks; it was driven by a bearded figure in goggles. We were seized, packed in and carried off to his very hospitable house, we were fed and his wife gave me a room where I could wash myself into the semblance of something more presentable after the grime of the night and we started at last for Fahtiabad, deeply grateful for the kindness we had received. We had a couple of more hours of waiting at Fahtiabad during which Captain Stewart and I played piquet with a pack of cards he had unearthed and we played straight on till Indore, where Wahid-ud-din and Mr Waterfield got out, and at Mhow A. met me and we took Captain Stewart home with us for the night, as it was past eight and it is a trek of many hours to Sirdarpur.

5th December

To tea at General Nicolson's and were constrained to stay for dinner. The Inspector General of Cavalry, General Grant, was there, a huge man, whose nickname is 'the Rogue Elephant'.

6th December

Rode to the riding school to see the inspection and dined again with the Nicolsons. After dinner General Grant sat down beside me on a long sofa but also on the end of a window curtain which brought the pole heavily on both our heads. It hurt, rather, but it enlivened the company.

7th December
Painted *Clerodendron phlomoides*. Women's hospital in the evening.

12th December
Mrs Barnes is ill at Indore and Dr Caldecott asked me to come over and see what I could do for her. She is in a dreadful state of nerves and I was there all day, but got home at night.

13th December
The 'Mhow week' is on us and festivities are beginning today. A great show given by the 20th Bombay Infantry on their parade ground at night representing the taking of Bushire in the Persian gulf at which their regiment had earned much distinction. They spent no end of trouble on it and did it splendidly with a torchlight procession to finish up.

14th December
Festivities go on. Captain Bannerman, the *Bankwallah* and his sister came to us to stay for them; she, Miss K., has come out from England on a visit to her brother. A horseshow on the gymkhana ground which I enjoyed, and a quite good little dance at the club.

16th December
First day of races. Three falls in a hurdle race but no damage except to Placid Joe, who broke his leg and had to be shot. Am awfully sorry both for him and Pat. Fancy dress dance at night which was excellent and great fun. I must say I like folly occasionally.

19th December
Col. Barr was telling me a curious story of his younger days when he was Agent in a native state where there lived two *Thakurs*, much of an age and very like each other, who were the closest of friends. They lived in a castle some little way from a town, inseparable, having all things in common and sharing the house between them; what one did the other did and it seemed as if nothing could shake

their friendship. Both were married. It happened that the elder one fell violently in love with a lady and took her to live with him in his half of the castle and this went on for a good long time until, quite unknown to him, the other *Thakur* conceived a passion for her too. One day, when the elder man was absent, the younger man seized his friend's mistress and transferred her to his own dwelling. The injured man returned to find what had happened, rushed off to Col. Barr and insisted upon seeing him. He entered weeping and crying on heaven.

'*Sahib*,' said he when he had told his tale. 'I am now on my way home and I swear that, before another hour has passed, there are two things I am going to do. I will kill my friend and then my mistress.'

No reasoning and no commands would stop him and after a long scene of conflict Col. Barr said, 'If, in two hours from now the lady is back in your part of the castle, will you give up your intention?'

'Yes,' said the *Thakur*, 'the thing is impossible, but if it *were* possible, I should spare them both.'

'I can't keep you a prisoner,' said the other, 'but if you will give me your word of honour that you will stop here for exactly two hours I will contrive to put things right and you will have to stay your hand.'

The *Thakur* promised solemnly.

Col. Barr rode as hard as he could to the *Diwan* of the state and said to him, 'Come with me at once and bring a couple of *sepoys* and a large blanket, or there will be trouble.' The *Diwan* obeyed and the two rode off to the *Thakur*'s castle followed by the *sepoys*, Col. Barr telling the state of the case as they went. A messenger was sent on in front to lure the younger *Thakur* out on some imaginary pretext and once he had gone, the *Diwan* entered with the *sepoys*, flung the blanket round the lady and carried her half-smothered to her elder lover's end of the castle. There they secured her while Col. Barr waited outside. When all this was done he rode back to the Residency, arrived under the two hours and told the *Thakur* that if he went home he would find his mistress in her old quarters. He then got a promise from him neither to injure her nor her purloiner and to say nothing of what happened to anyone, not even to his traitorous friend and the *Thakur*'s delight was such that he agreed and nothing more was heard of the matter. Within a few days the *Thakurs* were seen arm in arm, inseparable as ever. But what became of the lady was never known.

19th December
Drove with A. to Nandlia and painted the shrine there. Afterwards
I crawled through the hedge of the Maharajah's little bungalow for
I wanted some *Hiptage madhablota* that grows over the rickety
pergola. That creepy place, always shut and lost in the high grass,
was as silent as ever. I sometimes think the unseen presence of a
huge red idol — Hanuman, of course — that lives somewhere in
the scrub on Nandlia hill makes that bit of country feel odd.

23rd December
Left Mhow by the ten train in our riding clothes, for we are going
to camp for Christmas with Pat Bannerman. We boxed the horses
and got into the same carriage as General Grant and his A.D.C.[30]
who envied us. Pat joined us at Indore station. Got out at Ajnod
and rode fourteen miles across country to Baneria on the edge of
Depalpur tank, where we found our tents pitched. I loafed about
all the afternoon and saw a Jain temple not far off into which I
got by permission of its priest: it astonished me by having a round
top; unlike all others of its persuasion that I had ever seen, it was
not cone-shaped. But the Jain god Parasnath[31] was sitting inside
crosslegged in a recess. The floor was so highly polished that it
was difficult to keep one's feet and rats were running all over the
bare place and even over Parasnath; I sat there drawing and was
glad they did not run over me too. The *Bankwallah* arrived in the
evening on his grey pony.

24th December
Went out early and looked about the country with my drawing book.
The men were away shooting all day. I went on foot in the afternoon
but got no new flower. Cheerful dinner, as all camp dinners are,
though we had scant head room. To bed early.

Christmas Day
The others went shooting very early and I rode out to meet them
coming back. I met a lynx and saw a mirage of another beautiful
tank with palm trees as I rode away from the water. The *Bankwallah*
had to leave us before dinner because of some press of business, which
was a pity, and we three sat on the shore in the dusk talking. We had
a turkey and plum pudding for dinner and a few holly berries on the
table, quite unrecognisable, but they had been sent out from England
on the chance that they might retain some semblance of something.

We arranged them flat in the centre, where, their leaves having withered, they looked like cherry stones. The tent was small and we sat doubled up and drank many healths. I pictured the Christmas dinner tables, smug at home, and thought how infinitely I preferred the banks of Depalpur.

26th December

Up early and off to Indore. Whilst the tents were coming down I painted *Menyanthes cristata*, which I got near the tank. In the midst of this Trilby and Talisman both broke loose and galloped among the tent ropes till it made one's heart stand still for fear they should break their legs. Pat had started earlier and the *syces* had gone on so we had a dreadful time catching them; I got Trilby at last but had to lay hold of her from behind a tree trunk, she is so vicious. The arab looked very fine, his tail in the air and his neck arched, stepping up to his nose and snorting, but it was no joke. However we got off after some delay and rode six miles at a steady canter without a check and reached Ajnod in time to box the horses before the train came in; at five o'clock we were at Pat's house at Indore where we spent three pleasant days before moving on to the little state of Dewas[32] where we meant to spend the rest of our holiday.

1898
Diaries and Letters

The diary is continued throughout 1898; excerpts from letters to her mother appear later in the year. The first diary entry is a long account of her meeting with the two Ranis of Dewas state.

New Year's Day

At seven o'clock we breakfasted and were off driving in one of the lumbering landaus belonging to the state and taking neither saddles nor horses; Pat was due to be present at the Proclamation Day parade of the Dewas troops almost as soon as we got there. I went off to paint at the Chatri Bagh, the burial-ground of the reigning family, a curious old place, made more so by the water which was lying in it. They had some of the Christmas rain due at this time and the ancient stone cenotaphs stood up, reflected and doubled among long trails of the water-*convolvulus* that is in blossom during a great part of the year and was lying on the surface. Two Rajahs[1] rule this state, representing different branches, one an elderly man, the other a youth, and an Englishwoman, Mrs Cooper, lives in this out-of-the-way spot, the only white woman in it, as reader and instructress to their respective Ranis. She invited me to go with her to visit them and we drove into the little old city in a victoria of ancient build allotted to her use preceded by a mounted guard.

First we went to see Lelita Rani, the wife of the younger Rajah (who nevertheless represents the elder branch). We drove through the *bazaar* down a street of gaping inhabitants and drew up before a straggling, whitewashed palace with high black balconies and carved windows, its walls covered with gaudy figures of men and animals painted on them in wild blues and yellows. For a royal residence it was a ramshackle place; even in this land of incongruities it was surprising.

We were led in and mounted eternal flights of stairs so narrow that one's shoulder rubbed dust off the walls, we went down passages starting away at different angles like the tunnellings of a mine, we got sudden peeps of courtyards below and emerged on giddy balconies somewhere in the sky. Old women peered round corners.

On every hand dirt, lumber, squabbling servants and huddled-up soldiers who sprang to present obsolete arms as we passed. These were lounging and chattering about the very door of the room in which the Rani sat. Lelita is fifteen years old and very shy, a little, uninteresting-looking creature, though in her politeness she wore her best clothes to receive us and in her desire to accentuate what Jane Austen would call her 'consequence', many jewels. Talking was not easy, as my Hindustani, such as it is, does not enable me to speak correctly to a lady of quality and she either did not know, or was too shy, to speak a word of English. It was a relief when Mrs Cooper suggested that she should show me her bedroom and her treasures; this was much better than sitting stiffly on chairs, trying to look sensible, and Indian ladies love showing their possessions. We followed her up yet more narrow stairs; her room, as tidy as the unused parlour of an English cottager's dwelling, was very dark and full of cupboards with shelves on which lay her *saris* and other garments, all most carefully folded, and she pointed out a tiny doll's chest of drawers and looking-glass, evidently her great pride. It is extraordinary what the pleasures of Indian ladies are — the young ones, that is; I should not be a bit surprised if Lelita still played with dolls. Her husband is only twenty and good looking and he flirts with a youthful widow of his adopted father's who is about his own age and pretty. Mrs Cooper tried hard to make the Rani send for her but she would not. I was vastly interested to see three of the elder Rajah's mistresses, who also live in the palace; one was a very attractive girl; Lelita told Mrs Cooper that she is the only wicked one of the lot because she spends so much money. When we left, after the *attar* and *pan*, the Rani, according to the polite custom in palaces, hung a gilded *haar* round my neck.

We went on to call on Tara Rani, the wife of the other Rajah.[2] He is fifty one and looks older, and she is twenty, which is considered close on middle age for an Indian woman. But Tara does not seem at all middle aged, also she is clever and they say has managed to make her husband bored with his mistresses. I was very anxious to see her. She is a friend, and I think a relation, of Scindia's wife and when she goes to stay with her she enjoys herself, for the pair gallop furiously in the great garden of Gwalior palace. Old Dewas has no garden to his city palace so Tara never can go out except in a closed carriage and rumour has it that she meets that difficulty by starting out with a woman servant on the box seat and contriving to change *saris* and places with her *en route* and so see something of the world.

She received us very pleasantly and when she heard I had met Mrs Scindia she was much interested. I thought her a pretty woman. She is slim and rather tall and her eyebrows are joined with dark paint above her nose and her large eyes sparkled under the black bar, which was very becoming. She has well cut features but I wish the dreadful habit of *betel*-chewing hadn't spoilt her teeth, staining them with that terracotta colour, disastrous enough even in wall paper, but in teeth, a calamity; her hair was parted and dragged tightly back and gold earrings the size of half crowns, loaded with pearls, were in her ears. She had no nose-ring but she must have worn at least four necklaces, most of them of pearls and *cabochon* emeralds,3 and diamond bracelets were mixed with glass bangles on her wrists. The strangest thing of all was her footgear consisting of hideous black velvet shoes worked with red wool roses and purple and white embroidered stockings. Heavy gold rings encircled her ankles and the last touch was given by the Japanese silk handkerchief in her hand with its border of men fighting in semi-European uniform. I suppose to British eyes she was not an ideal figure, but I am a quarter Hindu by this time and I admired her. I am told the two Ranis are jealous of each other; that goes without saying. Jealousy is part of an Oriental woman's outfit and always has been.

Our conversation was not very inspiriting, made up as it was of long pauses and stereotyped politenesses but I felt more adventurous with her than I did with Lelita Rani, and aided by Mrs Cooper we talked a little about riding and she showed me her riding habit, a vast enfolding garment of black cloth covered with large roses embroidered in gold thread. How she contrived to keep it on in the saddle was what puzzled me and I did wish I could have seen her on horseback, if only to find out how it was managed, for it appeared to have no fastening of any kind. No one was with her when we arrived but a very small Indian lady in white who sat alone in the middle of a long row of chairs, like an island in an ocean. She looked so delicate that Mrs Cooper enquired after her health.

'Her husband beats her,' explained Tara in a voice of cheerful commonplace, 'and the last time he did it it made her so ill that the Rajah turned him out of the palace.' The lady's face remained unchanged while all this was said; no one could tell from her expression that she had heard one syllable though her eyes were fixed upon us all the time. I wondered whether it was apathy or good manners. In any case it was the best way of meeting the situation. Tara woke up after this and began to discuss with Mrs

Cooper the merits of various hairwashes. 'But,' she concluded, as the bottle that she had sent for for us to see was taken away, 'what does it matter to such an ugly elderly woman as I am? I, who am more than twenty!' I saw that she hoped to be contradicted and I had sufficient Hindustani to do so; and indeed, when I did not see her reddened teeth I spoke sincerely. All the same, an Indian woman is considered *passé* at eighteen. At forty, she is generally a hag.

The afternoon was advancing and the room became rather dark but not before I had taken in the rows of carved arches dividing it lengthways like an aisle in a church. The usual chandeliers hung between them and a line of pictures ran round the room. They were a strange collection, being principally made up of those old-fashioned productions called 'glass prints' and the most out-of-date German oleographs. Every possible kind of person was represented, from the Emperor Francis Joseph in uniform to long-haired troubadors smirking behind rosebushes; crowned heads jostled each other on the walls and crinolined ladies clung to the arms of offensive-looking men in pegtop trousers. Nearly all the glasses were cracked and all were draped in dust.

At last the quick-failing daylight had gone and black shadows came among the pillars; the crinolined ladies grew dim and Francis Joseph's truculent stare was lost in the dusk. It was lucky that we had made our visit so late because I saw a household ceremony enacted, a relic from the Aryan worship of the domestic fire. Now that it was time for the lights to be lit in the house, a man brought in a lamp and set it at the Rani's feet, prostrating himself before it. The palace servants came in by turns at the lower end of the long room and as each figure emerged from under the arches it threw itself down before the lamp. The whole made a picture; the gathering dark, the vista of pillars, the slim Rani leaning back in her chair with the lamp at her feet and the vague beings slipping out of the shadows and flitting like moths to the spot of fire to make their obeisances. I was rather surprised at the free way in which menservants came in and out of Tara's presence, for I did not realise that domestic servants were only a part of the house, so to speak, and therefore did not count. One episode amazed me, even in this land of incongruities. A smart young fellow, brilliant in a satin waistcoat of many hues, came in to do his worship after the others had gone. He had an assured air and his Maratha headgear sat rakishly over the curled lock that his race brush so carefully forward over the ear. At first he did not see that strangers were present but when he did, he gave a startled jump. This was not lost on Her Highness and she laughed aloud and shouted some chaff after him as he disappeared through the door. He threw her a backward glance and laughed too.

'Who is that?' I asked, forgetting my manners and supposing I had seen some favoured member of the family.

'Only the Rajah's dressing-boy,' she replied, calmly.

It was time to go and the *attar* and *pan* came in on a covered tray. The napkin was whipped off it discovering four things; a white handkerchief, a lovely silver scent jar with a long neck, a tightly tied bouquet of roses and jessamine and a plate made of silvered leaves with the spices and cardamom. Tara sprinkled the handkerchief from the vessel and presented it to me. I rose, *salaamed* to her and took it. Then she offered the leaf. This, one touches and gives it to the servant behind one's chair, who conveys it to one's carriage where it becomes a perquisite to one's domestics. We shook hands and parted. Next day we went home.

12th January

Rode out to a field day and got up on the hill of Richabada from which I saw everything well. Mrs Nicolson came out and sat with me while I was painting and came back to dinner as both our husbands were dining in the Mess. I laughed the whole way through the meal. Her wits were at their best. Afterwards she walked up and down the room, a tiny figure with a cigarette in its mouth, giving magnificent descriptions of all sorts of ridiculous happenings and I lay in the long chair and shouted with laughter. Presently a mouse came in and began running about behind the furniture and I whistled for Billy to come in and kill it but she was so horrified at the idea that I sent the dog away and I daresay she was quite right, for after all it could do very little harm and was very pretty. But that is the woman who, the General told me, was once in the garden and stepped on a *krait*. She had the presence of mind to keep her foot where it had lit on the *krait*'s neck, while she called to him to bring a pair of long scissors with which she cut the creature in two, holding it under her foot all the time.

14th January

Spent the afternoon at Bercha tank. The country lovely. Ranged about and sat painting near a well in a grove of mangoes. Golden lemon-grass half cut, blue hills, mist, hot road and heavy foliage. When dusk came on I went and sat high above the road looking towards Nandlia hill. Some peasants had gone to the well and were sitting by a little fire and having the communal pipe so dear to them. It is often made of a leaf rolled up and pinned together with a thorn of a stout sort (and never were there thorns of such length and strength as in this country) and it goes round the group from hand to hand, each man taking a puff and sending it on to his neighbour. Often its contents are merely a piece torn off the end of a man's *pagari* and lit. They did not see me and I watched the picture they made, one that never palls on me. I think today was, for sheer beauty, one of the heavenliest days we have had.

20th January
Went to the married quarters and women's hospital.

21st January
Got a sore throat and had a bad night.

22nd January
Cold better and went to Indore to the *Bankwallah*'s to see the eclipse of the sun, which is supposed to be better seen from there than from Mhow. A good many had congregated in his garden and we watched it from ten minutes to twelve, when it began, to three o'clock, when it was over. The sun was never entirely covered though only a very little edge remained light but the thermometer went down from 107° to 84° and the whole place looked as if a heavy thunderstorm was going to break. The world was livid. What astonished me was that the tree shadows on the ground changed their shapes, all the patches of light between the groups of leaves taking the form of crescents. Obviously, this was a natural thing, or it would not have been there, but to my ignorance it was astounding. There will be a good many black noses in the world today from smoked glass.

25th January
Today I went for a drive with General Nicolson, as he wanted to plant a banyan tree on the new 'Nairne' road and asked me to come out and choose a spot, but when we got there and had chosen it carefully, it was discovered that the servants had omitted to put the little tree in the carriage. I went back to dinner with him. He knows such a lot of strange stories of the people in bygone and John Company India4 that it makes a talk with him very amusing. One that he told me was about a lady whom I will call Mrs 'Vansittart',5

though that was not her name. Her husband, an officer in a native cavalry regiment, died and left her the very unusual legacy (for one of his profession) of twenty thousand pounds and she went back to England and there met an American doctor whom we will call 'Parker', though that was not his name either; he married her for her money and they went to the United States to live. A few years afterwards she turned up in England, having spent a miserable time with Parker, and told her solicitors that she wished to resume the name of Vansittart because she had found out that he had had a wife living at the time of his marriage with herself and was therefore a bigamist. On enquiry this proved to be true and after the necessary legal arrangements they separated and she took back her old name. Before very long Parker arrived in England and said he had come to claim his wife, as it had been discovered that the woman he had married first — his *original* wife — was in the same box with himself, she also having committed bigamy in marrying him because she had a husband living when their marriage took place. Consequently, at the time of his espousal with Mrs Vansittart he had not been legally married to the first lady. Therefore Mrs Vansittart was still his wife and he wished her to return to him. The poor woman was in despair and engaged in every means of getting out of his power. Her solicitors, acting on some rumours about in America respecting Parker, made enquiries which resulted in the discovery of the following fact. Parker's original wife's original husband was married to another woman when she became Mrs Parker. Consequently she was *not* married to him. Consequently when Parker married her she was free. Consequently the marriage was legal. Consequently, when he married Mrs Vansittart he was a bigamist after all. So she escaped him. She had one son by Captain Vansittart and when she died, shortly after leaving Parker, the young man inherited the twenty thousand pounds. He fell ill and died in General Nicolson's house and the money passed into chancery, he being a minor.

General Nicolson sometimes put things quite differently from other people in conversation. He was telling me how he had gone to Benares and been conducted through the temples by a guide who was determined that he should see and observe everything. Some of the *bas* reliefs at Benares represent scenes not usually found on the walls of religious buildings or indeed in any public place and the guide drew his attention to such outrageous indecencies that he could bear it no longer. 'And' (said the General) 'I turned to him and said "*Man!* have you *no sense of humour* that you should show me these things?".'

29th January

A. left for a practice camp and I went to Indore to get on with my picture of the Ranibagh near Rao.

30th January

To the Ranibagh. The temple in its garden that is occupying me now and to which the gilded dome belongs has the usual flight of steps running up to it and the arch at the top of them and the porch formed by this is covered, wall and sides, with a mass of painting of no great age or value but immensely elaborate. The high door facing you is surmounted by a frescoed group of gods, brilliantly coloured. Shiva sits surrounded by Parbati, his spouse,[6] Ganesh the elephant-headed and others, with a crude attempt at landscape spread behind his chignoned and serpent-crowned person, a green field with palms on the horizon. Paintings of various semi-sacred beings run down along the door jambs and every available bit of space is smothered in patterns and floral arabesques. Very rashly I have begun a drawing of all this though I can't imagine how I am ever going to finish it. It will be a chain round my neck and a clog to my feet whenever I come to Indore. However I can't help that. As I sat working away and cursing my folly a man came by, evidently a coolie belonging to the garden, and the *Bankwallah*, who had driven me out there and didn't know what he was in for, was trying to amuse himself by identifying some of the personages that stared down on us. 'Who is that?' he asked the man, pointing to the image of a stout, whiskered, turbaned gentleman smoking a hookah. 'That is Tookerji,' replied the coolie, naming Holkar's immediate predecessor. 'And who is that one?' continued the *Bankwallah* pointing to a prancing figure painted blue and holding up its four arms aloft. The coolie peered at it as if he had never seen it before and said, after a pause, 'The Maharajah.' I dined with the *Sahib* at Gwalior House. No one was there but Mrs Nicolson, who had come over from Mhow. It being a Mohammedan fast-day the Nawab and Jimmy might not eat until sundown but they had a huge meal the moment the sun's rims had disappeared over the side of the world.

In February 1898 Violet goes to Simrole with another officer's wife, and to Sadulpur with Arthur. Later the Jacobs visit Dhar again, and Violet meets the Maharajah.

1st February

A. being still away, M.K.[7] and I thought we would like to have a
few days at Simrole,[8] both our husbands being in camp, so we went
off to the little *dâk* bungalow at Simrole at the head of the road that
descends the Ghaut. It is just on the fringe of a bit of jungle and we
meant to hunt for new flowers. We left in the early morning in the
buggy taking some provisions and the *syce* Setul to look after Trilby.
In a couple of hours we had disembarked, thrown down our things
and gone out to see what we could see. The bungalow is on a dry
mound and has an attractive view over a long, uninhabited stretch
and across the way begins the thick scrub that grows wilder as you
go into it and a great *nullah* runs up from the south ending in a
deep ravine flanked by rocks. It is splendid standing and looking
down the chasm it makes. Westward are the Ghauts, cut clear and
blue on the sky. There is much bastard teak with its enormous leaves
and blossom like white plumes, and tracks wind in and out in the
undergrowth. We spent the day prowling about and I sat in a dry
ditch painting *Cylista scariosa*. In a particularly lonely spot we came
on a stone Hanuman set up looking across the jungle to the Ghauts;
I fancy his worshippers have long since ceased to visit him and the
Ghauts and the long grasses are the only things that he sees as he
stares westward. At night I settled myself in the southernmost room
of the bungalow and I hope no other traveller may have the same
ill-luck. The *charpoy* on which I lay was the home of myriads of
bugs and all night I never closed an eye though one of them was
closed for me.

2nd February

I had the *charpoy* put out on the grass and as much boiling water
as we could raise poured over it. M. had suffered nothing and slept
unattacked and at five o'clock in the cool morning we started for a
long walk and found ourselves about sunrise on the edge of a wide
basin of scanty scrub. Looking over it east, we saw the sun come
up and the mists disperse. It was glorious. All round were shrubby
plants with long heads of leguminous blossom, spikes of rose-purple
the colour of *mezereum*.[9] I did not know what they were and foolishly
brought none home, thinking we should come upon plenty more as
we went on. It is never worth while to do that (that I have discovered
from sad experience) though one generally does it with the idea of
bringing back the freshest specimens. We sat long, seeing the lights
grow on the stretch before us and then set off wandering again. After

a tour of nearly ten miles we got home with very little in the way of plants to show for it, and we spent the day resting our feet after the bad going and I finished *Cylista sacariosa*. When it grew cool again we took the buggy and went down the Ghaut road and were brought to a standstill by seeing some way below us in the tangle of undergrowth a beautiful pale golden flower about the size of a single hollyhock growing very high up on a slim, leafless tree. We marked it down to get hold of somehow and paint on the morrow.

3rd February

About mid day we heard hoofs on the road from the direction of Mhow and we saw Bobby R. approaching. I was not best pleased for I had meant to go for that yellow flower and hated being put off; and when he said that he had come out of curiosity to see how we were getting on I felt like suggesting to him that, having found us all right, he should go back again, but decency made me ask him to luncheon and he ate nearly all our ham. After this we all started on foot down the road admiring the great view towards the hills and after a few miles sat down to rest in the shade of a clump of bastard teak. Bobby lay on his back and recited yards and yards of Kipling and we listened delighted, for he did it so well, and I forgot the yellow flower and forgave him for coming. We talked long and long of this extraordinary and fascinating country, of soldiering and of everything imaginable. The buggy had followed us slowly and we drove back to the bungalow in a glorious moonlight. He set off home after supper, having pretty well cleared our larder, but as we have to return to Mhow tomorrow afternoon that doesn't much matter.

4th February

The minute we had sent off our small amount of baggage in the bullock cart we took the buggy and went to the place from which we had seen the yellow flower. There it was, quite safe and golden, like a star above the brown sea of undergrowth. We were out of the buggy in a minute, leaving Setul in charge, and down over the edge of the road, slithering and sliding down the thorny and stony side of the *khud*, not tearing our clothes to rags only because they were made of stout khaki; in the pauses of our descent we saw our goal looking more and more desirable the nearer we got, especially as it was the only blossom on the tree. When we stood under it at last we found it was far beyond our reach on an outstanding bough.

This was a cruel blow, for we had not realised its position from where we saw it so far above; but being absolutely determined to have it we climbed laboriously up again to the buggy, unbuckled the reins and telling Setul to keep a steady hold on Trilby's head till we got back, started down once more. There was a flat, smooth slab of rock thrusting up from the tangle just below our prey and we stood up on this to get to work. Then we found a stone and weighting one end of the rein with it, flung it up round the branch we wanted, with the idea of bowing it down — for it was not very thick — and making a leap for the flower. This done, we each took an end of our lasso and, at the word, pulled stoutly together. What we did not know was that the main stem of the kind of tree has a consistency something like that of a tallow candle. It snapped half way up and I found myself seated on the flat rock. But M. fared worse for she flew backwards into a thorn bush and lay with her legs in the air like the letter Y, unable to move and held in a vice. When I was able to stop laughing we managed to get her free, comparatively undamaged. But the miracle was that the precious blossom arrived on the earth intact. We climbed up, plus our treasure and a few bruises and scratches, and I had time to paint it before we left Simrole. Its name proved to be *Bombax gossypinum*. At Mhow I found A. had got home from camp.

6th February

A. is going to take a few days leave, which doesn't happen often, and we have settled to go to spend them at Sadulpur where he may get some duck shooting. We went out to get things together and provision ourselves for the trip. X—— has asked to come with us, and we shall start the day after tomorrow.

8th February

We are driving this time and left at cockcrow in the buggy having sent a *syce* on about dawn with the charger and a bullock cart. Before we reached Gopalpura hill we were stopped by the police, because a native infantry regiment was having a field day and firing across the road; so we had to pull up and wait while the day grew hotter and the chances of getting in unbroiled lessened. We were kept such a time that we could stand it no longer and drove in from the road to the open country, hoping to make a detour and come out somewhere on it again on the further side of the troops. We got on to tracks, when we could find any, and when we couldn't we bumped at a foot's pace among boulders and bushes, walking beside the empty cart. When we came to ditches we gave Trilby a slap, and each taking a wheel, shoved the thing over. It was hot work. After some time of this we heard piercing sounds behind us and feared that the police were going to hinder us again from crossing the area of some new military operation. But it was only X—— on horseback pounding along, and A. remembered that today for the first time whistles had been served out to squadron officers; X—— had brought out his and was using it with all the delight of a new broom and making a fantastic noise. He also had been turned off the road. What interested us a good deal was that his pockets were full of oranges and that we were streaming with perspiration and our mouths dry. When at last we got back to the road we were thankful to get into the buggy and were also enlivened by seeing X—— in front, raised skyward as his horse shied at a derelict roller lying at the wayside. By the time we reached Bagdoon tank the sun was overhead and we lay up for an hour by a stunted palm that was giving a patch of shade. We unharnessed the pony and put her in its shadow, tipped up the buggy, shafts to the sky, and got underneath it with our sandwiches and a couple of soda water bottles. When we had done our twenty seven miles and were nearing Sadulpur I smelt rain coming and was mocked in consequence. We were all tired at night.

9th February

Trilby had a rest day as she had done well yesterday and I remained on my feet as A. had out the charger. This is a disused mosque, now a travellers' bungalow, that we are living in. The main room is under its dome and there are little ones off it; its entire furniture is a table, two wooden chairs and a row of pegs in the wall. A. and I have a little dark hole with two *charpoys* in it. The mosque is on the north bank of the Chambal river — not that there is any bank to speak of — or any Chambal either, for the latter is almost dry with a bottom of flat rocks; an ancient aqueduct of many arches runs from the building to it. I found the small pink *Pladera virgata* growing between the rocks and took it in to paint; the others went off with their guns to look for small game. The rain I smelt yesterday came down and a great storm of wind and dust rose but I was so pleased at being justified of my derided warning that I did not mind it and when it was fair took the dog Billy up the river, for we had brought him out in the bullock cart to give him a change. Mhow is a dreadful place for dogs; so many die that it is best to give them *charpoys* of their own to sleep on, for it is supposed that the contact of the ground at night helps to induce the fever so many die of; Billy has his, though we did not bring it with us. There was a heavy thunderstorm in the distance. When the men came in we had tea and X—— ate so much that it made me shiver. A good pound of jam, chunks an inch thick of bread, which latter was rather ominous as we are carefully provisioned for a certain number of days only, and bread, in the wilds, is precious. Last night at dinner we thought he did his share but today it is becoming serious. They brought in quite a lot of duck that we hung on the pegs. X—— examined them all, pinching them to see which he thought the most succulent. We had a duck dinner.

10th February

Still a raging wind but fair. A. and X—— went off to shoot and I took the pony and accompanied them as far as Kesur village and then turned back. It was a very out of the way part of the world in that direction and I was amused to find that some women on foot whom I passed turned their backs and covered their faces and evidently imagined I was a man. They probably see no Europeans but occasionally gunners who come out for field practice and never a white member of their own sex.

As I went past a little village I saw a *datura*[10] I particularly wanted, a fine specimen, growing on a dust heap under the walls, so I made for it and told myself that, as it was a stormy day and I had had my only horse out all the morning, I would spend the afternoon on its portrait with Billy for company. So I went to get the thing and, as I approached, most of the inhabitants, who were watching me with much interest, began to shout in a very unfriendly way. But I did want the *datura* which is nothing but a weed and of no value to anyone, so I slipped off, darted up the dust heap and seized it, keeping tight hold of the reins, which I flung back over Trilby's head as I put my foot in the stirrup. But like the unblessed animal she is, she started off when I was half way up her side so I sprawled across the saddle very uncomfortably till the village was left behind and I could pull up and right myself. I pushed on to Sadulpur to get the flower painted before it should droop but it had begun to pour and by the time I had got something to eat such gloom set in in the dark mosque that it was hard to see and it was no easy matter to produce anything; it was bitterly cold and cheerless, and I wished I had brought out a book, for Roxburgh was all I had and it was dull when the *datura* was done and Billy was bored too and made injured faces when spoken to. The men came in, having been fairly lucky and bringing more game, and we sat down to tea. It was dreadful to see how the bread disappeared down X——'s throat. It was like snow in a thaw. It was there and it was gone, and afterwards A. and I went quietly out and examined the bread-tin to see what the prospects were. The result was not reassuring and he said to me 'if X—— goes on like this at the rate of a loaf a meal we shall be absolutely run out, so *you* have got to stop him'. At first I said I wouldn't, but thought better of it and having got hold of him, put the fact that the commissariat could not stand more than a certain deficit of bread as politely and firmly as I could. He took it quite kindly and I reported my success and thought all was well. But at supper he ate as if nothing had happened. We raged in our black hole at night.

11th February

Fair day but a high, cold wind. The others went out early and I rode to Kered village by the map and home across country, enjoying it, for the day mended and I saw several things I liked. The sparse patches of opium were lovely and I came across a bird that I think was a king-vulture. Lunched off teal which was very good and then went out to finish my drawing of the mosque from the river-bed. By tea time A. and X—— had not come back and as I had nothing to do I got out the pony and rode off to see if I could meet them; I knew pretty well what bit of country they had gone to and I jogged quietly along in the dusk that had already begun to fall. The crickets were striking up from every bush, it soon got dark and I made for the sandy track that I knew was there. All at once I felt the pony under me move in a particular sidling way a horse has when there's another horse advancing that he cannot see, so I stopped and whistled softly and A.'s answering whistle came out of the darkness. 'Hush-sh-sh,' said he as he came up, 'X—— is lost, and a good thing too, come on home and we can let him find himself.' We giggled the whole way back under our breath for fear he should be groping about near and hear us, and in a whisper the events of the day were conveyed to me. They had differed on the way out about the direction of the tank they were to shoot at and X—— had told him, among other things, that it was a pity that he, a cavalry officer, did not know his way about a country; after this they parted and took different directions. But it had been decreed that they should meet again and they appeared to each other suddenly beside the *bund* of a *nullah*. X—— crossed it and in doing so fell off it into the mud, and coming up covered with slime, started for home and was seen no more. We thought it possible that he might have arrived and got into the mosque without my hearing him, but the place was empty when we got back and it was some time before he turned up, having presumably wandered for hours. We all sat down quite civilly to supper though he did not say much about his day and I asked no questions. But the bread went as fast as ever.

12th February

Took Trilby, and some food in my haversack, and went out for the day. I got a *solanum* I did not know, painted a little and loafed and came back in the dark. Dined off one of the fat ducks in the larder which X——, after much pinching and prodding, chose from the pegs. He heaped his plate with chunks of bread while we looked grimly on, got a bottle of soda water — I suppose it was the coolest one because of its careful selection — and put it away under his own chair. The meal proceeded and peace reigned but the bread made us brood over our wrongs though we laughed and talked and were on short bread rations ourselves. All at once there was a noise as if a cannon had gone off and the dome over our heads echoed and resounded until we were almost deafened. The cherished soda water bottle had burst with a violent impact below the seat of his chair and sent him leaping sky high. It was hard not to cheer.

16th February

Mhow. — There is a domestic excitement going on. The sweeper-man is accused of being implicated in a supposed murder and was apprehended whilst we were away; it seems that the sweeper in B.'s bungalow died mysteriously not long since, taken ill it was supposed, with cholera. B., who is an angel in some ways and a devil in others, sat up with him all night till his death in the morning. After the funeral his widow ran away with her brother-in-law, about whom she had had words with the dead man, and the idea got about that the husband had been poisoned. What part our sweeper is supposed to have played I do not know but the examination is today and all our servants are summoned to appear with him. I know nothing against the man except that he is one of the most alarming-looking people I ever met, though that is nothing to his discredit. Karoo the cook is in a terrible fright at the thought of being in court. He is a great coward at all times and when we take him to camp I am told that he lives in dread of being overpowered by robbers and is a great nuisance to the bullock driver, for he sleeps in the cart and laments all night. This murder business will probably come to nothing as so many of these mysteries do here. I am going to Dhar the day after tomorrow with the *Bankwallah*, his sister and Captain Stewart who is there on business from Sirdarpur and has asked us to meet him. We shall all live in the little guest house I like so much. Miss K. who is very much interested in what she sees, is looking forward to it.

19th February
Dhar. — This morning we went up to the Temple of Kali Mata, high on its conical hill; the view from its ramparts carries your eye across the plain below, partly cultivated, with its lakes like looking glasses lying on the expanse that ends in the blue hills of Mandu. It is a long ascent of steps that takes you from the shore of Dhar lake to the white building but the priests and their satellites welcome you in a friendly way, for the Maharajah of Dhar is a loyal man and British people are liked here. We were allowed to look at everything we wanted to see and we stayed some time enjoying the wonderful landscape and admiring the giant frangipani tree that grows out of its walls as though hanging in mid air. The temple covers the whole hill top and from below makes an extraordinary outline against the sky. We wandered about the town in the afternoon.

20th February
Today we went to visit the Maharajah, for when he is well enough he likes to see his English guests. The palace is squalor itself and a labyrinth of narrow dark passages; I think nearly all royal palaces are that except those in the large states. We were ushered into a room that was darker than any of them and in the centre, in the dim light, the Rajah sat, a tiny being, in the very middle of a plain *charpoy* with various nondescript people in attendance; round three sides of the room were small wooden cages of canaries whose voices made those of any other created being inaudible. The Maharajah is a dwarf, a cripple and paralysed in his legs, but his disabilities have not prevented him being a good ruler and loved by his subjects. He sat like some strange, half human creature with wholly human eyes, shaking

hands with us all before we took our seats on the four chairs, two on either side of His Highness. Close to him sat the heir, a boy of perhaps eleven years old who is his nephew, very grandly dressed. It was rather trying, for the Maharajah said nothing after some mumbled civilities and we could not think what to say and some of us were not able to say it even if we could. Captain Stewart seemed nonplussed; the *Bankwallah*'s sister knew no word of Hindustani, except perhaps how to ask for hot water, I, very little and that not of a sort to suit Maharajahs. The *Bankwallah* made some effort but His Highness' replies were hardly audible; I thought I ought to do something to try to relieve the strain, so, having carefully spread it out in my mind, I lifted up my voice and said '*Ap ka misag kaisa hai, Maharajah Sahib?*'* There was a kind of murmur and silence fell again. By this time I was flattened out by embarrassment and the pathos of the sad little figure on the *charpoy* and the loneliness and gloom of it all. We felt at our wits' end and I think the feeling ran round us like hysteria. Then, without the smallest warning the youthful heir, who had not uttered, prompted I suppose by some satellite behind the Maharajah, raised a piercingly shrill voice and screamed (there is no other word for it) in one long, sustained breath 'Howdyoudumadam!' It was as sudden as the stab of an assassin's knife and almost as fatal, and we could not imagine what this cryptic cry could mean till it dawned on us that it was a belated acknowledgement of my words to the lad's uncle.

After this we took our leave and, as we left, His Highness gave me and Miss K. each a couple of silver bangles and we were wreathed with jasmine and tinsel garlands. We were all rather shattered. We knew that the old man liked visits and took them as a compliment and we had meant to please him, and felt at the same time that such a posse of fools as we must have seemed could please nobody. It was Captain Stewart's fault for he knew the language well and was the responsible person among us. The Maharajah drives every day in the same direction along the road past the guest house but at a certain point he turns back because a few paces further on would bring him in sight of the cenotaphs of his forebears and he considers that unlucky.

21st February
Back to Mhow.

---

* 'How is your health, Sir Maharajah?' (Violet Jacob's own note)

Apart from the account of a nautch, Violet's diaries from March
to June 1898 are dominated by the problems of hot weather and
disease. The Royal Fusiliers leave Mhow on April 14th.

6th March

We drove to Haselpur tank, A. to shoot for the pot and I to get a
flower I had chanced to see there and in no other place, a beautiful
thing growing in the fork of a *gular* tree a few feet above my head;
white, not very large, trumpet-shaped and faintly shell-pink in the
throat. Its great beauty is its very pale green bracts veined with a
darker green. It took me some time to find the particular tree in the
wilderness of others and the shrubs and tangle and grasses, but after
much tramping about and comparing little landmarks I had learned
for the purpose, I discovered it.

The trouble was that, approaching from a new direction, I found
there was a drop between me and it, the edge of which was fringed
with not very tall nor very wide thorn bushes. These stretched for
a good long distance and it seemed that I should have a longish way
to go to get round it. I knew that below the *gular* tree was flat,
sandy ground with a shallow trickle of water hardly to be called a
stream and that the drop was not deep, so I just leapt out over the
thorns (through which I could not see) and lit on my feet within a
foot of the dead body of man that lay, wound up on a brushwood
bier and half burnt, by the water. It sobered me a good deal and
I felt rather sick and when I took a look round I realised that the
spot had evidently become a recognised one for these perfunctory
cremations and that several scraped-up mounds round me suggested
yet more perfunctory finishings-up to them. However, there bloomed
the lovely *Pedalinia barleroides* above the rather horrible scene like a
star, so I clambered up to it with great difficulty, for I am not good at
that sort of thing, cut it out of the tree, slid down picking my way very
carefully and put all the ground I could between me and that sandy
place as quick as I could. That brushwood bier with the shape — or
what was left of it — on the top of it was best forgotten. We went
home with partridges and pigeon.

8th March

I drove out to Palassi village to see the poppies for there are acres
of them out now, and for the first time since coming to this country
I had a disagreeable experience with a native. It was silly of me not
to remember that it was a feast day and as I neared the village it

struck me that the people seemed to stare at me rather rudely so I did not go near the houses and merely stood admiring the flowers. I had left the buggy on the road which was out of sight. A man came towards me and told me very insolently to be off. I answered him quite civilly that I was coming no nearer and was only looking at the poppies. At this he stepped up to me flourishing a stick and at that I was so enraged that I rushed upon him, seized it and twisted it out of his hand before he had recovered from his surprise; he fled, astounded, and as I saw that the village was watching, I chased him for a short distance to produce a good effect upon it. It did, and before it subsided I walked away with all the deliberation necessary to round up the affair. I fancy my assailant had drunk a little too much of what the servants call 'countree liquor', for as I say, I have never had anything but civility from the people in the fields before.

The 4th Bombay Rifles[11] had a *nautch* at their Mess in the evening to celebrate the feast of the *Holi*, which occasion I am certain was the cause of the episode of this afternoon. Personally I am not bored by a *nautch*, as many are, though one may often get too much of it at a time. The girls do not dance as we should understand dancing but posture stiffly and they are so much loaded with different coloured stuffs that one might think they could hardly move. Every time their feet stir their anklets clink and mark time, much like the triangle and bells in a band; they sing with shrill nasal voices but their impassive faces and long eyes please me much, and the extraordinary character in their hands. One girl I saw gets a hundred and fifty rupees for one *nautch*; she had her hair plastered and parted and done up in a bob at the back and gold dangles hung down on either side of her face. Her little jacket was orange covered with gold and a dark red skirt of I should think a hundred folds swung below it, a mass of tinsel too, so she was a glittering object; below this again appeared tight white trousers and over the whole was a green muslin *sari* with a tinsel border at least a foot deep. As she postured, singing at the same time, men held torches round her and poured oil out of scented vessels from time to time. Behind her was her tom-tom player and other musicians who played those monotonous stringed instruments that always go to my head and keep a time so perfect that there is nothing I have heard to match it. Each girl of any note has her own particular band. This one rather spoilt her effect by chewing *betel* all the time and spitting occasionally; even I can't stand that.

The next dancer who came on was, purely but unintentionally, comic, and it was all one could do not to roar with laughter the whole way through the performance, though we had to keep serious because all the Indians looking on took it seriously. As a matter of fact I think they preferred her to the first one. She was rather elderly and fat and wore a huge silver thumb ring with a looking glass in it. The terrific part of it was that she sang in English and as this was supposed to be a great attraction and a compliment to the British present it was absolutely imperative to keep a straight face. The whole song consisted of the following words, which began quite suddenly, like the shameless, indecorous outcry of a cat's love-making on the roof; and it was in much the same key and pitch.

> *'Whar ees my darlin' whar eess she-e-e-eeee!*
> *Whar ees my darlin' whar eess she-e-e-eeee!*
> *Whar ees my darlin' whar eess she-e-e-eeeeeee!'*

Here there was a pause while the last syllable decreased in volume until it died down into silence, then with the same appalling suddenness there burst out:

> *'Shee has gone away from mee-e-e-e-eee-eee!*
> *Shee has gone away from mee-e-e-e-eee-eee —'*

This was repeated, as above, four times and the performance went on for a good ten minutes by which time I was, between my agonies of stifled laughter and the noise and heat, almost fit to be carried out for dead. After this came supper and I went home shaken to the very marrow and thankful to get to bed.

21st March
The first day of the week's festivities into which we quiet people burst twice in the year. There was a polo tournament in the initial event of which the regiment beat the Royal Fusiliers, as well as a concert in the evening which was but dull work after the *nautch* of a fortnight ago.

25th March
Rode the mare. The regiment gave a dance which was quite good and the supper was excellent. Dr Malcolm Moore and the eldest Barr boy arrived today; we are putting them both up in our verandah. I have been counting the days till Dr Moore's arrival, having heard of him as a first rate botanist. He has a brother, another Dr Moore, who

is head of the Royal Botanic Garden in Dublin. I haven't had one knowledgeable person to speak to about botany ever since I came to the country and have had to teach myself from Roxburgh's *Flora Indica* as best I can and I have been two years grinding at it alone, knowing no Latin and having no means of correcting my mistakes, so I am looking forward to seeing Dr Moore with excitement and dread, as he will probably be very learned and I shall find out how ignorant I am still.

26th March

Polo finals and the regiment won the cup. Dr Moore is a really delightful man but I have had a cruel blow. I have been learning everything on an obsolete system; the Linnaean System[12] is dead and superseded by the system of Natural Orders and I must begin all over again. I knew Roxburgh's *Flora Indica* was an old book but I did not know that it was a dead one and after all my slaving and groping it is hard, but Dr Moore says that it is something to have the Linnaean System at one's back and he thinks I have done very well for nearly all my identifications are right. He has told me of other books, but there is not much written, so far, and nothing on the large scale of *Flora Indica*. So I shall have to readjust all my ideas that I have battered into my head with such difficulty. If I'd only known a little botany before I came out! He was very comforting in other ways for he tells me that he has a brother at Kew who employs a woman to paint new specimens and that she is not as good as I am. I hope that is not a polite fiction but I fear it must be. He would like me to publish my collection but I told him that it would be far too expensive to think of, and there's no fiction in that! He is writing to Major Prain who is in charge of the Botanic Garden of Calcutta to introduce me, and asking him to identify anything for me that I can't manage to find from books. I hear the P. and O. *China* has gone down in the Straits of Perim.

29th March

Rode very early. Much farewelling. So many are going home for six months.

30th March

Went over to the Residency at Indore. Evelyn has been very ill and is up, but weak. The usual fever. There were people to dinner at the Residency, including Mrs Moore by whom I sat. Very hot night.

31st March
Went back to Mhow and painted *Gloriosa superba*. Tired.

1st April
Rode Trilby early. Horrid night of heat and mosquitoes. Glad to get up.

4th April
Went to Jamli and found the white moonflower I saw in a *nullah* at Mandu and marked it down. Very, very hot, so slept on the roof. Everyone is taking flight to England or Kashmir or the Hills.

7th April
Evelyn Barr arrived. It is a little cooler here than at Indore and the change though only from ten miles off, may help her.

9th April
Drove E. out in the morning. She is very weak.

10th April
Finished painting the blue *Ternatea*. The Royal Fusiliers leave on Thursday and everybody is sorry; so many, jolly, friendly things will be over and we shall miss Bobby. The men hate it too as there has always been such a strong relationship between the two regiments. Some Royal Irish have appeared already.[13]

19th April
E. was well enough to ride and we jogged quietly to Pitumpur. Coming back we had to make a wide detour to dodge a loose stallion.

9th May
Early ride. A raging wind and very hot. The roof very acceptable at night. A most agitating thing happened last night. A. had a brother officer to dinner and they sat outside in the garden near the porch. I went early to bed, being glad to shed my clothes, and went up on the roof where I sleep now always. Billy followed me and we walked round the flat roof together. Even the chain mattress with a sheet over it gets too hot to be comfortable so I thought I'd wait a little before committing myself to it and Billy and I continued our parade. There's one place where there is an interruption in the low

parapet and here Billy stopped and looked over and in so doing overbalanced himself; I was close by him when he fell and it was horrible to see the little white figure dropping to earth like a stone; I shrieked and the two men came rushing along to where Billy lay but he was up soon afterwards quite happy and yet he must have fallen over twelve feet on to the ground which is hard as concrete at this time of year.

12th May
Cooler night. We are getting on very well for May is nearly half over. A. and I went to Indore for the weekend to stay with the Nawab and the *Sahib* at Jaora House. It is Jaora House now, for the residence that has been built for the Nawab is ready and he and his retinue are in.

14th May
Canoeing on the river. A. went back to Mhow but Harry is still here. They are so good to him and he has his big football with him. Col. Barr has done some very good snapshots of him with it. It is his greatest delight.

24th May
Queen's birthday parade. Liked it, as I always do. Found the Nawab and Jimmy, who come over for it, on the way there in highly coloured *pagaris* which flew in the wind. We galloped furiously to One Tree Hill and they came back to breakfast with me. It rained. The *Chota Barsat*, I hope.

25th May
Rainstorms.

1st June
To Indore for the *Mohurrhum*, which we saw from an elephant.

2nd June
Home to Mhow after dinner. A grand moon.

5th June
Sunday, and awfully hot. Bad night with the moon shining like fire on my head so that I had to come down from the roof at four in the morning and finish the fag end of the night inside the walls.

8th June

Think our trials are nearly over. Began to paint *Canna warascsawizi* and rode out early to meet E. who is coming in from Indore for a bit. Went past Rao and waited behind a bush a mile beyond it in the shade. Here I heard hoofs and waited to see her go by. She went thundering past followed by Mana Singh with a lance and I emerged and followed them with shouts till they stopped and she sent him home and we trotted home quietly to breakfast before eight o'clock. Very much excited because the sky looks really businesslike.

9th June

Both went out at cockcrow to see the young horses jumping in the riding school. A great rain and the monsoon broke. A tremendous relief.

10th June

Pouring. Got out a little in the evening under an extraordinary blue-black sky, but we had a very hot night. E.'s room was cooler than mine so I slept on the floor there, was driven out by mosquitoes and finished the night in A.'s room.

13th June

Rode but felt pretty ill and went to bed on returning. Stayed there all day. E. very good and looked after me. Sister Lloyd to dinner but I did not get up and she came in to see me.

15th June

Big rain with thunderstorm. E. left. Am much better.

16th June

Our first day out with a gun since we stopped for the hot weather. Batkheri tank. Not much of a bag. The *Sahib* came in from Indore. A snake was killed in the dining room at dinner. Skipper, the new puppy, discovered it in a corner. It gave me a horrid shake for Harry had been playing there not long before. It was not a poisonous one but we are going to have jagged tin fixed on all the outer thresholds like they have at the Residency, for there is no denying that Mhow is a snaky place in the rains.

20th June

Painted *Thevetia nerifolia*. Sat in the Club garden after tea. The band is back from the Hills and it is nice to hear it again.

26th June
Went with A. shooting into a shallow *nullah* in the Ghauts and saw
a sounder of pig.[14] Great promise of blossom in all the creepers.
Met a country lad we had come across in these parts a year ago;
he remembered us and we managed to talk a little. A nice day.

27th June
Rode and saw a large cobra near the burning *ghat*.

28th June
Did women's hospital.

3rd July
Went to Indore. Hot and steaming. The Residency is like an oven.
Both E. and I felt very washed out. Went for a drive with the *Sahib*'s
Bagli horses; I like driving a pair and don't often get the chance
nowadays.

I got another history from Col. Barr that I don't want to forget.
In one of the native states a certain man was accused by government
of a fraud — swindling money, or some such offence — and the
police were out after him. There were at that time seven Ranis of
varying degrees of relationship to the reigning family and in the
house of the most important of the seven the culprit took refuge,
claiming her protection. The Ranis, with one exception, lived in
fortified palaces and had the privilege of all jurisdiction within their
own gates; they had the right of looking into each disturbance that
happened and dealing out punishment or acquittal. The chief Rani
harboured the rascal and when desired to give him up to be tried,
stoutly refused to do so. At this time Col. Barr and two assistants
were about forty miles off in camp, and when they heard what was
going on they rode into the town and demanded in the name of the
Raj to have the man surrendered.

But the lady, who was one of the sun-descended house of Udaipur,[15]
was anxious to try her strength against British rule and refused; so Col.
Barr sent for a squadron of Indian cavalry to come from the nearest
station and see the thing through. The regiment was commanded
by a man who had no stomach for the matter and brought every
inch of red tape he could find to prove that he had no justification
for acting. As cavalry would be of no use in the siege that seemed
imminent he was ordered to dismount his men and force an entrance
into the palace. Col. Barr and his two Englishmen had transferred

their camp to a place just outside the town and the argument was going on when a priest of the Rani's family, who had charge of the tombs of the reigning princes and was consequently empowered to enter the palaces, came out and said that he would arrange the matter and see that she came to her senses. So the soldiers bivouacked round the walls and the holy man entered. He went in and had an interview with the Rani and when his request for the giving-up of the fugitive was unavailing he lay grimly down at her door announcing that he would refuse all meat and drink until his desire should be attained. But the Rani held steadily to her course and each day, as the holy man's vow was kept, he was reported to be growing weaker and to be within measurable distance of death. When things had gone on like this for nearly a week Col. Barr sent an ultimatum to the palace and late in the evening a messenger went to tell Her Highness that, in twelve hours — at eight the next morning — the palace would be fired on and entered by troops no matter at what cost if the culprit was not brought a prisoner to his camp. After this everyone turned in and awaited events. At midnight they were awakened by the priest, much emaciated but leading his captive who was promptly secured, pending trial. In a short time he was tried, found guilty and punished and after the expiration of his sentence, set free. Peace then reigned, for the Rani had learned that there are limits even to the power of a daughter of the house of Udaipur. But the gravest thing from the Indian point of view was that she had come near to having caused the death of a Brahmin.

4th July
Back to Mhow. Rained and poured. Hear we may be ordered to Lucknow but I hope not. The great attraction down here is that it is so much less social than up north and there's no doubt in my mind that the native states are twice and three times as interesting as British India.

8th July
I saw a nest of young cobras today, a revolting sight; I was riding down the Mall before breakfast when the Cantonment Magistrate, standing at his gate, asked me if I would like to see it and I went in. The thing had been discovered in a little bamboo fern-house in his garden and the gardener had just killed the brood. They were the horrible livid colour of blindworms, with that sickening, unbaked look and not much longer than very long earth worms. But what was

lovely was that the fern house had just been watered and was dripping and the white single petunias with which it was filled were dripping too and smelt as they smell in this country, with a hint of primroses. They are wonderful flowers as you see them here, velvety and of a different white to anything else, almost as if they had originally been green and then bleached without losing any of their texture. Some are pale pink but all the best ones are white with an undercurrent of pale canary yellow laced with black, in their throats. The old fashioned sticky, stodgy petunia of our youth ill prepares us for such exquisite things as these. With the emerald green of asparagus fern and the clear sound of dropping water they were like a foretaste of Paradise in the hot morning, and it was of them and not of the vile litter I had just seen that I thought as I rode.

12th July

Rained most of the time. There has been a great to-do in the house of Yessoo, the hero of the *borah* episode, today. He has been married for some time and his wife is now of an age to take up her abode with him. He asked for an afternoon off to entertain his guests and also asked me to look in on the festivities, a thing I was longing to do. I consulted Rachel as to whether this would really be acceptable to the party, and as she said it would, I stepped across to Yessoo's house amid the braying of the *bazaar* band, which was playing in the compound with our permission, clashing and banging and blowing out that absurd old tune 'The Captain and his Whiskers', sung with luscious archness by nurse-maids at the firesides of one's childhood, and accepted by the native as the true representative of the best English music. Entering the dark little place, it was rather a shock to find Yessoo and the girl sitting with the motionless stolidity of graven images side by side in a sort of green tabernacle bedecked with tinsel and hung with a labyrinth of festooned garlands; and looking exactly like idols; it was almost dreadful to see the quiet young man who had waited at a prosaic British breakfast that morning and brought in one's eggs and tea and been so sensible and understanding always, transformed into this barbaric heathen creature, this figure of wooden solemnity, bedaubed and bedizened into another atmosphere altogether. Odder still when he waited at dinner a few hours later, trim, businesslike and domestic.

13th July

Went to Indore for the day to Jaora House and found that the

Sahib was ill with fever. Yar Mohammed Khan was there and he, I, Jimmy and the Nawab dined together without him. He is not really strong and he has been too long in this country without a change. Dr Caldecott has always been telling him to go home and take a little leave, which could be managed quite well. Evelyn and her people are off home, which will be a loss to me.

14th July

A. and I went to Bercha, left the buggy at the watergate and went on foot up the temple hill, a nine mile walk over very rough ground. Some rather wild looking Brahmins were reading and praying round the place and we exchanged salutations. I found a mauve and white ground orchid.

15th July

An officer died yesterday and was buried this afternoon. Took the mare out, she is getting much handier. Painted the orchid and found it to be a *Limodorum*. The old Maharajah of Dhar is dead; I expect he finds he need not have been so much afraid of the tombs of his ancestors.

16th July

Went shooting with A. on the Mhow side of Bercha and returned just before dinner to find a telegram from Dr Anderson at Indore asking me to come at once as Captain Napier had become very ill and there were no nursing sisters to spare and most of the Indore people had gone home. I just caught the nine o'clock train and found Jimmy, the Nawab and Dr Anderson at Jaora House. We dined together, the boys very silent and subdued. I went upstairs afterwards with the doctor and found the *Sahib* desperately bad, though he just knew me. I put my things in a spare room and prepared to sit up for the night.

When Dr Anderson went away late he left an old Eurasian woman they had got in from the barracks who was supposed to look after him but whom he would not listen to, and it was this difficulty that had decided them to send to me. The Nawab's Mohammedan doctor was in the house too. All one could do was to sit quiet and be ready if he wanted anything. The boys went to bed and the house was very still; the *Sahib* lay tossing and restless and as the night went on he became delirious and would not allow the Eurasian woman near him though he took his medicine quite passively from me; he said there was a mutiny beginning and that she was a German spy. The sight of her distressed him so terribly that I made her sit where he could not see her, but he seemed to know she was near whether he could see her or not so I sent her out into the passage and he grew quieter. But the thought of the mutiny obsessed his brain and he was troubled because there were no British troops at Indore but the Royal Irish of the Residency Guard. I reminded him of the Mhow garrison within a few miles and that soothed him a little and he got a snatch of sleep and I thought he might quiet down. But he sprang up quite suddenly and I had a terrible business to get him back into bed for I dared not call anybody in for fear of upsetting him; the Eurasian woman, hearing a movement, looked through the door and it had such an effect upon him that I forbade her to stir from outside.

I sent his servant, whom I had kept within call, for the Mohammedan doctor but he could only say that he must be kept perfectly quiet; so I pushed everybody out, thinking he was easier with me alone, for I was convinced that he recognised me and I knew that Wali Mohammed, his servant, would be on watch if I should need him. A dreadful thing was that his bull terrier, in the compound, howled all night and it made one's blood run cold. Once again I had to grapple with him but got him quiet and in a little time he grew more easy and less excited and he fell asleep at last and lay for some time and I hoped and thought he was resting. So I sent Wali Mohammed for the Nawab's doctor again and leaving him with these two I went next door to get a few minutes' sleep if I could, for I was tired and footsore from a long tramp when I left Mhow and did not know how many days and nights I might have to go on at my post. I had just laid down and shut my eyes when I heard a sound and dashed out to find the *Sahib* struggling with Wali Mohammed, but I got hold of him and led him back to his bed and persuaded him to lie down. Then after a bout of delirium he fell into a sleep so quiet that I told myself we had seen the worst. I asked the doctor whether I was right and he said he believed the sleep would continue and begged me to go and rest. I was immensely relieved by the turn things had taken and went to my room leaving him to watch.

But it was a false hope and in a few minutes a sound brought me out to find the *Sahib* in the passage. I determined that whatever anyone said, I would never leave him for a moment. He slept again with intervals and though the doctor assured me he was no worse I sent for Dr Anderson in the small hours. The dog never ceased howling. Dr Anderson said he did not give up hope. Just after daylight the officer in command of the Residency guard sent to know if he should send an orderly to help me; he had only just heard what was happening. I should have been so thankful for one earlier in the night. It was now evident that the end was coming. The *Sahib* knew me, I think, and I held his hand till it came. After that I left him with the doctor and an Englishman who liked him and who had come in and was kneeling beside him, and went to my room. As I sat there trying to be calm I heard a step on the verandah and the Agent at Bhopal, Captain Newmarch,[16] who had just come by the morning train, called out to Wali Mohammed to know if his master was in. Wali Mohammed said 'He has been dead a few minutes'. I called him into my room and told him everything. Eugénie Barnes came later, packed my things and took me home with her and I went back to Mhow in the evening.

17th July
A. left very early to go to Indore for the funeral and follow the *Sahib* as chief mourner. He had so many friends but they are all away. I walked to Rao to meet him coming back. It was a military funeral,[17] as I hoped it would be, for though he had left the army he was always a soldier at heart; I could think of nothing else all day but the poor fellow. It has been a terrible time.

25th July
Went to Indore to meet the *Sahib*'s brother, who has come down from the north, and tell him all I could. I went over to the Residency. The Bayleys seem uncommonly nice, kind people.[18]

26th July
Began to write *The Sheepstealers* again. I wonder, will it ever come to anything or is it a vain imagining?

27th July
Wrote. Painted *Jasminum auriculatum* and went for a ride, nosing about for any unfamiliar flower, but saw none. Much illness. Two more enteric cases, one of them the vet.

3rd August
Went to Indore for a few days to Eugénie Barnes.

4th August
Rained all day. Mr Barnes went to Mhow by train and coming back

found himself in company with a funny bearded old boy who turned out to be the ex-sergeant Forbes-Mitchell of one of the Highland regiments who wrote his experiences of the Mutiny, a book I have possessed and valued for years.[19] Went to the railway station to meet Harry and take him to the Residency, for he has been invited there with Rachel and the Bayleys. Holkar was arriving too and with his usual politeness spoke to him and, seeing that he was hugging a ball, took it from him and began to throw it to him along the platform; this suited Harry exactly and they played solemnly for a few minutes, the huge, fat Indian in mauve satin and the small child; I never can make out why Indian royalty — the male part of it — seems to keep its grand garments for ordinary occasions and its ordinary garments for grand ones. Old Forbes-Mitchell came to luncheon and was most entertaining. Ernest Barnes had never seen his type before, being an Englishman; but, being a Scot, I knew it well; he might have been a burgess of Montrose of the old-fashioned sort. He said he was sixty eight. It was amusing to see him arrive at the door for he came in a *shigram*; and as all must, who drive in that astounding vehicle, he came out backwards, as though from a tunnel, and very nearly stuck. He was massive and encased in black broadcloth with tails and wore a chimney-pot hat; a contrast to the smart young kilted non-commissioned officer one had pictured, years ago, when the book came out. How he can wear such clothes in this temperature is a marvel. He went into business in Calcutta when the Mutiny was over, very successfully, and actually lives in the same house he had admired when landing in 1857 and thought he would like to possess. I went over later to see Harry and how he was getting on on his first visit alone and found him very happy. They are so kind there. Eugénie Barnes is a remarkably good artist and we went sketching on the Dewas road. The Nawab sent over his mail phaeton for us to use, so we took the opportunity of going out there, but it made one sad, thinking how often one had been in it with the *Sahib*.

7th August

Up the hill of Rala Mundl on an elephant and the Jaora boys came too. I long to talk to them about the *Sahib* but don't know whether they would like it, so I don't. I can't imagine they can forget him, he did so much for them and taught them to ride and to do all the things they like best. It was beautiful up the hill. Two things happened. I got a — to me — new *convolvulus* and the elephant spat in my face, backwards through his trunk. Drove home from the foot of the hill with the Nawab; something of a risk, for he never could hold 'Child of the Desert', who was in the shafts.

8th August
Out to the Ranibagh and finished my endless picture of the temple doorway. The *convolvulus* I got yesterday, which was only in bud, opened in the bath to which I had committed it.

9th August
Painting the *convolvulus*, then went to see Harry at the Residency where he is extremely happy and laying about him with a bat and ball. His precious football has gone visiting with him.

13th August
Back to Mhow.

17th August
Am plunged in Nairne's *Flowering Plants of Western India*[20] which Dr Moore advised me to get, and struggling with the Natural Orders; it is very interesting but my love for Linnaeus remains intact.

19th August
Furious rain in the night and water coming in streams into my dressing room.

23rd August
House leaking copiously and it still pours.

25th August
Harry's third birthday. He was charmed with his presents.

26th August
Two little boys came to play with Harry; he was very polite, offering them his new toys to play with.

29th August
Am dividing my plant drawings into Natural Orders. Hospital.

30th August
I've got a new leguminous plant whose name I can't discover. I found it in rather an odd way a few days ago. I've always made it a strict rule never to pass one of those thick straggling patches of scrub one meets

so often when on foot and off a track without examining them, and coming home I was so footsore that I *did* pass one and when I had done it, blamed myself and went back. I parted the brushwood and looked in and there lay along the ground, in the very middle of it, a long trail of cream coloured pea-flowers with brown markings, in racemes. Neither Nairne nor Roxburgh can enlighten me and I shall take advantage of Dr Moore's introduction to Major Prain and write to Calcutta.

2nd September
Painting the beanflower. It takes a lot of work.

3rd September
Beanflower finished.

7th September
Took Harry over to Indore and went to the Chatri Bagh, the old burial place of the reigning family. Harry was immensely interested because he saw there the images of the Hindu gods in my books which he is never tired of looking at. Some Brahmins were there too, whom the *Bankwallah* knew and they took the friendly notice of him that Indians always have ready for children and he asked them questions about everything he saw. They were highly astonished, much amused and very kind, taking him by the hand and showing him the place.

18th September
Eugénie has asked me to go to Bhopal[21] with her to see the place. Slept in the train in Mhow station till 3 a.m. when we started.

19th September
Eugénie got in at Indore which woke me up. Arrived late after a dusty journey.

20th September
Out early to paint.

LETTER TO C.K.E.

Violet writes to her mother in late September 1898, describing her visit to the Muslim city of Bhopal. She also recounts, in her diary, her meeting with the Begum Shah Jehan, female ruler of Bhopal state, and her visit to the great Tope *at Sanchi.*

Bhopal.
September 1898

. . . This is an old Mohammedan city and if one met the Prophet himself in the street one would not wonder. The streets are narrow, very narrow, and so many of the houses are half tumbled down; old staircases grown over with grasses and creepers stand out in ruins against the sky among heaps of filth; birdcages are half out of the windows and half in. Turbaned heads and faces of venerable old men look out over ramshackle shutters and balconies; flowers are planted on roofs and hang down in trails and bits of broken and unbroken mosques peep out of side alleys and between houses. The sons of Islam prance below on weedy horses with their reins dangling and red litters containing ladies one can't see go about the streets. When we arrived here we went for a drive in the city, latish. There is a carriage of what I call the *berline* description put at our disposal and in this, with two ragged men in attendance, standing up behind on the footboard or running along bawling to clear the way in front, we set out to see what we could of the place.

We got out at the Jamma Musjid, a large mosque, just as the sun was setting and it was the prayer hour. At a street's end we came to the narrow market place in which it stands with a high gateway of old red stone at the top of a flight of steps and we went up and looked through a door into a court where, with their faces turned to Mecca, knelt or stood or lay about four hundred men. On the tower above them the tall minarets were topped with gilded balls; the sun struck on them and on the warm stone and the white pigeons flew about like flashes; just in front of us, inside the door through which we looked, a young man in a ragged shirt and trousers lifted his hands to his head and cried in a voice that rang over the sounds of the city outside. 'Allah! illah Allah!' We stood as near the door as we dared and listened to his high wild voice. The kneeling men prostrated themselves.

We went back to the carriage and told the coachman to drive us a little way out of the town, for we wanted to see what it looked like when one is outside the walls; and it was well we did for when we pulled up and looked back at it lying in the dusk the sky overhead was green-blue like an aquamarine and a young crescent moon that was turning golden as the light went hung above the Muslim city with one star just over the horns of the half circle; the very emblem of Islam. It was exactly as if it had been set there for the purpose of proclaiming the faith of the place below. But it was a wonderful evening, cool and delicious, and besides the crescent, another great display arose. We looked across the plain to the north and saw a dark purple cumulus cloud coming up, one of those that often rise at this hour at the end of the rains. First, out of the translucent green of the horizon there swam up a cloud-castle, high and steep, then out of the same sea rose the head of a serpent that seemed to threaten it; but it melted away and there came a horseman all of cloud with a spear and a flying cloak who travelled along just above the junction of world and sky. I have never seen such a sight.

It was nearly dark when we got back to the guest-house. The Waziri *Sahib*'s palace where we are now painting has a white façade picked out with blue that ends in a high gateway and here the green parrots scream and perch everywhere in its *niches* and the world passes below, soldiers, beggars in plenty, country people and the town population. The guest house is pretty, a low straggling building in a garden near the shore of the lake. It is a common experience, if one goes about in the native states (as I have the luck to do) to live enjoying hospitality that has no visible source, waited on by decent serving-men and finding one's meals ready and one's bed made. I hope we may see the Begum before we go. The Agent is here, a pleasant man and we are to dine with him tonight. This morning I got a little silver box shaped like a pineapple that I am going to send you. Our verandah is a mass of blue *convolvulus.* . . .

(Diary)

23rd September

Went to the garden of Secundra Begum[22], a rambling very attractive place with tall trees and a riot of old fashioned roses straggling about and a few peacocks straying in it. When we are by ourselves Eugénie and I often talk French; she is bi-, or rather, tri-lingual and it is very good for me, who have not had to speak it for ages, to get a little practice. But last night in the guest house after dinner as we sat talking we remarked the many framed photographs of groups of men on the walls, some very much out of date and others more modern; they all suggested the Indian Political Service. Eugénie, who is a little creature, stood up on a chair to examine them through her lorgnette. When I asked her if she found anyone she knew among them she shook her head at first but suddenly pointed to one and exclaimed 'Mais oui

— voilà un—. J'ai oublié son nom, mais je m'en rapelle de Lui —
il nous a donné un exposition de tableaux et de chansons obscènes!'
At my loud shriek of laughter she descended. 'Dieu! que je suis bête!'
she cried as she stepped down, 'je voulais dire, *comique*.'²³

24th September

Painted. We went with the Agent, Captain Newmarch, to see Shah
Jehan Begum.²⁴ She was very gracious and we women were summoned to sit beside her behind the *chik* that hid her from our view.
Though we could not see her she could see us, as we found when we
got to the other side. It was so odd to be looking straight into Captain
Newmarch's face and to realise that we were perfectly invisible to
him. A *purdah* has an advantage that never occurred to me till I
got behind one, though it is obvious enough; it doesn't matter how
untidy and dishevelled you may be, or how frightful, for your guest
will never know it. You may laugh at him, shake your fist in his
face, allow everything you may tthink, however uncomplimentary, to
appear on your own and he will be none the wiser. This *purdah* of
the Begum's being made of straw was transparent, looking from her
side into the light, and opaque, looking from his side into the dark.
She is small, very shabby and rather dirty, not good looking; a thin,
positive, lined, old woman. Her one beauty was her hand and of this
she was well aware, for it was constantly allowed to appear round
the edge of the *chik* where Captain N. would see it. It was evident
that she liked men's society and she talked away to him with great
verve, whilst we, who could see both, looked on and thought how
curious it was to watch the expression of one who is talking into a
blank wall and to notice what an advantage the situation gives to
the hearer on the inner side.

25th September

Only a fool would go to Bhopal and not see the Sanchi *Tope*,²⁵
which stands on a low rocky hill in the Bhilsa jungle. It has a
station of its own now, so we went to one of the oldest and most
celebrated Buddhist buildings in Asia, prosaically, by train, got out
at Sanchi and lay up in the *dâk* bungalow till the heat of the day
was over. When we came out an elephant was waiting for us and
we mounted and made our way up the hill with a crowd of odd
coolies and come-by-chance followers who seemed to have arrived
from nowhere. The *tope* is shaped like a beehive and has many
smaller ones near it on the hill that were built to hold the relics

of the Buddha. The large one is encircled by massive stone railings formed of enormously thick blocks and at each point of the compass there is a stone gateway over fifteen feet high bearing huge, heavy lintels thickly carved in relief with scenes from the great saint's life. A few paces in, under each portal sits a cross-legged Buddha looking fixedly out over the country; two of them are much broken but all have a remote grandeur about them that no damage can entirely mar. A little path meandered away among brushwood to a building far smaller and differently designed which contains another cross-legged figure, inferior in size but the finest one of them all.

When we went down from the hill it was dark and for part of the way we descended a flight of steps cut in the hillside. The elephant walked down with most meticulous care and, swaying on the top of the great creature, one felt as if one were in mid air; a half-naked man ran in front with a torch to show it the way. Tall bushes and creepers grew at each side which made the darkness darker and all the coolies and people came after in a shuffling procession. The *mahout* said to the elephant (who was a lady) '*Aré*, sister, be careful. Watch your steps. Go gently, sister elephant', and when we had got over some particularly steep bit, 'O fine elephant!' It was pleasant seeing our procession come winding down the hillside into the very silent plain below with the stars coming out overhead and the crickets throbbing and twanging from the brushwood enclosing us all.

We stepped back into the modern world when we were picked up by a train stopped for us by signal. Getting about is an easy matter under the *aegis* of a Begum. As we waited on the platform of that little shed of a station we thought of the five great stone Buddhas sitting up on the hill in the moonlight as they had sat for two thousand years.

26th September

Today we went to the *bazaar* with the Begum's treasurer to see the chief jeweller's shop. There were some wonderful things to be seen. One in particular, a head ornament for a Rajah, was made of a spray of flowers in rubies and diamonds about eight inches long and nearly as broad; from it hung a tassel of rubies a foot long, all the fringes of the tassel being plaited into each other as thick as those on old fashioned bead mats and quite as stiff. There was one exactly like it in emeralds and diamonds, and a belt of rubies, diamonds and enamel, all the stones cut flat, Indian fashion.

The shop was very low and the verandah filled with divans; all the jeweller's male relations seemed to be there. Some of them wore jewels themselves. We sat on a divan and while we waited for the wares to be displayed we saw a little boy sitting cross legged with a tablet before him on which he wrote with a bamboo pen. A venerable old man was beside him, dictating Persian. All the time he did this he held up a small box covered with looking glass into which he gazed as he trimmed his moustache and elaborately curled grey beard with a pair of scissors. We went over to him and asked him if we might come and listen to what the little boy was learning. He put down his box very politely and said in the most cultivated Hindustani, 'I am teaching him Persian; it is well that he should know it, for he who does not know literature cannot have true communion with God.' A murmur of assent ran through the shopkeeper's relations and even the passers-by who had stopped to look in. We also joined modestly in it. 'Child,' he said to the little boy, 'read your lesson. Ladies, it is poetry. The *Gulistan* of Sadi.'[26] The little boy obeyed in a pretty, childish voice, but as it was Persian I could only recognise a few words here and there that are embodied in Hindustani and Eugénie, who knew a great deal more, could only follow him occasionally. We expressed our interest and said we had both read Sadi, translated. The old man was pleased at that and Eugénie told him that her husband could read it in the original, which pleased him still more. Then he began a sort of recitation or address to us, the jeweller, his relations and the people outside. The following is the general gist of it, gathered from as much as I could take in myself and what Eugénie told me afterwards. 'He who would govern a country must know the poets and be learned in the manners and customs of the time. To him who knows the poets and has studied literature the things of this world are displayed to his eyes as the merchandise is laid out in the *bazaar*. Literature is as salt and life is not good without it; without salt mixed in his food, who can enjoy *ghi* and Marsala?' There was much more that I can't remember and the discourse was full of proverbs and sayings and after each of these he would pause that all the listeners might express their approval and say '*Shabash. Ye achcha bat hai!*'* which was duly done. When this had come to an end the inevitable plate of cardamom appeared, of which we partook, and the usual sprinkling of scent followed.

Just as we were leaving a terrible hub-bub arose in the back of the shop; a man replacing some jewels in a box had found a deadly adder,

* Well done. That is good talk! (Violet Jacob's note)

a *krait,* curled up in it but when we expected its death warrant the jeweller explained that no life could be taken in his house as he and his family were Jains. Our hair rose but we could say no more, it being against the religious principles of the Jain to destroy so much as a gnat and the reptile was carried away with a pair of tongs and put I don't know where, and I don't know what those of the onlookers outside who were *not* Jains felt about it. We departed, having thanked the treasurer, the jeweller and the learned man for our entertainment. In the evening we left Bhopal and were sorry to go.

Violet does not leave any record of October 1898; but in November she and Arthur go off to camp, where they are joined by some fellow-officers.

6th November

Mhow. — Out to Jamli. A. got a certain amount for the pot and I got more than I bargained for, for I saw an odd looking plant hanging in a tangle above my head, jumped at it and pulled a bit down with my bare hand, ignorant that it was covered with virulent stinging hairs, though I am not likely to forget it again for my palm is swelled and stiff. The thing has a name that suits it well. *Mucuna pruriens.* Leguminous, with a plum coloured blossom. A. and I have planned a little private camp a fortnight hence, if he can get away.

24th November

A. has got his leave and we were up at half past five and off in a *tonga* to the tenth milestone that is such a popular jumping-off place with us. Trilby and the Waler had gone on overnight and were waiting beside it. He took the mare and I the pony and we went on through Betma to Senauda tank where we breakfasted and pitched our two tents under a tamarind not far from the water and near an oddly shaped *gular* tree with a Mohammedan saint's tomb underneath it. Idled about and rested and A. went off to get duck and snipe for our maintenance. There was a lovely evening light and we dined in the open at our tiny camp table in a brilliant illumination, for the moon is near the full. This is a roguish but charming little camp. We only take bare necessities with us. My extra baggage, that used to be Roxburgh, is now Roxburgh, plus Nairne.

25th November

Struck tents and were off again at seven. A long wait under a banyan tree for the bullock cart to come; we had to wait for it as we had changed our minds and our intended direction and meant to make for Depalpur; when we got to the old camping ground there it looked so snaky and there were so many shed skins lying about that we chose another more open spot on good ground with a few trees. Near at hand was a beautiful Mohammedan well which I made a drawing of. A. went off shooting for the pot and we sent a *syce* to Depalpur village to cater. Karoo was very funny that night in his bullock cart with the cooking things; whether he feared robbers or not I don't know but his scolding voice ran on unceasingly. I wonder the other man stood him but, being an Indian, I expect he liked his jawbations better than no talk at all.

26th November

B. and P.M.[27] arrived having come out from Mhow and went shooting with A. I took Trilby and found a pleasant mango *tope* where I tied her to a tree and sat on a root looking over the country. In the afternoon I rode the mare who has had too much edge on her lately and galloped her to take it off. A great bonfire after dinner round which we all four sat in its pleasant blaze, talking and laughing at P., who has a merry tongue.

27th November

Depalpur. — The Waler threw herself over a heel rope so I had to stay in camp all the morning. I had meant to take Trilby and go out in the afternoon but the others came in at mid-day bringing specimens of the much desired blue lotus, *Nymphea cyanea*, so I had to attend to that instead and worked hard all the afternoon in the shelter of my tent. It is a most lovely, not very large lily, of so pale a lavender blue that in full sunlight you might almost think it was white. It does not open out wide and cup shaped, like the white water-lily of the Thames backwaters, so that its gold stamens are generally hidden; and if you turn back its flat green leaves you find that the under side is richly purple. I have wanted that flower for a long time and now I have its portrait. B. and P. left to go back to duty and I had time in the evening to get the pony and go across the water to an attractive village with a pool by it and banyan trees, but there was no time to paint there. We had cherry brandy for dinner tonight to console us for the loss of our companions.

28th November

Up betimes, moving camp to Senauda; went by Jalanda and got in before the noon heat. Wrote a mail letter and sat on the *bund* watching A. trying to get ducks and listening to the curses of a little Bhil when they would not come over. Dined off snipe.

LETTER TO C.K.E.

November 1898

. . . I am writing this from our camp and as I have no ink it may be harder to decipher than ever. . . . We didn't get much sport at Depalpur and we left it this morning early. . . . I have got the blue lotus at last! It is the same sort of blue as an *agapanthus* but far paler. Our days are something like this. Just before daybreak, about quarter to five, our camp stirs; fires begin to burn and pots to clatter and one wakes up. It's nice to lie in one's tiny tent (I can't stand upright in mine except close to the pole) and see the sky getting red and the world growing light. About six A. comes in in an overcoat, for the mornings are pretty chilly, clasping a teapot, and sits on my bed whilst we drink. Then we have a cat-wash and dress and breakfast at our faithful folding table and are very hungry. A look round at the horses picketed close by and we arrange our day. He goes off to shoot and I get on one of the horses and make for any point of the compass I happen to fancy with a sketch book in my pocket and a botany book in my haversack. I stay out sometimes for hours going through wastes of grass burnt straw-colour, through villages with red idols set up outside them. Often I come across some pleasant, shady mango grove, or *tope*, as they call them, and tie my horse to a tree and either sketch or read, if I have a book with me, or perhaps see some plant I do not know and hustle home to paint it before it droops. We lunch off bread and potatoes and anything that A. may have shot and then off again on foot, if the other horse has been out already. Home about dusk. A tidy up and bath in my tent. The dark comes down suddenly and we dine in the open with one lamp on the table and one at our feet to keep off any crawling thing that may be about. Moonlight here is clear like a searchlight and you see a great distance and objects keep some of their colour. We are generally asleep by nine o'clock. A good life.

There was frightful bawling this morning over the loading of the bullock cart but at last we got it off. We have now gone back to our first camping ground, which we had on our way to Depalpur, and I am writing while they are pitching the tents. We are in a grove of trees and my tent is under a *mowha* — a tree you often see mentioned in Kipling — and the horses are under the shade of a *gular. Gular* trees grow curiously sometimes with irregularly shaped holes piercing the trunk like windows and their odd outlines make them look rather sensational. This one has an old Mohammedan grave under it; right among its roots, is the grave of a *Pir*, or holy man and there is a little ragged white flag stuck in the ground. . . .

(Diary)

28th November

Made a black and white drawing of the *Pir*'s tree; I can see it from my bed and it looks very ghostly at night. Only one more day here and we shall make for the civilization that will be dull after this. Went out to prospect this morning but found nothing to draw, but luckily had a Balzac in my pocket and sat with it in a fine shady *tope*. Today under a tree near my tent I saw a large chameleon begin to go up it; he stepped off the ground and proceeded very deliberately up the trunk and when he had arrived at a height a little above my head he stopped and remained still, as if he was dead. After a long period of thought he decided to go on and continued his way spirally, going round and round the stem as he mounted. Happening to look up into the branches I saw a grey squirrel emerge from the leafage and set off downwards, also spirally. Neither creature seemed to be aware of the other's presence and I wondered what would happen when they met; at last they came face to face, for the stem was not thick and they popped suddenly out on each other. As though worked by a spring, the chameleon spread-eagled himself on the bark and made a lightning grimace of such parts and magnitude that the squirrel turned and fled upwards as though he had seen the devil.

30th November

Painting early. The cart got off before noon and we rode home through Betma and Mota Billod.

December is taken up mostly with Christmas celebrations. Arthur is appointed Brigade Major.

1st December
Have got fever.

3rd December
Got up but returned to bed.

6th December
After five days of it, am out again.

11th December
Well again, but not exactly very strong on my legs. The polo week will soon be on us with its gust of gaiety. Personally I think it far the best plan to have a big burst now and again and then go back to normal life until the next jollification comes round. There is going to be a fancy dress dance and I am busy with my own and A.'s clothes. I took the buggy and the dogs today and went to the mango *tope* near Harsola village; there was some rough ground but I got the cart over it and found a new way home. I moored up near a fine Mohammedan well with an image of Hanuman hard by and started painting; a large magnificent tree spread its branches over the masonry and added to this, a passing man came and sat on his heels on the well steps, holding a fold of his garment carefully over his mouth, so that a devil, summoned by my presence, should not leap down his throat. His pose was perfect and he was just such a figure as I wanted in exactly the right place. The dogs shared my luncheon.

15th December
Quite good races and a fancy dress ball. Had a black Pierrette dress with a high extinguisher hat and A. bloomed into a canary yellow Pierrot with a huge ruff and had a small drum which he beat in moments of expansion. There were various other Pierrots, and H. who had procured himself the outfit of a low church parson and a pair of side-whiskers, was mobbed by the whole crew of them. There was a long passage leading to the supper tent and H. and I, feeling light-hearted and light-heeled, raced down it hand in hand and sprang like Harlequins into it. Some frowned upon us and some shouted with laughter. Anyhow, we cared nothing.

16th December
Eleven of us were photographed in last night's attire.

17th December

Races. A picnic with some of the choicer spirits near the judge's box. Dined and supped out. End of the polo week and return to sanity. A rather funny thing happened at an extra dance there was the other night; during the evening a woman came in whom I had not seen for a long time and believed to be in England. We were glad to meet and sat down in a quiet place to talk. There was much to hear and we were deep in conversation when a figure crossed the empty floor between the dances with something of a dancing master's airy gait and an elderly man who she knew slightly and I not even by sight, stopped in front of us. He put his head on one side and shaking an arch forefinger cried 'Scandal, dear ladies, scandal!' I had not the presence of mind to say 'La! monster, you are incorrigible!' as I should have done, and he pirouetted away and was lost in the shades of that Early Victorian world which he supposed to be still round him.

Christmas Day, 1898

Harry was much occupied with his presents and sat with us to partake of his first luncheon with grown-up people, pulling crackers and enjoying it very much. Dinner at F.B.'s, we providing the goose and another guest the plum pudding. The dinner would have been very cheerful had we not heard of Mr S.'s death in hospital from enteric in the middle of it. A dreadful silence fell on us and it was a relief when a cat that had got in and was lurking under the table clawed one of the guests by the leg, making her spring up with a shriek and changing the atmosphere.

26th December

Young S. was buried. I rode some way out today and was far from any road when I heard the sound of the horns that the Brinjara people carry with them. It's a high, clear note that comes floating across country when they are on the move; I've heard it when I've been awake in my tent at night at Mandu and always thought of 'the horns of Elfland faintly blowing'.[28] There is none of the blare of brass about it. It's more like a disembodied voice in the air. I had never seen the instrument that produces it till today, for my only sight of Brinjara *log* moving was some months ago when they streamed by outside our compound wall and I was standing inside it. They are the grain-carriers of India — or used to be — and I rather think they carry other things as well in the way of trade. They are little, slight people not unlike the Bhils in appearance but better looking and their women can be extraordinarily fascinating figures. What is so attractive is that many wear a kind of thing like a pointed horn on the top of their heads, slanting a little backwards and covered by the *sari,* which makes them rather like Spanish ladies on a feast day in their towering combs and long mantillas.

I once saw a Brinjara woman at Sadalpur when I was grubbing for a plant; I looked up to see her walking among the trees not far off. She moved beautifully with her *sari* drawn about her in one long, undulating line from the top of her pointed headdress to the hem of the skirt that splayed out round her ankles as she went in and out of the light and shadow, looking back at me over her shoulder. I did not speak to her, for on the day when they went by our compound I ventured a mild jest which met with no success. They were passing along with their grindstone — they always carry them with them — roped together in pairs and slung across their cattle like panniers. Upon most of these sat hens, tethered loosely on the backs of the little bullocks and swaying easily with the paces of their steeds. I said to a man who walked beside them '*Tumara murghi bohat achcha sawari hai*'* but received a look of haughty contempt. But today I was luckier. As soon as I heard the horn I pulled up to listen and saw on the skyline a party of Brinjaras collected on the top of a conical hill, so I made for it and arrived in due time in the middle of them. They looked a little surprised but quite friendly and I explained that I had come up because I wanted very much to see the horn. So one was handed up to me to look at, a long straight metal instrument, very light. When I gave it back I asked them to blow it again, but at the first sound the mare backed and then made as if she would stand up on her hind legs, a trick she's liable to. I didn't want the risk of being rolled on up there on the very edge of the hill and I was just going to ask them to stop when a couple of them jumped to her head and held on to either side of the bit while a long blast went out over the country; she didn't mind it once it had begun and stood quiet till the last echoes had gone. The little men pleased me by seeming to think it perfectly natural that I should wish to hear the horn; I am sure if I'd had a *syce* with me he would have thought me crazy.

27th December
A. went to Delhi manoeuvres as Brigade Major to the 6th Cavalry Division.

* 'Your hen is a good horsewoman.' (Violet Jacob's note)

29th December

Had a long solitary ride towards the Ghauts. It was latish and there was the beautiful light on them that one sees so often. The air was so refreshing that I went on and on, enjoying it. Next month we are going away for some weeks' change to the Kumaun lakes.[29] We were entirely averse to going to the real, official, dreadfully social hills, and kicked against the idea, and by a stroke of luck, a brilliant idea of Col. Barr's saved us and we have taken a fishing hut on the shores of a lake called Naukuchia Tal. It belongs to a man who built it up there, far from any white habitation.

1899
Diaries and Letters

Violet's accounts of 1899 mostly take the form of diary entries, with a few letters to her mother at the end of the year. There is no record of the first few months of 1899. Presumably the Jacobs' trip to the Kumaun lakes, first mentioned in December 1898, and planned for January, was postponed. They depart in April, and Violet recounts their pleasant time in the hills, by the lake Naukuchia Tal, where they stay until late June.

10th April

Packing all day. Had dinner early and went down to the station. A good many came to see us off. We have never been away for more than a few days before, so I suppose they came out to see the marvel of our departure. General Nicolson was among them. He is always so nice to us. By some carelessness on our part the train was just in motion before we realised that it was starting. Fortunately Harry and Rachel were settled in and we ran like hares and sprang in without saying goodbye to anybody. The General was so agile he ran along with it and we managed to shake hands with him and one or two others. One would think they did not expect to see us back. It grew very hot as we went down the Ghauts and we turned in and slept.

11th April

Khandwa at three in the morning. Hotter than ever. Changed to the broad gauge. It cooled a little and we stretched ourselves out and slept till daylight when we got up and made some sort of a toilette; but at Itarsi, where it was baking, we took off nearly everything we had on. The *tattis* would not work and we got through the day as best we could. Another fearfully uncomfortable night and the dust and black dreadful.

12th April

Cawnpore just before daylight.[1] There we changed and made for the Civil and Military Hotel for breakfast and the bath we longed for

and then went off to see the place we had always so much wished to
see. The memorial church impressed us, as it must impress anyone,
with its walls covered with tablets and the marks of 1857, rows and
rows of names of those who had died of their sufferings at the hands
of the mutineers. Going through the scene of these horrors nothing
short of ferocity was in one. The *Suttee Chowra Ghât*, where the
sand stretches for miles on the further side of the Ganges bed and
where those who had escaped to the boats were shot down, seemed
to reek of blood and terror and death. We had much time to spend
but we went to the garden where the well is into which corpses and
those who were not yet corpses were thrown. It is railed in and no
Indian is allowed to approach it. I thought it rather spoilt by the
large white angel standing over it; it needs nothing but itself to
speak of the solemnity that is round it. The house where so many
women and children died horribly made one shudder, with its bare,
sinister walls crowding upon one, kept spotlessly clean and all the
more suggestive for that; every angle and corner was revealed round
which the murderers must have chased the defenceless creatures. It
is unforgettable. We started on again in the evening.

13th April
Woke half an hour off Bareilly and changed to the Rohilkhund and
Kumaun line. There was a dining car on the train, quite new to us
who had never seen such a thing in India, extremely comfortable
and well appointed, and we breakfasted in what seemed almost
sinful luxury; we got to Khatgodem at noon, nearly an hour late
and thankful we were to get out on the platform and see from it
the beginning of the steep, tangled way to the hills rising straight up
before our eyes. *Dandys* were waiting with their teams or crews, or
whatever they are called. It seemed a marvellous thing to be really
starting for the hills. The heat was still pretty strong and we crossed
a little river and got up some distance before we felt the coolness that
increased as we went on and was like a breath of new life; after three
hot weathers we need it. I could see all sorts of things growing that
I did not know and the only trouble was the impossibility of getting
at them. There was a creeping *Bauhinia* with a clustered blossom
reminding one of rhododendron flowers, that hung in trails with
very large leaves; the clusters were white with a lemon-coloured flush
and the curved protruding stamens added a touch of light grace to
each blossom. The ordinary tree *Bauhinias* were out in pink flowers
marked like *pelargoniums* and as we wound up the hill we passed

places where the rock was lime white. That, with the *Bauhinias*, was like a piece of fairyland. After a long climb through woods and by rocks we drew near Bhim Tal, the biggest of the Kumaun lakes, and came out on flat ground. The place was thick with rose bushes, starry with white single flowers rather like the English *Rosa arvensis* but larger and flatter. There was a little old *dâk* bungalow by the path, empty and solitary, and as a tremendous shower of rain came suddenly down on our heads we made for it and were kept there three hours. When it began to clear we went on through dripping tracks among the press of bushes; how cool it looked! At the open bits we were almost knee deep in small blue *delphiniums*; these with St John's Wort, golden yellow, and the galaxy of white roses that covered every twig and spray were a feast to eyes fresh from the plains. At last we came upon the grubby little temple at the beginning of the Naukuchia lake and, winding along the shore, reached our hut.

14th April

Up at cockcrow to examine the world. There is no food so we are doing the best we can with some sardines, bread and tea from our tea-basket. We've got coolies who will run between this and Naini Tal,[2] which is our nearest civilization, for provisions, taking a day to go and another to get back. In the afternoon A., Maula, I and two of these set off for Bhim Tal to see what food could be got there but were not very successful. The sun was fierce but we had a fresh wind. I got dead beat before we got home and when we reached Naukuchia temple we shouted for a man to bring over the boat that is ours with the house and is moored up at a little landing place near it. Being short of food we were rather dashed in spirit to hear from him that he had caught no fish but one was pulled out before dark which we had for supper. I enjoyed my day and the views of the mountains that we saw. At one place where the track ran across a piece of wet ground with shallow running water it was thick with English buttercups. I believe the white roses here are *Rosa pubescens*.

15th April

Painted St John's Wort. We can't get much food yet, as 'Jones-*sahib*', the more or less European personage who lives at Bhim Tal, cannot supply anything till Monday but we managed yesterday to get a little mutton from him and did our best with potatoes, tea-basket bread and onions. One of the coolies, fishing with dough, got a fish that we devoured gratefully. I wish the fishing tackle would be quick and come from Allahabad; it has been ordered some time. Harry is very happy and is building a temple on the shore to Bhiru, the god whom he affects at the moment. He and Umar sometimes make really wonderful ones; they build them with stones, odd bits of wood, toy-box bricks, cigarette cards and anything coloured or shining that comes their way, and when the structure is finished they take any small branch that has twigs or thorns and stick it up in the middle; they then collect single blossoms — frangipani flowers for choice — and set a blossom on each protuberance; the effect is fantastically charming despite the strange things they make use of. They'll get no frangipani here, but they'll find something else. Today we heard that bird that makes a noise like the whirr of a fishing reel being run out and would have been completely deceived if we had not known of its existence before we came.

16th April

Roamed about generally. Neither A. nor the boatman has caught a single thing. A meagre commissariat, and supplies can't come till tomorrow. I found a track which took me up to the top of a hill and sat looking down on the lake above a creek where there is another temple; these are dull affairs after the Central Indian ones but this particular little building is conical and makes a better feature in the landscape than the squat box at the top of the lake. Sat out in front of our mansion after tea while Harry turned somersaults for our amusement. A very frugal dinner.

17th April

Painted *Delphinium ajaccis*. Out trawling and got nothing. The Allahabad man seems to have forgotten us. Thunder and heavy showers and fish evidently not taking, and if they were, we have nothing to catch them with. At least we have got milk and butter and today we have had enough to eat, which was pleasant. The bookseller in Bombay has sent me Crooke's *North Western India* instead of his *Religion and Folklore of Western India*[3] that I ordered. Tradesmen seem to have a grudge against us.

18th April

Squally and no rises. Painted *Rosa pubescens* and rowed A. out to fish, the flies having come at last. Walked to the other end of the lake; rain came on and I sheltered under a large *peepul* tree and was only liberated from there by a man coming out from behind the temple to tell me that he thought a great storm was rising; he unearthed an umbrella from a hovel hard by that looked as if it could contain nothing human and insisted on my taking it, urging me to run my best. This I did and got home a few seconds before a perfect deluge, with lightning and crashes of thunder came on, quite dry, thanks to my friend.

19th April

Harry has been longing to see the temple so I took him along the shore and then carried him on my back while he carried the umbrella to return to my benefactor. There was a strange *sadhu* sitting in front of it with whom we exchanged civilities. We strolled slowly back round the base of one of the small hills that have their feet almost in the water and sat watching a jackal come down to drink; Harry is a very good companion despite his extreme youth for he is interested in everything except his alphabet (which he is determined not to learn) and misses nothing. It was so damp that we had a wood fire after supper.

20th April

Up the high hill west of us with a field-glass and looked down into the Gola valley and river. I saw places I should like to explore later and a way into the big ravine where *Bauhinia candida* is growing and I think *Bauhinia racemosa* may be there too. Looking down on Naukuchia, I could see A. fishing. Came across a piece of the wistaria-like flower that grows at Mandu but it was far too much faded to paint. There were orchids sprouting on several trees but none yet in flower and I built little cairns of stones on my way down to guide me back to them and I shall go back in a week or so to see what is happening.

21st April

Painted an unknown pink flower and rowed A. out to fish after supper; we hugged the shore all round the lake and stayed out till it was a sheet of black and silver. Home in the dark. Lovely. Am beginning to understand the manoeuvring of the boat more shrewdly and silently. If A. takes the oars to go in at night and I have the rudder I find if I steer straight on Corvus[4] I can always bring her direct into the landing stage. The stars are wonderful now.

22nd April

Painted the small blue gentian. A. got a decent fish which helped the pot. Up the hill behind the house and saw into a new country with bare blue peaks like craters. Got some *Bauhinia racemosa* which, though it was almost over, had some paintable sprays left. The pods are most astonishing things like black puddings, over a foot long and so hard and impenetrable that they can neither be cut, broken nor hacked open. Took a few home. It is evident that there will be a whole crop of orchids on the trees, especially on those overhanging the water, but none are out yet. An ominous thing has happened. A white man has appeared on the other shore, right opposite, and has sent a coolie over to ask for a boatman, which shows he knows this place. Rage and horror fell upon us; but, talking it over, we decided, as the man had come a long way — so the messenger said — we would send the boatman across with the extra boat. I took his place and rowed A., filled with the martyred sense of my own virtue, for I had intended to fish, myself. The man has pitched a tent and lit a fire which is smoking away among the bushes. Our kingdom will no longer be our own if he doesn't march on. At any rate he has decent manners for he sent over in the evening to say he had not known there was anyone in the hut and had not intended to usurp our man. His name is Lewis Hyde Baker and he has brought a small boat with him. All this depressed us very much.

23rd April

Up at 4.45 to fish, A. got one, I nothing. We had a council of war about the enemy opposite and decided that we must find out what he is like and whether he intends to stop. That little camp has a permanent look. So a collar was put on A. after breakfast, the boat was pulled out and he rowed across to call on him. I took the field glasses and lay in the shadow of a bush at the water side, agog to watch the proceedings and I saw A. land on the slope of grass below the camp. As he went up a tall figure came out followed by a little black dog. They shook hands like Livingstone and Stanley in the picture and disappeared into the tent. They were such a long time in it that I was getting bored when they emerged and A. re-embarked, escorted to the boat by the enemy, but I hung about till he landed and I could ply him with questions. Does he mean to stop? How old is he? Where has he come from? Does he look as if he drank? 'He's coming to supper tonight,' said A. 'You'll like him awfully.' We set to on our larder and got out all we had. Supper was a great success.

He is an uncommonly nice fellow, somewhere in the forties, I should think, quiet-mannered, with a grizzled head and highly amusing, a Major in the 3rd Bengal Cavalry, on leave, and he has marched a long way from the north. As we sat at supper I saw him eyeing a half finished drawing of mine of the Indian strawberry. My cup is full, for he is a botanist, among other things; I rose like a fish, and quicker than they rise in this place. We had out all my drawings and he is going to lend me Brandis' *Trees*,5 which he has in his tent. He stayed late and when he had gone we decided that we'd like him to stop and that he'd be a fine addition to life.

24th April
Finished painting *Fragaria indica*. The enemy sent over Brandis' *Trees* and a Botanical Dictionary and I read for five hours without stopping but for meals.

25th April
Off behind the temple and down a bank to get some of those pink roses that are, apparently, wild. Met the enemy as I returned and made the acquaintance of Topsy, the dachshund. He came over to tea and we all went fishing after, I rowing A. We are planning to go up the high hills on the west to see the other side and look for Mallowa Tal.6

26th April
I went up to the orchids guided by my little cairns; one of them is undoubtedly over and one has produced something which may or may not be a blossom and is most superlatively hideous.

27th April
We and Major Baker set off for the top of the hill east of us and were over the water by 5.20. A fresh morning. Topsy came too though it seemed very stony going for her little feet. Saw a new yellow balsam, a golden cactus and various other plants. A great pull up and a fine view lying below us. We zigzagged up and arrived at the saddle of the hill at eight o'clock to find no sign of Mallowa Tal; the other side was very disappointing. For the first time in my life I saw rhododendrons wild, tall and strong and rich with crimson blossom. We scanned the plains with our glasses. Going down we came upon the most awful specimen imaginable of the vegetable world, a fly-eating *aroid* coloured like

blotched raw meat and filling the air with what one might almost call a blinding stench. Knowing what it was, we cut it open and it revealed a mass of imprisoned flies turning a livid colour by their long seclusion from the light. Its carrion-like hue and filthy smell attract them and once they crawl down into its middle they cannot escape, as it has a long, india-rubber-like *spadix* furnished with a ring of excrescences like stamens and set downwards against which they cannot move up from their prison. I think it is a *Sauromatum guttatum*. Had a drink at the enemy's camp on the way back — at least I did. A. was haughty and would not have anything, nor let me. But I was parched with thirst and had one behind a bush while he was getting into the boat.

28th April

Took things easy, being footsore. In the afternoon when A. had gone out to fish I took out *The Sheepstealers* and settled down to work and getting well under way, never raised my head for hours. At last I was tired and looked up and found it was dark outside, which the lamp Maula had brought prevented me from noticing. The clock was standing at twenty minutes past eight. I was horrified and had visions of A. drowned in the lake, so I got the hurricane lantern and called Maula; his face was rather long too. We ran along the shore in the direction we thought A. had taken, shouting and getting tangled up in the scrub and trees of the wood that borders the water. My heart was in my boots as we ran and yelled and heard nothing. Once out of the wood, A.'s voice in the distance replied in shouts that he was in difficulties and to come out to him. Maula and I ran back for the *chowkidar* and he and I embarked with the lantern in a leaky old tub, guiding ourselves by the sounds, for one couldn't see anything in the darkness; as we drew near a perfect volume of orders and expletives met us. 'Don't come here! Where are you coming to? Stop where you are! Mind what you're doing! Get out of the way! Don't make a noise!' These did not sound like the remarks of a drowning man and I began to laugh, and had to keep that quiet too. The *chowkidar* didn't laugh because he knew no English and Maula, who did, was probably laughing on shore. At last it was conveyed to us that A. had been at grips for three hours with an enormous fish that he almost despaired of landing, a mammoth *mahseer* that he was contending with still. But things got no forrader and after cruising about under a hailstorm of directions more bewildering than any other part of the affair, we were suffered at last to come alongside with our lantern and the leviathan was found to be a submerged, waterlogged piece of a tree which, with fiendish ingenuity, had been making little lifelike dives up and down the undulating stony bed of the lake. In a cloud of jeers and sighs the procession made for home. The lights which had now begun to move about the hillside made it look like the scene of some gala and we wondered what Major Baker, should he look out of his tent, would make of it. A. spent a thoughtful evening.

29th April
Painted *Murraya exotica*.

30th April
Major Baker to supper, full of great prospects. Even while the combat between A. and the log was going on, word was carried to his camp that a twenty pound *mahseer* was being landed and, dazzled by the news, he sent off this morning to Naini Tal for a selection of the largest flies. He arrived with the great news on his lips and we hardly dared to tell him the truth.

1st May
Did a lot of useless plant hunting and book searching but could discover nothing I wanted. Wrote a lot of *The Sheepstealers*; useless work, probably.

2nd May
The man came from Naini Tal with my rod, mended. Rowed A. out late. He hooked a good fish near the temple creek but it went off with the hook, the gut being worn. To supper with Major Baker in his tent and afterwards had a glorious evening with his bird books and botany books and talked till ten o'clock. He is a nephew of Sir Samuel Baker, the traveller and writer.[7] Home in the boat. Very late hours for us.

4th May
Went to get some of the large golden cactus and took a short cut to the place where the buttercups grow and up the stony track. A. got plentifully pricked getting the flowers and had to sit down by the wayside with his shirt over his head whilst I extracted the prickles from his back with the pincers out of his knife. Saw a new white *Trichosanthes*. Home by water and dawdled along the right bank

of the lake enjoying the scent of the Indian vine, which is out now. Painted the cactus far from well. Fished from the shore in the evening. We've had a curious dust storm, quite motionless and airless; more like a blight. Terribly stuffy and no fish rising.

5th May

Up at 4.30. We and the enemy want to prospect at Bhim Tal. Walked round the lake there and saw some small bungalows built for possible letting purposes by the ubiquitous Jones-*Sahib,* on whom be curses. He will spoil this sanctuary up here. We all hated Bhim Tal and returned to our own place more pleased with it than ever. Got some *Cedrela toona* to paint, it is a tree with a lovely lemon coloured flower like that of the tulip tree one sees sometimes in England and they say that it is much used in Mandalay for offerings at the Shwe Dagon temple.[8] It has a delicious pale smell. Saw some *Jasminum officinalis* wild and a lot of *Trichosanthes palmata,* scented like cloves. Rested till evening as we had been going from 5 a.m. till 10. Both fished and neither got anything.

6th May

My new 'Roxburgh' arrived from Bombay, the old copy being read and battered to pieces. It has had a stormy life for a book, but though it is obsolete in its science it is still more precious than any other. Saw two badgers in the dusk.

9th May

Very hot and am beginning to loathe fishing.

10th May

The heat is pretty trying and I feel rather wretched. We had no idea Kumaun is so hot; one might almost be in the plains. Up at 5 but could hardly crawl. Better by afternoon and crossed to the temple, taking the course of the stream that runs behind it. It was nearly dry and in some places we walked down the bed till we came to pools. Some of these were bordered by lemon bushes growing almost in the water; the fruit was not yet coloured but the great cool-looking green leaves and the white flowers were lovely, scenting the air and forget-me-nots grew at their feet, half submerged; a sight indeed for panting people. The clove scented *Trichosanthes* was tangled above in the branches under which we had to duck. When we emerged from the vegetation and could follow the stream from the bank we came upon a series of small water mills, many were dilapidated and deserted but some were grinding away with little men sitting crouched by the wheels and looking like goblins in caves. They charmed us very much, imparting a sort of fairy-tale atmosphere to the place and one almost felt as if one of them would start up and give us three wishes. After we had left the last of them behind we saw in front of us a V-shaped split in the hill we were approaching, and remarked that it looked as if we had got to the outer edge of the world; because though the split came down to the level of our stream we saw nothing but the atmosphere beyond it. True enough, we reached it to find ourselves gazing into space. The ground stopped dead and the stream made a dive hundreds of feet down over the escarpment and we were looking down on a misty country far below. Home very tired but the walk was well worth it.

11th May
Painting orchids. A thunderstorm broke which has dispelled the heat and is more than welcome. A barber came from some fastness of civilization today and made a visible improvement in the appearance of the establishment. We sent him on to Major Baker, who came in to tea looking quite smug. All fished afterwards and he got a four and a half pounder.

12th May
A. got a good sized fish. Rowed him out in the morning. Two Europeans appeared and fished, which angered us all. More lightning today.

13th May
Finished an orchid. Am going to give up fishing. I haven't enough patience. A great excitement at night, as the cow-herd up the hill found a panther sniffing about his shed and yelled warning all over the lakeside; the village above us lit fires and cried aloud from the going down of the sun to the rising up thereof; the servants are disquieted as it is said to be coming down to us. A. and I ran out and could hear it grunting. The noise in the village went on, making sleep difficult.

14th May
Finished another orchid. Major Baker to supper; he dines with us every Sunday and we dine with him every Wednesday. He told an amusing story of his uncle, Sir Samuel Baker, who was justly proud of the many books he had written. At a dinner he was telling his fellow guests some of his experiences, which were all the better for his being a wit and a good mimic, when an old gentleman, delighted, exclaimed

at the end of the evening, 'Delightful! Delightful! really, with all you've seen, I wonder you have never tried to write a book!'

16th May
Walked up before breakfast to a high point overlooking the Gola and the way down to the plains. No orchids out yet of the sort I want. Came on the ruins of a small fort and a bush covered with a mass of the strangest looking insects, collected in great numbers on the leaves of a shrub, so many that in the distance I took them for rich sprays of some blossom. They were pure white with long, feather-like tails which they would raise like peacocks and then put down while they jumped as grasshoppers do. I managed to catch one or two and sent them over to Major Baker. Got a belated but splendid spray of *Bauhinia racemosa*. Storms have hung about all day and the clouds gathered as if for a terrific one before sunset. A towering mass rushed over the sky with a gale of wind but did not break. Dined with the enemy, who has moved his camp and come to a place near us in a cove of the lake on our right, close to the water between the brink and the trees. We call it Baker's Creek. The lightning went on all the time. We each cast a fly into the pool in front of the tent but no one got a bite. These insects I brought down have astonished him, for he has never seen or heard of them before and can make no guess at what they are.

17th May
Painted all day till five, when I thought some watercress might make a variety for our meals and went to look for some at the big spring. Going round a thicket I came up against a very tall handsome young man whose hair was cut square from nape to jawbone and very thick. His face was painted and he had an immense coloured paper mitre-shaped headdress. This sounds comic, but wasn't. Tinsel hung on either side of his head — that sounds *more* comic, but it wasn't either — and a yellow cloak over his shoulders. Behind him came two men with a tom-tom and a litter, striped and slung on a pole; he was evidently a bridegroom on his way to bring his bride home. I asked a man who passed whether that was so and he said it was. Home with no watercress. Rachel and Harry were also out somewhere and met the bridegroom and she told me he was sitting sideways in the litter with his legs dangling. Then, I fancy, all his accoutrements *had* become comic. A lovely moon. A. out after dark and he got a fish. The lake beautiful and still and the mountains looking huge and like some magical scene.

18th May

The wedding party with the ornamental bridegroom came down the hill today and I had another look at them through the fieldglass. He was on foot this time and the bride in the litter lying flat and wrapped up like a corpse; she must have been almost smothered. I hear she is thirteen and he twenty five, which with us, would correspond to about eighteen and thirty. A woman went in front of them carrying a bundle of what looked like household utensils, among which I could see *lotas* and other brass vessels and a buck skin. I took Harry over in the boat to the temple, as he wanted to see the three stone Nandias there; he had never been in a boat before and he was much interested. 'This *is* a big water!' he remarked as we started; he was not frightened, but a little awed. I left him on the shore with Rachel and went on up a hill to search for some *Taberneamontana* bushes that I was told are there, but could not find any.

19th May

Both went up the hill behind our pitch to look for orchids, which are beginning to excite us a good deal. Saw several new ones coming out. We met the enemy and began discussing Sath Tal. He and A. settled to go there tomorrow. I don't think I can face eighteen miles rough going after all this heat we've had without being knocked up. Saw a lovely tree today which I think is *Eugenia caryophyllifolia*. A jaw-breaking name.

20th May

A walk in the morning up a hillside and met a woman who asked me for medicine for a cut on her leg and was much surprised when I told her that quinine was no use for it. I suggested a thorough washing with warm water and a clean bandage which appeared to be a new idea to her. She seemed impressed but the difficulty will be that she doesn't know what cleanliness means. The two heroes came in latish from Sath Tal where they have been today and I couldn't get much out of them about it. Plainly, I think they both got drunk. They found the heat a lot greater than they expected and early in the day, a place where they could get beer. After that, they told me, they lay down under the shadow side of a thorn hedge where they slept for some hours, returning as soon as they woke. Rowed A. out to fish in the dark and he got a good *mahseer*.

Whit Sunday

Idle day. Found *Phlomis montana*. Major Baker came in. There is evidently trouble in the stable at home, for a letter is come from Yessoo:

'Dear Sir & Madam,

I am very sorry to tell you, that I always says all the syices you don't take the horses for exercise by the market ways but the Vailer (Waler) syice Algoo he left our syice Moonshami & Yeloo & Baloo, and he goen out by his self alone at his house and he did not inform the other syices, and he went by hidden ways, when he returen from his house & before his house was one small Nala and after he gave to the jump, when the Vailer jumped the Nala & he fell down from the horse & he got some hurt upon his head nose and hand. And the Captain Adverds syice told the Moonshami that your syice is fell down from the horse & that time was quiet evening. Moonshami is alone run away at his house & he found the syice Algoo is fell down & Vailer was stand along his side & and he catch the horse & he brought with safly in the stables.

But please sir, I found the horse alright. But after I gave the report to Lt Cowley & he ask me mare is alright then I told him yes sir alright when he ask for syice where he is than I said yes sir than I told him he is at his house and after he told me you kept the syice than I said yes sir & he told me he dont want again that syice in Compound and after he told me bring that syice here but he not went & I told him you come with me because Cowley Sahib want you & he gave me the answer I not want to go.

But after Algoo he went to Doctor Magil for medicine & he ask him whose syice you are than he told I am syice of Captain Jacob & after he gave the medicine. Please sir I change the syice of Col Bar's for the Vailer because he done his work very neatly & he kept it. the horse is good & another syice new one his kept it for the white horse. And after I waited for your order, what Master giveing the order & I after I doing the same Master's order.

My best salams to Sir & Madam & give my loves to Baba.

Bungalow, horses & Dogs is alright.

& please Memsahib say my Slams to Rachel.

Your most obedient

Servant

Yessoo Butler.'

I think Yessoo must have written this with his own hand, or had a most literal secretary for in minuteness of detail and determination to reproduce ever shade of an occurrence, it reminds one of his account of his dealing with the *borah*.

23rd May

Dreadfully hot. Went over the lake to see if the lotus bed is budding in the temple creek. Had a letter from Major Prain, curator of the Calcutta Botanic Garden. Harry drew a really wonderful flower. A new tent has appeared on the further shore in the same spot where our late enemy, now our boon companion, had his, and there is great excitement in the allied establishments; we hear it is a Major on leave from Meerut and he is going to be here a week. The delight of Harry's life is a large leather football, but here, at our end of the lake, there is no flat ground to use it on, so we crossed to the temple today which has a level bit of turf behind it. Maula and Umar came round on foot, for they are awfully good about Harry, and the three disported themselves whilst the thuds of their kicking resounded over the water. Figures came stealing out from all sorts of places, boys and a sprinkling of men, and soon there was a knot of natives looking on with the greatest interest and I almost longed to ask them to join in but didn't know whether this might not knock up against some prejudice of the servants' so I didn't. Besides, if they all fell to, I thought Harry might be overpowered by them. They stayed on watching until it was time to take boat and get home; Maula and Umar ran round the shore and went so fast that they were there when we disembarked.

24th May

The Queen's birthday. Major Baker to supper. A rather grander supper than usual in honour of the royal occasion and we drank her health, standing, quite solemnly.

26th May

Major Baker says the interloper is a Connaught Ranger and has a friend with him. We haven't seen either except in the remote distance, but the same authority tells us that one of them is 'an old gentleman in a flannel shirt, disreputable-looking and running after butterflies'. Went to paint a willow down the shore. A note came from Baker's Creek enclosing one from the butterfly hunter's companion the signature of which the recipient could not read, but we deciphered it at last and sent it back to him remarking that he, of all men, should have no difficulty with it. Writer's name was Oven.

27th May

Thick fog over everything. Gasped and panted through the day and went to bed early, but I hadn't been long there when I was awakened by A. standing over me, adjuring me to get up at once and row the boat, for the fish were rising in hundreds. I leapt into a dressing gown and pulled on a pair of old riding boots and we were out on the lake in five minutes, but the moment we were afloat every fish subsided into stillness. Being out, we persevered and skirting the willows by what we call 'Snippet Point', got a good one. The atmosphere was so thick it seemed as though we were being suspended somewhere in mid air in an absolutely featureless and unreal world. No land, no stars, no anything. We got home more by luck than judgement. The survey people say that this lake is a hundred and twenty five feet deep in the middle and I can well believe it for its bed is shaped like an inverted foolscap.

28th May

Supped at Baker's Creek. The water was running so high and the wind so strong that A. could hardly get the boat across and there is no decent landing place at the enemy's camp but he was out on the shore to meet us and give us a haul in. We were rather wet. Our last feast with our cherished companion as he is off on Thursday to the Pindari glacier. The tent is a tiny one and just holds us three; I sit in the place of honour on the bed, and A. and he on a camp chair and a wooden box respectively, and the supper sits on another box in the middle. The trouble is the terrific holocaust of flies round the lamp. Stayed late talking and got home more easily than we had come, for the lake had calmed down. This afternoon an offensive-looking, stout Eurasian appeared and said he was the man who licensed rods; finding our boatman fishing, he hammered him and both came up before A., who referred the Eurasian to Captain Colvin from whom we have leased the hut and its rights. In the end the man gave the boatman two *annas* to try to prevent A. from reporting the affair; such is the dignity of the dusky-white official — though, as a matter of fact, I imagine he was not an official at all but an inspector. Anyhow that was the end of him.

29th May

Harry goes on well with his drawing and I've given him a little colour. More football, with Karoo joining in this time, and more natives appearing from various points of the compass to look, seemingly much attracted. Some rain.

30th May

On one of the islands I came across an enormous swallow-tailed sea-green moth hanging like a bat on a rock. It was so surprising that I rowed off full speed and ran to Baker's Creek to see if the enemy could give any information about the creature, each of whose wings was as large as my hand, but the camp was empty but for a boy, so I went to the hut and found A. He thought we ought to let the butterfly hunter know so we rowed about till we saw him appear with his net lying in the boat, so we accosted him and told him what it was like and where it was. He rowed away, landed on the island and, I suppose, caught it but he never troubled to come and tell us its name. We were very much disappointed and longed to duck him in the lake. Perhaps we had sent him on a wild goose chase and he found it gone. The air grew lighter with afternoon and the clouds began to disperse. Major Baker sent over two orchids he had found, one beautiful, *Saccolabium guttatum,* described as the 'Foxbrush' orchid. It is not rare. A raceme of spotted, thickly clustered mauve blossoms.

31st May

Painted *Saccolabium*. Rowed out to see what the lotus is doing and got one superb flower besides a seed vessel to add to my drawing of 1897. Had a splendid walk up the hill, along the top and down by the orchids I have been watching, but found nothing in blossom. They are very slow. The ex-enemy to supper for the last time for he starts for Almora tomorrow. All rather sad.

1st June

Up early to say goodbye. Major Baker came over. We went down with him to the landing stage and stayed watching him through the glass cross and land in Kingfisher Bay, followed by Topsy; one of the best companions we ever had. Went for a walk towards Bhim Tal and saw his boat being carried back there by coolies, a dismal sight. Home by dark and rowed A. out. He got two fish.

2nd June

Over to the temple with Harry and found some boys behind it lustily kicking a bundle of rags made up into a ball about the size of ours. I went on for a long walk up the hill and in a wood met two beautiful pheasant-like birds which ran up against me in terror and seemed to be fleeing from something I could not discover; all the other little birds screamed in sympathy. Not far from the lake I found a liliaceous plant I had never seen before growing in a dry ditch with a bank on the further side, so I began to gather the treasure and was busy with it in the ditch when I heard a sound and looked up to see a large old boar standing on the bank and looking me in the face. I stared too and wondered what I had better do next, so I said 'shoo!', which seemed the only thing to say, and he fled in horror. I can't think it was he that the birds were afraid of, for I've never heard that they mind pig. I got my plant home in good condition to paint and found it was a near relation of Soloman's seal. The 'natural order' system is becoming more natural to me now.

4th June
Took Harry out to see the *Vanda cristata* that I've discovered on a tree in the lake then climbed the hill to see my other orchid plants and rowed A. to fish after dark as usual. Got one good *mahseer*. We had a great talk at supper about old fashioned coach horses.

5th June
Painted the Soloman's Seal. Rowed out to the island and cut *Vanda cristata* out of the tree; it is not uncommon, I know, but it is curiously coloured, a mixture of green and brown. A hot, rather uninteresting day. Our friend has gone and we are out of whiskey, both bad things.

6th June
Still at *Vanda cristata*, which is tedious painting and needs much accuracy. Wrote more of *The Sheepstealers*.

7th June
Wrote. Crossed the lake for a walk towards Bhim Tal and up the hill met a woman outside her hut who asked me the usual questions; whether I was married, where I lived etc. When I had satisfied her she said 'But why does your Honour walk? Where are your horses?' I replied that I liked walking and had come out to eat the air. 'Your Honour has thick legs,' she observed, politely. Never had I so strange a compliment, and it was reassuring to remember that I was wearing leather leggings.

8th June
English mail and finished *Vanda*. Very hot. Too much so to sleep comfortably.

9th June
Too hot to dress till 5 p.m. After that took Harry over the water to see the boys kicking their rag ball at the back of the temple. He has a bad leg, poor little fellow, and cannot join in himself, but he was amused all the same. We saw a snake which fled up a tree incredibly quick.

11th June
Read the first seven chapters of *The Sheepstealers* to A. after supper.

12th June
Rain. Cooler. Very thankful.

13th June
Pouring morning with mist low on the surrounding heights and everything thick about us. It cleared late, and I, hearing there was a dead cow in the wood above us, went up and got into the fork of a tree to study the vultures and get a drawing of them. It was a shocking sight. They were, from wing-tip to wing-tip, longer than the cow. They fought over their feast and buried their necks so deep in the carcase that one could see the movement of their heads inside it; I tied my handkerchief over my nose and got on with my drawing as quick as I could. They quarrelled and screamed and mouthed at each other. One old veteran had a wing broken and had evidently been hampered by it for a long time, but he was the largest of the lot and seemed to dominate the rest, never swerving from his place near the best bits. The action of a gorged vulture trying to rise off the ground is the most ungainly thing in the world. The greed, the grotesque lack of dignity, the devil-take-the-hindmost of it all made me think of the words of an old woman I knew in Scotland, who, speaking of the crowding relations of a rich man just dead, said 'Where the money is, there will the blayguards be gathered thegither!' Some men passed by but never saw me up in my tree though I was not much above their heads; it is strange how seldom people look upwards out of doors. I got a successful pencil drawing of the birds. Walked round the lake and when I got home and A. heard what I had been doing he said I made him feel sick.

14th June

Off to look for orchids in the trees I have marked. Some were out at last but I found it difficult to get up near them without dropping my knife. One wants as many arms and hands as Kali⁹ when pursuing orchids.

15th June

Painted yesterday's haul and afterwards we went over the lake and down the stream where the water-wheels are. Gathered some *Citrus media* with the fruit still green, though far on towards maturity; a pity there is no more time to wait for it to turn yellow. The boys were hard at it behind the temple with their rag football. We heard today from the servants that the headman of one of the villages above us has sent to Calcutta for a real leather one, so Harry will have introduced the football into the Kumaun district! Unluckily we shan't hear what comes of it, but if the youth of the district play they will have either to evolve or procure rules; I suppose the enterprising headman will step in and get an expert from Nani Tal. Fishing closed today. We had a fire before night to dry up the damp and as we sat at supper a report like a rifle shot close by made us leap from our chairs and rush out for it sounded as if someone had fired at the open window. There was nobody about, not a movement outside though we looked everywhere, so we went in puzzled, to find an odd curled up, leathery-looking thing on the floor in a corner. It was the burst pod of *Bauhinia racemosa*, impenetrable by knife or even hatchet, that had been lying for weeks on the mantel piece and had exploded in the unaccustomed warmth of a fire. The seeds, rather like flattened horse chestnuts and bigger than half crowns, were lying about; they might have done us a real mischief had we been hit.

16th June

Painted *Citrus media*. Walked round the hillsides. Wonderful clouds rose in the valley over Bhim Tal. I am making a little map to leave on the wall when we go with all the names we have given the places marked on it; Baker's Creek, Kingfisher Bay, Snippet Point and so on. I wonder will anyone ever come here who will look at it? Probably it will be torn down by the *chowkidar* as soon as we are gone. I read the last of what I have written of *The Sheepstealers* to A., who is very appreciative. I wonder will anything ever come of that either? I expect not, but one can but try.

17th June
Took Harry out in the boat to see the *Saccolabium* which is now
hanging in profusion from the trees over the water, rich mauve and
cream colour with tiny carmine spots.

18th June
Packing. Painted some seed vessels. The boatman brought me a pink
lotus and I gave Harry a pencil and some paints to see what he could
make of it. It kept him quiet in this turmoil and he did wonderfully
well for a small boy. He has a tremendous facility with the pencil
and, like me, finds paint very difficult. Everything is upside down
and we all went over to the temple for the last time. A holy man with
long hair was walking about with the *patel* of the nearest village and a
man came out of the temple and gave Harry some sweets. It was very
kind of him but I didn't let him eat them, for heaven knows what
native sweets are made of. I did a little drawing of our abode just
to look back at afterwards and remember the good time we had in
it. The fishing has been scarcely worth the name — and it has been
much hotter than we expected, but we've had a lot of fun.

19th June
Did up my orchid roots in a basket. *Celogyne cristata* is just ready
to flower. What will happen to it I don't know, for it won't like the
plains. Harry and I and A. played ducks and drakes with stones in the
bay, for there was nothing else to do and we've taken our last looks
at various pleasant things. Then we sat before our door and listened
to Harry, who entertained us with stories of his own invention, now
in English, now in Hindustani when he used such native gestures and
threw such absurd pathos into bits of his discourse that we had to
hold ourselves tight in hand for fear of laughing and offending him.
Tomorrow we go.

20th June
Started at 7.30, the prospect complicated by the baggage porters,
who, it appeared, had run away in a body from Bhim Tal in the
night; and only seven turned up. I set off on foot, putting Harry
into my *dandy* and Rachel into A.'s, for he decided to take the
coolies' route to superintend the baggage and see that it wasn't
dumped and abandoned by the scratch crew which had been raised
from the villages. I set off last and alone and, taking a wrong turn,
found myself some distance off the way to the plains. I can't imagine

how I could have done such a thing and must have been thinking
of something else when I came to some cross track and took the
wrong one. But I suddenly saw that the horizon was on a different
level to what it ought to be, and retraced my steps very hurriedly
till I recognised a piece of the way down. Once on this, I made all
haste dog-trotting and passing all sorts of flowers unknown to me
that I longed to stop and gather, but I had to keep on. Lots of small
landslips and banks giving way owing to the recent amount of rain.
Overtook the *dandys* after some miles and got into one of them and
did the rest of the journey in luxury; earth and stones came rattling
down round the coolies' feet very often but they were wonderfully
clever in dodging them. We had been one hour in Katgodam station
when A. footed it in, dripping with heat to such an extent that he
looked like a man in dark clothes, or even Neptune himself, instead
of a man in khaki. He got a few orchids coming down. We got into
the train and off at last reaching Bareilly in the evening. Awfully hot
night with many mosquitoes and much difficulty in sleeping.

21st June

Cawnpore in the early morning. Breakfasted in the refreshment room
and got a paper. The Transvaal news looks very bad indeed.[10] Fear
there is war coming on and we are wondering if the 20th will go.
Looked out as we passed the fascinating country near Jhansi, basaltic
rocks rising in fantastic shapes out of the dead plain. Dined at Bhopal
in company with Captain Newmarch, who was in our train though
we had not known it.

22nd June

At dawn, I found that *Celogyne cristata* had flowered in the night
in the rack over my head and produced a lovely white blossom
fringed at the edges and with a faint straw colour flushing the
throat. Even though it may not reach Mhow alive, I have at least
seen it. After Khandwa we had a couple of hours sleep, but I got
a sight of the holy Nerbada as we crossed the bridge spanning it.
Juggernath, the railway guard who has his headquarters at Mhow,
came to see us at Khandwa and brought us a fresh fish, which I
fear will not be fresh long. After we got home, several men came
to see A. No one appears to think much of the Transvaal business
but I wonder they don't. Is it that we have been so many weeks
away from the news of the day that we overestimate things? I
hope so. Went in the evening to look round the women's hospital

and found none of our own women in it which was satisfactory.

23rd June

Busy getting things going. A. went to the square and to the club to look at the newspapers. A man brought news from Indore (Reuter) of an ultimatum gone to the Transvaal and a call for 15,000 troops from India. One does not know what a day or an hour may bring forth nor how soon we may be all scattered to the winds, for all say a wire may come any minute. It seems very grave and we must face it as best we can.

24th June

Things seem to have been exaggerated yesterday, they say.

25th June

Slept long, having been very tired. A. and I drove along the Indore road when it grew cool and talked of many things and possibilities. The country is very green and the plains are a great rest to the eye.

26th June

We hear that the South African trouble is likely to be settled satisfactorily.

29th June

To Bercha tank; nice fresh day, soft and blowy. Went about looking at favourite places. Got some *Iphigenia* bulbs for Major Prain, who has written for some. I do hope we are left in peace here, I love this country so. The *Celogyne* has lived long enough for me to paint it, which is a great piece of good luck that I hardly expected. An ugly white cat has been added to the household and I have christened it 'Katgodam', and any time it transgresses the mere mention of its name will relieve my feelings.

4th July

The *syce* Setul has been dreadfully ill. His senseless family and our foolish servants told us nothing of what was happening and we merely thought he was having fever and so did nothing for him, but this morning early he went off to hospital in a *tonga* but was so bad that he died on reaching it. He said '*salaam*' to us as he was lifted in. It is very sad, for he was a nice fellow and a good *syce* and had been long with us. It is dreadful to think that if he had had more care he might have recovered. In the evening his body was carried away to the burning *ghat*. Rachel says they covered him with flowers.

27th July

I have written nothing for over three weeks and must begin again. If I live to be old I should like to be able to look back on the sights and sounds of this — to me — beloved country and the good days we had in it, and even on its trivialities. We went to Jamli village, having meant to go to Haselpur to sketch and shoot respectively, but it started pouring and we sheltered under a tree and smoked and got wet. Our only diversion was an old countryman selling vegetables and a man on a pony with a tattered umbrella who shared our refuge; the old man amused us with the history of his affairs.

29th July

To Akolia to shoot for the pot. A boy ran out of Pitumpur village on the chance of beating for A., who took him on, and he was an excellent lad. We had our drink in Hanuman's grove near Palassi. A. smoked a pipe and I and the beater had cigarettes and a little conversation; I suppose he had never smoked one before but he accepted it with some caution and seemed to like it.

1st August

Today a child in the *bazaar* rushed straight across the street when I was driving through it and fell right in front of the white mare. She stepped over it most neatly and I just managed to pull her up before the wheel was on its neck. These things are shattering. For the sake of example I made a great row and sent for the police inspector and Rachel, who was with me in the buggy, called everyone for miles round *su'ars*. I have never used that word to a native myself and heartily despise those who do, but if Rachel did, it was none of my business and it was extremely funny to see her shaking her fists and being so unlike the Rachel of civilization.

22nd August

A gymkhana, which we eschewed, going out to Simrole instead with a gun. A few new plants but it was so hot that we lay out under a tree and did nothing until it grew cooler.

23rd August

Took Harry to see the squadron football which he liked very much.

24th August

A highly exciting cricket match, the last game of the first round of the cricket tournament now going on. It was the 20th Hussars against the Gymkhana Club team and had a disastrous beginning. The Gymkhana, in first, made 193; the regiment lost eight wickets for well under 100, with only Nulty the schoolmaster to go in and Private Harvey of the band. They crept up but Nulty got very beat; he is a weedy, delicate-looking fellow. Harvey played steadily, stolidly and with caution. Nulty made one or two big hits. When the score reached 150 he was nearly done, but was plied with soda water and held on. By this time everybody connected with the regiment, and some who were not, were congregated outside the tent shouting encouragement, and as the score went slowly up the excitement was great. When it reached 192 it was tremendous and when it got to 194 the noise was perfectly deafening and Col. Irwin,[11] leaping to his feet, thrashed the bench in front of him with a bat till one thought it would collapse. It was a funny sight for he is very small and he attacked it as if it was his enemy. A great game. Nulty looked like a rag at the end of it.

25th August

Col. Irwin has sent to Calcutta for two cricket bats of the first water for Nulty and Harvey as a remembrance of the fight they put up. This is Harry's birthday; he had a tea party and Karoo made him a cake with his name on it in sugar and his age, four years.

26th August

To Indore for the weekend to stay with the Curzon Wyllies, who are at the Residency while the Barrs are at home. Drove with my hostess in the afternoon and felt very smug, not being accustomed to take myself so seriously. The other guests are an officer of the Royal Irish and a General of no particular interest. Hot night. Mosquitoes and other hateful flies. The Transvaal looks more threatening again.

27th August
A. arrived and I was very glad, for it was very dull. Spent the morning showing drawings to Mrs Wyllie. To tea at Jaora House with Captain Cameron, who has replaced the *Sahib*. It was an effort, for I hadn't been there since his death but I am glad I went, as it had to be, some time; I thought of him much. Went to church with my hostess. She saw a pink hollyhock out of the window and was torn between her intensely devotional bearing and her desire to point it out to me. A very hot night and there's no doubt that Mhow is cooler than this place as a rule.

28th August
A.'s birthday, also the god Krishna's[12] and Parag the cowman's little girl Natia's. Returned home. Went to hear the band and talked to Mrs Neil Gordon and to Col. Irwin, who is getting very sad as the last days of his command run by.

Around this time many people are leaving Mhow and India. News from the Transvaal continues to be ominous.

1st September
My birthday and to celebrate it we took Harry out to the bridge on the Indore road and had tea in a mango grove. The aged *patel* of Umria village came out and sat by us and gave us a head of Indian corn which we roasted and ate at dinner. I got some *Crinum* today in a ditch.

2nd September
Awakened in the night by Harry who has got fever and a cold and sent for the doctor this morning who said he had a touch of bronchitis. But as he became quite normal in the afternoon and immensely cheerful I went out to dinner. B., the new commanding officer,[13] was giving a farewell dinner to the departing one.

3rd September
Harry very well.

4th September
A couple of visits to the married quarters and then went to the club and sat with the Little Man,[14] whose departure is very sad; we have always been such good friends. He told me his dressing boy asked

for leave to go out and when asked where he wanted to go said 'I go to my Devil-house', for he knew little English and mistook God for the devil, as indeed many more enlightened people have done before him.

6th September
Went to hear a gramophone, which is a wonderful invention. It played many tunes extremely well.

7th September
A. went to the Little Man's official farewell dinner; he has been eating himself out of Mhow for some time. Mrs Neil Gordon dined with me. Had a *punkah* all night but did not enjoy it as I ought, having neuralgia. The nights ought to be cool now but they're not.

9th September
War seems inevitable in the Transvaal. The 6th Dragoon Guards, 9th Lancers and 19th Hussars are warned. Col. Irwin came to say goodbye. Drove out to see the Royal Irish play the Royal Fusiliers; their team have come from Nasirabad to stay with the 20th whose indecent roars of joy, whenever their old friends scored, were loud and I wished I could have roared too. To the station late to see Col. Irwin off. Cheers, 'Auld Lang Syne', and I was sorry for him. Two doctors, Sparkes and Dove, are warned for the Transvaal, also Neil Gordon, who goes with his battery. It will hit her hard.

11th September
Painted *Barleria prionites* which I found in the next compound. Took the Waler mare out for an hour's walking exercise and met Mrs Gordon, very sad but very plucky. She says she will stay out here till October, for which her passage home is taken. They expect the final wire any minute.

12th September
Neil Gordon got his wire in the middle of the night.

13th September
Out to Jamli for plants on the Waler mare. Got fever quite suddenly as I sat doing some mending after tea. The wind rose all in a moment and blew it at me, or so it seemed, for I had not time to finish my job before I had to lie down. In half an hour I had ague and was in

bed. Five hours steady rain which is a great boon. Better towards evening but had a headache that lasted all night.

14th September
No fever but pretty weak. A. drove me out in the buggy in the cool of the evening. But there wasn't much 'cool'.

19th September
Took Mrs Gordon out in the buggy. We went out beyond the Towers of Silence and sat under the mango trees for a long time. The moon got up, pale yellow, over the plain covered with lemon grass and a boy came along and sat on a bank rising out of it; he was just like a faun. At dusk two teams of white bullocks came up out of the fields and trailed slowly over the bank; the grass smelt as only Indian lemon grass can, aromatic and sweet, and the faun got off his rock in front of the huge low moon and followed them slowly home. All disappeared into a dove-coloured horizon as the very last light went.

20th September
Alan Goring said a very funny thing today.[15] He is distrustful of the new regime since the Little Man went away. He said, 'I feel as if Mother had gone away and left me all alone with Nurse.'

24th September
I went to Manpur, driving the little white mare. Mrs Gordon and a friend had gone off there for a change of a few days and invited me to come out; I have often heard people talking about it as an odd, lost sort of spot. Dr Sparkes, whose orders have been cancelled for the time being, was going there for the day so I offered him a lift and we started so early to avoid the heat that we got there before the occupants were up and had a long wait for breakfast. The place is the most ramshackle old travellers' bungalow with a wild native garden choked with weeds and rambling, half obliterated paths. We did not like to go in and disturb the house so we sat on the only seat we could find that would bear us and smoked patiently for we were very hungry, and soon a rustling sound became plain and squeals and we saw that a Russell's viper was killing a bird hard by. The brute had curled itself round its prey and had got its fangs buried in its breast; there was no good interfering, for the bird was past everything and the viper slid away when we moved. It struck us

that this must be a snaky spot, with the place so much neglected, and we hoped there would be no more reptiles about. The country round is open and there is a conspicuous little old temple crowning a conical hill where the wild zinnias, or rather those which have escaped from the garden, are covering the place with every sort of colour and half colour. The variety of shades is greater in them than in any other flowers I know. These press up round the foot of the temple. Wandered about most of the day.

25th September

Got up before the others and walked till I found Manpur village and there I met a policeman who told me he was the local constable and a pensioned 4th Bombay rifleman; he produced his papers and was anxious to show them. I told him I knew officers of his regiment at Mhow and often listened to its very fine band and this seemed to please him so much that he offered to show me the sights of the village. I knew there were none but I went, because he was such a pleasant fellow, and looked at the school where a begoggled man was holding forth to a handful of little brown boys, the hospital and an absurd little gaol. When we parted I promised to tell Major F. of his regiment, that I had met him. Dawdling along I saw a small jungle cat the exact colour of a lion cub and admired the hedges wreathed with scarlet *Ipomea phoenecea* and white *Convolvulus calcynus*. I got a new *convolvulus* too. Up the temple hill in the evening and saw a glowing sunset spread over the hills by Mandu.

26th September

A rather disturbed night for when I was comfortably asleep Mrs Gordon appeared looking like a ghost and woke me to say that there was a snake in her room. I went in and saw it, a fat, sickening thing, that I think was a Russell's viper from its stubby blunt tail. Her friend rushed in with a lantern followed by the *chowkidar* with a stick to kill it. While this was being done the two women (with the friend's dog) jumped into my bed and pulled the clothes over their heads. After I had turned them all out and also turned a toad out of Mrs Gordon's room — which probably was what had lured the snake it — I settled to sleep once more. At five o'clock I was awoken by yells and, not knowing what might have got in this time, put on a pair of long boots before going out to see. There was another toad and after its ejection there seemed to be no use in getting into bed again in case something else should turn up; so

I dressed and departed home in my buggy, which at least contained no reptiles.

I hear that plague is bad in Poona. A little girl, daughter of General Burnet there, has died of it as well as another European and many Indians. There has been another death from enteric in the hospital. Plague, fever, war and approaching famine — which is now certain — are not cheering.

8th October
We took the early train to Patal station and went down the big *nullah* on foot, A., Maula and I, for I wanted some oleander seeds to paint and knew they must be ripe. Climbed down the sloping side of the ravine to the pool below the big waterfall, hanging on to the hot rocks and getting our hands rather sore. After I got what I wanted below we started climbing up the other side, frightfully hot work and I was dead beat at the top. Rested under trees and home by train. Maula was very good and helped me up gallantly though he probably thought I was mad. But he's a youth of imagination and always ready for anything. I had wanted those seed vessels for a long time, for I am trying to paint each flower of my collection with its own ones.

19th October
To Killod with A. and walked down towards Bercha. Near a patch of cultivation I sat down to paint surrounded by cucumber plants trained like vines. A man who said he was the son of the *patel* came along and stopped by me and began consulting me about his children's health; he brought his son, aged four, for advice about his eyes. It was easy to see the poor little thing had ophthalmia and I advised him to take him without delay to the Mhow native hospital and he seemed inclined to do so but was afraid of his wife (or so he said) for her suspicions were in the way. He finally promised he would, though I doubt him. He brought some vegetables as gifts and asked me much about Queen Victoria. He said his grandfather remembered Sir John Malcolm.[16] My Norwegian knife interested him very much.

27th October
Fifth anniversary of our wedding day. Champagne.

Violet and another British woman go camping together to Harsola.

31st October

The little camp at Harsola that Lily Edwards[17] and I have talked
about so long has really materialised and we are here in the mango
grove by the big stone wall for a few days' sketching. She has brought
a couple of tents and we've both brought food. The foliage is like
a roof overhead and I can look up from my tent door through an
opening in the trees and at night I shall be able to see the spangled
sky through the branches, a thing I love. The well near us waters
a plantation of beans which are in full bloom, trained like hops
on five foot poles; irrigating channels run between their rows and
the flow rises in them when the leather buckets are drawn up by
a pair of white oxen and tipped into the main sluice. I've been
told that this system of watering is what was used by Abraham.
Paddy birds walk about the cultivation, fearing neither God nor
man, and following any tiller of the soil who is likely to turn up
a succulent grub.

On the flight of steps going down to the well there is a stone vase
on either side holding a plant of the sacred *tulsi*. Near by is a rough
stone image of Hanuman, stained red and raised on a plinth from
which he stares out with his monkey face over the sugar canes. He
is an interesting person, this monkey idol, Ram's[18] faithful follower
and friend, who was not exalted enough to be a real divinity but had
that which raised him above ordinary beings. His story is set forth in
the Ramayana. When the demon Ravana dragged Sita from Ram —
Ram being on a pilgrimage — the despairing lover asked help from
Sugriva, king of the monkeys, and Sugriva's general, Hanuman, a man
with a monkey's head, led Ram's invading army through the Deccan
to the coast. Sita was imprisoned in Lanka (which is Ceylon) and the
rescuers were brought to a standstill by the sea that lies between the
mainland and the island. But Hanuman was not to be beaten and
sprang in one mighty leap from India to Lanka, where he began to
build a bridge across the water. His followers on the Indian shore
began to build too and when they joined hands in the middle the
whole army passed over; some pictures represent the bridge as being
made entirely of monkeys holding each others' tails. Sita was restored
to her lover and in most Hindu paintings in which these arch-lovers
in Hindu lore appear, Hanuman is seen standing near Ram. I have
a great weakness for Hanuman and like camping in his grove; he is
a gallant fellow, full of resource; perhaps the man part of him had,
by long struggle, got the better of the ape; perhaps he is a prototype

of the human race engaged in the same fight to get the better of the man and reach the god.

In the evening we sat outside our tents in the dusk of the mangoes. Today is the Hindu feast of the Diwalli when every town and dwelling place displays its light. We watched the gradual illumination creeping out all round, and the little lights came out, one by one, some far away across the fields, some in our grove. There is a *chatri* between us and the well raised to the memory of a late headman of Harsola village who was rich and whose relations could afford to build it of stone, a dome on four carved pillars springing from a high plinth; steps go up to the emblem of Shiva and the sacred stone bull, Nandia, kneels before it. The lights burn round him. In all this glow the servants sitting round their fire made monstrous shadows on the tents. We strolled about among the trees to enjoy the Diwalli and to see Hanuman, who had a lamp at his feet, a wick swimming in oil in an earthen saucer and making a greenish shine on the red monkey figure. His priest had been all day putting offerings before him and now sat on his heels attending to his prayers and keeping up a running hum of devotion just above his breath. He had a light beside him over which he stretched out his arms from time to time; his brass *lota* was full of water and he poured a libation from it and taking off his amulet, waved it over the lamp. His duties finished, he rose and turned to us who were standing by, a thin, brown man, naked but for his loin cloth and the string of *tulsi* beads round his neck. We said that we preferred the Diwalli out here to the one in Mhow. He smiled indulgently and said, 'We do our best, but what will you? It is only the jungle!'

We sat up late watching the *chatri* ablaze; it looked rather like a scene in a theatre. A pious villager came out from between the trees and went up the steps to trim the wicks and stood transfigured in the brilliance. Just before midnight a pariah dog sneaked from behind the grass hut in which Hanuman's priest was now lying asleep; he was a noiseless, skulking creature stealing up the steps, unperceived but by us, to sniff his way among the lights, guided by the savoury smell of oil and *ghi* pervading the offerings. Poor wretch, he was thankful for anything he could pick up and he looked furtively behind him as he swallowed his loot. We were glad he had found what would be more useful to him than to Shiva. Presently he put his feet on the principal light and it went out. We went to our tents and lay watching the other lamps sputter themselves into oblivion, listening to the tom-toms beating in the village like the pulse of the great

Hindu world round us. I had a touch of fever and not a very good night as I had more than once to shoo a pi-dog[19] out of my tent; and as I was just settling to sleep a rat ran over the pillow.

1st November

Out to paint and then breakfast under the trees. The white bean that is cultivated here I find from Roxburgh is *Dolichos lablab,* a shocking name for such a piece of decoration as it is. As we strolled to Harsola village today we met Major Edwards' Sikh orderly coming out with letters. No Transvaal news. The village was vastly impressed by the Sikh, who thought it right to attend us there and added the only touch of grandeur we had. Supper under the trees and an idle stroll afterwards. During this we sat down by a rough track and having struck on an abstruse subject, sat there discussing it for ages, oblivious of everything else and got back to camp in the dark terribly late. Pulled our beds outside our tents, mine under a mango. Fine, cold starlit night and most refreshing.

2nd November

Woke just after dawn with the animal world. Had an early cup of tea and went off to draw till breakfast, but did nothing interesting and then settled down to do a picture of Hanuman. Harry was brought out to visit me in the afternoon and the moment he arrived he said, 'Let's go into your tent,' so we did and he seated himself cross-legged on the floor. I suggested that he might have a more amusing visit if we went out. 'No, sit down,' said he, 'now let us talk.' I said, what about? 'About Hanuman,' he replied. So I went into Hanuman's history and when that was done he examined all my sketches. Then we had tea at our camp table and he went home, having enjoyed it.

3rd November

Awful war rumours reached us. We heard it was reported that Sir George White[20] had committed suicide and the garrison at Ladysmith capitulated. We were sure this was pure nonsense of the silliest sort, and probably started in the *bazaar,* but we are beginning to feel being out of the reach of immediate news, so have decided to go in tomorrow.

4th November

An orderly arrived bringing word of the rumours being unfounded but we are going in all the same. It wouldn't do to be out of the way should any orders affecting either of us come, so we put up our few belongings, and I made a rough sketch of the little camp whilst Lily went to the village to see a child with fever whose parents had come to her for quinine. We bade our jungle acquaintances goodbye, had our tents struck and the bullock cart packed and were off in my buggy to Mhow. A., Lily and I had tea and discussed the situation under the *peepul* tree.

7th November
Celebrated our fifth wedding anniversary by having a whole day out at Haselpur, as A. had not been able to get away on the 27th. Did no drawing and was unlucky flower hunting but walked many miles over new ground and returned at dusk footsore and brick coloured.

8th November
The Barrs have returned to Indore and I went over to the Residency to see Evelyn who met me at the station. Dined and returned by last train.

10th November
No African news.

30th November
It's nearly three weeks since I attended to this diary. It seems now that there is no chance of the regiment going to Africa for it is considered necessary to keep one cavalry regiment here; so A. and I think we can go off to Mandu for a few days and we are off tomorrow.

Violet and Arthur set off for Mandu.

1st December
Started at 7 a.m. Took Kulloo's *tonga* as far as that favourite jumping-off place, the tenth milestone on the Dhar road, to which we had sent the horses. We started straight across country and rode steadily along, but being puffed up with what knowledge we have of the map, decided to take a short cut to Mandu, feeling sure that there was such a thing and that we had lit on one end of it. As a result we soon found ourselves in a very deep, wide *nullah*, all rock and undergrowth, and it was not long before we saw that

the best thing we could do was to get out of it — somehow. We were stifling too, for the sun was getting high, and we attacked a possible looking bit of the *nullah*'s side. Our struggles up that place were like those of earwigs drowning in a deep bath and trying to save themselves and we cursed the folly that had led us to such a pass. We stumbled and slipped, we staggered over and round boulders half buried in the thorny scrub; long, tangled arms of bushes lassoed the horses' legs and ours, and we slid out of our saddles and led them, pushing along with the perspiration running down our faces.

At last we did emerge and got over the lip of the *nullah*, panting, streaming and much humbled, having wasted time we could ill afford, for it was getting hotter every minute. When we had rested ourselves and the horses we started, resolved that nothing should tempt us from the tracks again, and rode at a hand-canter, one behind the other, just far enough apart to evade the dust cloud that trailed after our respective heels; we passed Keri village, Guljeri, Silotia, Saggeri, Baggeri, Kunda and Lunera and then struck the Dhar road three and a half miles from Nalcha, the last *dâk* out of Mandu. At Nalcha, after a hard morning that had stretched well over noon, we dismounted and looked about for shade. A whitewashed Mohammedan temple stood up like a square-built, protecting angel and threw a bar of blue shadow across the dust; mid-day being well past, we knew it would lengthen.

We off-saddled by a sandy patch and sat watching Talisman and Trilby roll in it, which they did with avidity, the arab especially. Beautiful as horses are, they look grotesque on these occasions and quite extraordinarily misshapen with their amazing breadth of body underneath and comparatively slim legs waving above. One wonders how they can carry it all with a saddle and oneself in it into the bargain. Then we tethered them and sat ourselves down with our backs to the temple wall and our legs stretched out in front of us, blessing Allah whose house we leant against. The villagers were hugely interested in us. Then A. held out his felt-covered waterbottle filled with cold tea and said 'Drink honestly'. It was a real feat of integrity to take my lips from it when the half of its contents were down my throat, but I did. When he had drunk his share and we both had some food and a smoke we changed horses and were off again. What a relief a change of paces is after thirty miles of sun baked ground! We got to Mandu well before the sun dipped behind the hills. The bullock carts were there already, having started overnight; we had thought to catch them at Nalcha and should have done so but for the *nullah*. The scenery coming in was splendid. We dragged our beds outside our tents and were in them early.

2nd December

An easy day after the strenuous yesterday and we didn't stir till eight. Spent the morning wandering and looking for things to paint. I sat under a *khirni* tree and got a sketch of an old building behind the camping ground and A. shot duck. We had one for luncheon and ate every bit of it. When the light began to turn I worked while it lasted for the great domes and tombs looked marvellous. Surely there is no life to compare with this one in camp and no place I have ever seen has the charm and grandeur of this one. We idled by the shores of the tank.

3rd December

Stirring earlier than yesterday and went to a place I have spotted where the morning sun comes through a broken window of the Dai Mahal. Found some *Hiptage madhablota* which, though wild in many parts of India, is scarce here, and wise from experience, painted it at once. There was only one sprig left in flower and I got it. Such luck. Teal for luncheon. In the evening I took Trilby for a short, slow turn, remembering her stout effort of yesterday, and went as far as Baz Bahadur's palace. There I had a great hunt for that mauve flower that I once saw growing in a tangle just outside its ruins. Not a sign of it now. It is a foolish thing to put off painting a plant you want and I shall always regret having been so silly as to leave it undone the only time I saw it. The chance has never come again. There was not so much as a withered stem of it though I examined every bush and thicket. A grand sunset and we sat by the tank watching the birds homing till darkness came down. Teal for dinner and much talk.

4th December

Slept late and woke to find A. stoning me from his bed. Painted till breakfast and then was lucky enough to come on some Sarus birds in the low ground where I hid and got portraits of them without their being disturbed. In one place I saw a piece of beautiful old wall down which a tangle of banyan roots fell, almost engulfing it. Marked it down and returned to it after the usual mid-day feast of

teal; but I had the misfortune when sitting down to paint to take my
seat firmly on a fleas' nest. I only discovered the situation when half
through my drawing and though I had the fortitude to do much of
the work where I was, I had at last to flee writhing to finish it from
memory. Oddly enough, it was a little more successful than usual.
Saw many grey apes. A.'s bag today was moderate; seven duck and
two green pigeon. Good supper and liquor.

5th December

To the Lal Bagh. I found a Bhil who was willing to stand for me and
got a drawing of him with his bow and arrow. We rode afterwards
to look for the Lal Serai, a large building in the thick of the seven
miles of jungle that this place is swallowed in. We found it with
some difficulty and admired its great beauty and the blue and green
Multhan tiling that adorns it, then A. went off with a gun and I
made for the Hindu village that is set in the middle of all these
Mohammedan remains; the main track was such a river of sharp
stones and boulders that I had to leave it and so got into all sorts
of thickets till I struck it again. Once in the village,[21] I left the pony
outside the Jamma Musjid and went into the most majestic of all
these majestic Mughul buildings, accompanied by an old man who
had suddenly joined me and who carried a large handful of twigs.
He was almost naked and for some unguessable reason he beat his
legs with them as he went, rhythmically and incessantly. It was as
though we marched to tuck of drum. Two other decent looking
men passing came too and when we had gone through the Musjid
we went to the high great building which contains Hoshung's tomb.
The man who lies under its vast floor was the first King of Malwa, a
turbulent character, always at enmity with someone; he died in 1432,
after reigning for twenty seven tempestuous years, at Hoshungabad,
whence his body was brought to this spot. His tomb, austere and
flat, like all those of his creed, has a white flag at its head and
round it lie the smaller tombs of his women. The dome above him
is high and the only light comes in through the door and the pierced
stone windows; an old, old woman who has been here for years is
its guardian and she sits crouched in the semi-darkness every day
and one night in the week, Thursday the Mohammedan vigil, when
she keeps a light burning by Hoshung. I asked her her age; 'I do
not know,' she replied, pulling forward a wisp of grey hair. She has
attached herself to the place and will probably be there till her death
for she has outlived her husband and children. I suppose someone in

Dhar state maintains her, probably some members of her own creed, but whoever they are she cannot cost them much.

6th December
Painted and rode to the Ship Palace, so called because it is built between two tanks and so, in the rainy season, stands in the midst of water. I took Moonaswami with me, riding the arab, and we came across a crowd of monkeys; one was sitting meditating on the sill of a carved and broken window and the sight of our approach made him leap from it like a harlequin across the way right into a window of the banqueting hall opposite. The whole drove were close to us and I made Moonaswami dismount, for Talisman looked on them with misgiving and he is no horseman. This is our last day here for A. has only a few days leave. It has been glorious but it's over now, worse luck.

TWO LETTERS TO C.K.E.

Violet writes to her mother telling of another visit to Dhar, this time with Harry and Rachel; she climbs the Hill of Devi, and meets the Rajah and Rani of Dewas Senior again.

17 Dec. 1899

. . . I have been to Dewas again and took Harry and Rachel with me. We were put up in the guest house. I don't think I ever told you about the hill[22] that rises just outside the city and the cave temples that surround the summit. Tara Rani sent an elephant to take us to them and on waking, the day after our arrival, we found it waiting with its *mahout* at the guest house door. There was a kind of sedan chair too that was ordered to follow us. When Harry saw the enormous beast kneeling there with me climbing up it, it was almost too much for him and he shrank back, but I told him he must follow and he did, rather white; I knew he would like it when he found himself riding along with me and Rachel and I was right, for he was delighted. The hill was very steep and the huge creature that looked as if it ought never to have survived the deluge, walked up the long flight of steps we met on the ascent as neatly as a human being. We went along narrow places where every tread was near the edge and looked down giddy slopes with a pleasant thrill, for it is impossible to feel nervous on an elephant, it is so much more like riding a building than an animal. We passed under a line of trees and there I made Harry and Rachel take to the sedan chair for the branches hung so low that I had to lie on my face on the *charpoy* roped on the beast's back to avoid being swept off. At the top of the hill I met Gotu Ram, priest of Kali's shrine, an old acquaintance; he stood on the paved platform before it and I left the elephant. We went up the steps cut clean in the hillside and I stopped at the door of the shrine, being an unbeliever and, moreover, shod with leather, but I could see everything from the threshold; Gotu Ram went in and brought me out a gift of dried raisins and I took them and sat down at the door.

It was difficult, looking at Kali, mother of terrors, not to laugh and with the European side of me I did, inwardly. To our eyes she would be about as alarming as a child's drawing on a slate, a thing she much resembled; for her face, with its wide, elementary, staring eyes and innocent, silly expression of mouth and eyebrow, cut in bas-relief on the grandeur of the naked rock, was confounding, considering what she stands for. I suppose in no country do the horrific and the *banal* come into such close quarters as in India, for there is enough civilization to make the contrast doubly sharp. The huge, gaudy devil with her four ungainly arms wore a little green jacket such as Indian women wear today; that, and her lower garment of the same colour were covered with a lattice of gold tinsel paper and a tinsel crown was on her head. One of her left hands held a disc, the other hung at her side. A sceptre was in her lower right hand, in the upper, a club shaped much like a bolster case. Iron tridents stood before her, sacred to Shiva, her husband, that were painted red, like most things in the shrine, and small heaps of offerings, rice and raisins, were lying on a stool in front of them. All this time Gotu Ram, who had noticed my sketch book, sat inside the wooden railing by his deity; not for the world would he have missed being portrayed and as I drew he threw me a polite word now and again, from his sanctuary. There was a large stone smeared with red paint and oil outside the cave representing Bhairon — or Bhiru, as the village people called him — one of Kali's twin sons and a tree stood above it with twisted roots sticking high out of the hard ground, as tree-roots do here, that looked like a knot of snakes. A heavy bell hung from the branches for worshippers coming to the shrine to sound, to call the attention of the great one within, or to scare away any demons that may be hiding about to interpret their prayers. When the drawing was finished Gotu Ram and I sat side by side on the ramparts of rock and looked down on the chequered cultivation far below. Crouched on his heels, he was as still as the images we had left, his old, fierce eyes staring out on the vast plain. Far on the horizon, very dim, we could see the towers and temples of the holy city of Ujjain, unreal, like a mirage. One great advantage about an Indian is that, though probably the greatest talker on earth, he can keep you company in a silence that need never end till you break it.

'Who built Ujjain, Gotu Ram?' I said at last.

'Your honour, the Rajah Vikram. He also built these temples for Mother Kali; one thousand years ago or perhaps two thousand. And I have served Mother Kali for twenty five years, though I receive but six *rupees*, four *annas* monthly from our Rajah.'

'And where did Rajah Vikram live?'

'In his palace at Ujjain, but he also comes here.'

'But how can that be, seeing that he is dead?'

'I do not know, but he comes.'

'Have you seen him, then?'

'No, no, but I have heard about it.'

At this I mentally applauded Gotu Ram for he might so easily have spun me some marvellous tale with himself for hero; and yet I was sorry too, for it would be a wonderful thing to think of the old man sitting alone up there, perhaps in the darkness, listening to the footsteps of the dead Rajah coming up the hill. When I got up and said I was going he proposed we should walk round the summit that he might show me the shrine on the other side of it and he took his shoes and staff and we set off over the rocks.

By this time Rachel and Harry had arrived in their sedan chair and now appeared at the top of the path. Harry insisted on coming too; he likes to see the originals of the stories I tell him from the Hindu pantheon; the accounts of these beings are to him what the story of the Sleeping Beauty and Jack the Giantkiller are to other children. He would not be left behind and said he was going with me and Gotu Ram. The path was very rough but he went with us step by step and when his legs were too short to manage the high levels he went on his hands and knees. Wherever I went he clambered after me. Nothing daunted him and at giddy places I held him tight. We looked into one shrine in which an image of Kali rose knee deep in the floor and the old man explained how she and the one I had been drawing at the other face of the summit were sisters but had quarrelled years ago and how this one had flown through the rock in a rage and appeared in the spot before us where she had stayed, unreconciled, ever since. It was about half a mile round the top and we were two hundred feet up and I wondered at Harry's enterprise; the one drawback to his pleasure was that there was no figure of Hanuman there.

Talking of the Sleeping Beauty and Jack the Giantkiller reminds me that I've always forgotten to tell you a funny thing that happened the other day. Sometimes I vary the Hindu mythology with the ordinary fairy-tales and 'Cinderella' is one that he particularly likes. I had come to the part where she appears in all splendour at the palace and was rehearsing the time honoured situation, which has always to be told in the same way, 'and there was the Prince *Sahib* dancing with Jane and Susan (for these are our names for the cruel sisters) and when he saw the lovely Cinderella come in he said "Go away, wicked Jane and Susan, I will not dance with you any more!"' 'Oh!' said Harry, thrilled, 'and did he kick them?' When I told him it was not thought right for Princes to kick their partners I think he was rather sorry. . . .

Mhow.
23 Dec. 1899

. . . My letter of last mail reached such lengths that I had to break off without telling you all I intended. I saw the Rani Tara before I left Dewas for Mrs Cooper drove me to visit her and thank her for her hospitality and the elephant and the sedan chair and the entertainment generally. She was at a white stucco villa she has outside the town and as we got out at the door the Rajah was standing on the steps to receive us in his boat-shaped scarlet Maratha hat with his grey whiskers brushed fiercely upwards. But he was anything but fierce and most polite. He took us into a large centre room in which we found Tara sitting on a green velvet sofa and I was invited to take my place at her right hand under the enormous chandeliers that hung from every part of the ceiling. She has rather fallen off in looks since I saw her and that shocking habit of *betel*-chewing has utterly ruined her teeth. She was anxious to take me into the garden and we parted from His Highness and went out to a round grass plot with a path round it and a fountain in the middle. As we emerged from the house all the women in it, and there seemed to be a good many, crowded on to a balcony to look at us. Some of them I had already seen watching privily from above; finding themselves at a safe distance they chattered and giggled ceaselessly. But it was not so very safe, for Her Highness grew exasperated, 'What are you staring at?' she cried, 'are we a show?' They fled. One thing that puzzled me was a highly decorated armchair of white pierced marble, so small that no one but a very young child could have sat in it, which seemed to be fixed in the ground close to the rim of the fountain. One might suppose it to be used for sitting in an outdoor showerbath when the fountain was playing, but that even the proportions of the slimmest Indian woman could never find room in it.

Tara said she was learning to ride a bicycle and I must see her do it; I am sure it was this that made her so anxious to take me into the garden. So the bicycle was brought out by a man evidently a servant who helped her to mount and then ran beside her holding her on till she made him let go and started by herself. She looked very insecure but went as hard as she could, her draperies ballooning out behind her and the machine wobbling so that I was thankful to see her stop and await congratulations; I really wondered how she escaped disaster and why her streaming muslins did not catch in the wheel and send her flying to eternal smash on the hard path. As she stood panting she was summoned indoors to see some ladies who were leaving Dewas for a few days and had come to bid her goodbye; Mrs Cooper said quietly to me that if I wanted to see one of the Rajah's chief mistresses I should go in too, as she was among them. So we all went back to the house.

In the room where the ladies waited the farewells began. There were five or six of them and they all fell on the Rani's neck, one after the other; there were no cries and howlings, such as I have seen in the street on similar occasions and I suppose that Court manners are a little quieter than those of the bourgeois. I watched them with interest and when one of the group precipitated herself into Tara's arms with an extra fervour I saw Her Highness look over the woman's shoulder at Mrs Cooper and make a grimace of such sarcastic impudence that it did not need that lady's meaning glance at me to explain who the embracer was.[23] There's something very attractive about Tara Rani and I feel sure that the gossip about her changing clothes with the maid in order to see the world for herself is true. She is what we in Scotland would call 'a card'.

New Year's Day 1900

1st January

We came here to the Residency last night to spend the New Year and when the heads of the family had gone to bed its younger members conceived the idea of going out as 'waits'. So we put on other people's coats and drew other people's hats over our faces in the best traditions of villainy and went round to the first Assistant's house. There we collected some sympathisers and a youth called Tony Martin who, as a stranger, would be invaluable to send forward to parley with suspicious people and those who might be moved to enmity by our voices. I said to Evelyn that I should be useless because I could not sing a note, even in church. 'That's nothing,' she said, 'you can always boo.' We went back to the Residency and taking our stand under Col. Barr's window, began our roundelay. In a short time there was a movement above and the contents of a jug of cold water came down on our heads; we dodged them by stepping under the balcony but the sounds of wrath behind the shower made it wiser to move on to less august circles so we made for the bungalow of a lesser light, who had a large garden with flower beds, and at a safe distance we collected again and raised a new strain. This time it went better, for a tall figure came out into the light of the verandah, evidently holding that bribe that, with the poor spirited, moves itinerant musicians on. So Tony Martin was thrust forward, but he had not quite negotiated the flower beds when the real, official waits made up of soldiers and other Europeans, suddenly set up a piercing note from the shadows close by. Tony Martin fled into the bushes; some — I among them — ran; some lay down upon their mother earth and watched between the stems of the zinnias and geraniums the waits receive the reward which, as they said next morning, *they* had earned. I had run in a different direction from anybody else, making for the back premises of the Residency; and hearing steps and voices approaching and being determined not to meet the waits (among whose ranks there might possibly be privates of the 20th on leave) I stepped aside into a thicket till they should go by. A large, pot-bellied object stood in the darkness of the bushes — the watercart; I crawled in under it and as I lay in my sanctuary, face downwards, I heard the gong strike from the native infantry lines in the town, and the twentieth century come in.

Notes

1. Parsee or Parsi: Persian in origin and followers of the ancient religion of Zoroastrinism, Parsis worship in fire temples. They played an important part in India's industrialisation and in the movement for political independence.
2. Dun Kirk: the church at Dun, Violet Jacob's family home in Angus.
3. Rachel the *ayah*: despite her name, the Indian nanny.
4. Native infantry regiment: at this time probably the 20th Bombay Infantry.
5. The Western Ghauts (or Ghats): an important range of mountains, running from north to south parallel to the west coast of India.

1. *ewigkeit:* (German) eternity.
2. Indore: Indore state was a large (9,519 square miles) Hindu state in the Central India Agency. The city of Indore was the nearest big settlement to Mhow, and was ruled by the Holkar dynasty from 1733.
3. Nawab of Jaora: Jaora was a small (601 square miles) Muslim state in the Central India Agency. The Nawab was Iftakhan Ali Khan Bahadur Saulat Jang. Born 17th January 1883, he succeeded his father in 1895, as a minor, receiving administrative powers in April 1906. He joined the Imperial Cadet Corps in 1902, and in 1903 married his cousin, the daughter of his uncle Yar Mohammed Khan.
4. Scindia: Maharajah Scindia of Gwalior. Gwalior was a large (26,382 square miles) Hindu state. The Maharajah was Madho Rao Scindia Bahadur (1876-1925). He succeeded to the throne in 1886, and was granted ruling powers in 1894.
5. a cousin: This is presumably the boy 'Jimmy', mentioned again frequently later.
6. Maharajah Holkar (of Indore): Shivaji Rao (1859-1908). He came to the throne in July 1886, but abdicated in favour of his son in 1903.
7. Colonel Barr: David William Keith Barr (1846-1916) of the Indian

Army entered the Political Department, Government of India, in
1869. Served in many parts of India, and held position of Agent
to the Governor-General in Central India 1894-1900. He retired
in 1905.

8. landau: four-wheeled carriage with adjustable top.

9. Dr Caldecott: Randolph Caldecott was first appointed to the Indian
Medical Service in 1869, and was at this time Resident Surgeon and
Medical Officer for Central India.

10. Heir apparent of Indore: Tukoji Rao Holkar III. He was born on
26th November 1890, and succeeded in 1903 on the abdication of
his father.

11. really a man of low descent: the Holkars, like the families of Scindia
of Gwalior and Gaekwad of Baroda in the area, had humble origins.
Apparently the Holkar dynasty was established by a shepherd, Malhar
Rao Holkar (born 1693).

12. *Lalla Rookh*: a series of four 'oriental' tales in verse linked by a prose
narrative, by Thomas Moore, published in 1817.

13. *The Second Jungle Book:* by Rudyard Kipling (1895).

14. Roxburgh's *Flora Indica:* William Roxburgh, known as 'the father of
Indian botany', was a Scot from Ayrshire. He went out to Madras in
1776 as an assistant surgeon, but pursued botanical research which
resulted in several publications, with many of the illustrations by Indian
artists. His *Flora Indica* appeared in several editions, the complete
three-volume edition coming out in 1832. Although in some ways
outdated, it is still a significant work.

15. F.B.'s French maid: F.B. is probably Captain C. Fowler Burton of the
Royal Fusiliers.

16. Shiva, the Destroyer: the Hindu triad of gods comprise Brahma, Shiva
and Vishnu, who may be seen as representations of the many attributes
of one god. Shiva embodies the cosmic paradox; representing opposites,
he is both destroyer and reproducer.

17. Hare's *Two Noble Lives:* Augustus Hare (1834-1903) was an English
writer of biographies and travel books. His *Story of Two Noble Lives*
(three volumes, 1893) deals with Lady Charlotte Canning and her sister
Lady Waterford.

18. Lady Canning's diary: Charlotte Canning (1817-61), elder daughter
of Lord Stuart de Rothesay, was married in 1835 to John Canning,
First Earl (1812-62). In 1856 her husband became Governor-General
of India, and in 1857 dealt with the Indian Mutiny. In 1859 he became
the first Viceroy of India. Charlotte accompanied him in India, and
she died in Calcutta. Her diary of her time in India has been partly
republished in recent years.

19. eight-year-old wife: as matrimonial alliances were considered of special
importance for Indian royal families, betrothals and even marriages

were often arranged when the royal children were still extremely young.

20. adjutant: an officer appointed to each regiment as assistant to the commanding officer.

21. Matabele: Matabeleland in Southern Africa, now part of present-day Zimbabwe.

22. Jimmy: some Indian royal children were brought up by English or Scottish nurses, and were known by western names. 'Jimmy' seems to be the cousin of the Nawab of Jaora, the son of the Jaora Prime Minister.

23. The Viceregal visit: the Viceroy was a Scot, Victor, 9th Earl of Elgin, who held the position 1894-99. A somewhat unwilling Viceroy, he nevertheless developed the system of railways in outlying districts.

24. phaeton: light open four-wheeled carriage drawn by two horses.

25. 20th Hussars . . . full dress: this was a blue uniform with a crimson busby-bag and a yellow plume.

26. Ujjain: an ancient city, holy for Hindus, on the bank of the river Sipra (or Sepra). It has a varied history. Once an important city in the kingdom ruled by the Emperor Ashoka's father, it was also the favoured seat of King Chandragupta II (380-414 A.D.), whose court encouraged Hindu literature. This one-time capital of Malwa was ruled by both Rajputs and Mughals, finally coming under the power of the Scindias of Gwalior.

27. Hanuman: Hanuman is a monkey chief of near-divine status in Hindu culture. Known for his learning, his agility and his loyal service to Rama (the god Vishnu's personification of the ideal man), he is the subject of many legends.

28. Captain Bannerman: this seems to be Arthur D'Arcy Gordon Bannerman of the Indian Army, at this time assistant to the Agent to the Governor-General in Central India.

29. Anarkalli: the Mughal Emperor Akbar buried a girl alive for smiling at his son in the harem. Her name was Anarkalli. Akbar's son, Jehangir, raised a cenotaph to her in Lahore (Pakistan).

30. Akbar: Mughal Emperor who reigned 1556-1605.

31. Bret Harte: Francis Bret Harte (1836-1902) was a widely travelled American editor, poet, dramatist and writer of popular fiction which, at its best, recreates life in the western United States, especially California, in idiosyncratic style.

1897: DIARIES AND LETTERS

1. A.J.-B.'s dog: A.J.-B. was 2nd Lieutenant A.W. Jennings-Bramly of the 20th Hussars.

2. Bhiru: sometimes called Bhairon; originally worshipped as a protective village deity, but adapted into Brahmanism as Bhaivara, 'the terrible one', one of the most awful forms of Shiva.

3. Kali: the fearful goddess who is the bringer of disease and war; the god Shiva's wife in her most terrifying form.

4. Chambal (river): this river today forms the boundary between Rajasthan and Madhya Pradesh.

5. Nerbada: a river which runs through Madhya Pradesh.

6. Patinir: the picture is probably 'Landscape with the Rest on the Flight into Egypt', of the Studio of Patenier, undated. Joachim Patenier (also called Patinir) was active in 1515, died not later than 1524. Of the Dutch school, he specialised in landscapes.

7. B. and F.B. and Bobby R.: B. is unidentified, but could be Major (later Lieutenant-Colonel) H.G.P. Beauchamp of the 20th Hussars. F.B. is Captain C. Fowler Burton of the 20th Hussars. Bobby R. is an officer in the Royal Fusiliers, possibly Major R.P.B. Rodick.

8. pergola: arbour or covered walk, formed of trailing plants over a trellis.

9. Reckitts' blue: proprietary blue laundry powder for whitening linen.

10. Maharajah of Dhar: Anand Rao Puar III (adopted) (1844-1898). Ruled 1857-1898. His Highness Udaiji Rao Puar, born September 1886, succeeded on adoption in 1898 as a minor, and ruled until 1926.

11. Mandu: standing on the Vindhyan mountains, Mandu was founded in the 10th century as a fortress and retreat by Rajah Bhoj, who also founded Dhar and Bhopal. It was conquered and held by different rulers down the years, including Mughals, Afghans and Marathas. One-time capital of Malwa, it was deserted when the capital shifted again to Dhar.

12. Multhan tiling: Multhan is in the Punjab, south-west of Lahore (now Pakistan); an ancient settlement, it is known for its pottery and enamel work.

13. 'Ain-i-Akbari': This was written in 1593 by Abul-Fazal (1554-1602), historiographer of the Mughal Emperor Akbar, as an appendix to his *Akbar-Namah*. The book, written in Persian, gives a detailed account of Akbar's administration and is one of the main sources of information on Mughal government in the 16th century.

14. curricle: light two-wheeled carriage, usually drawn by two horses.

15. General Nicolson: Major General H.M. Nicolson was District Officer of the Bombay Command based in Mhow 1895-1900.

16. *On the Face of the Waters* by Mrs Steel: Flora Annie Steel (1847-1929) was a Scot who went to India in 1867 with her civil servant husband. This best-known of her many novels, which included several about India, was published in 1896, and deals with the Sepoy Mutiny.

17. Diana of the Crosthwaites: a reference to the novel by George Meredith, *Diana of the Crossways* (1885).
18. Dandie Dinmont: a character in Walter Scott's novel *Guy Mannering*. His two terriers, Mustard and Pepper, are supposedly the progenitors of the Dandie Dinmont breed.
19. the Towers of Silence: Parsis do not cremate or bury their dead, because this would pollute the elements. Instead they leave the bodies on tall 'Towers of Silence', where they are generally consumed by vultures.
20. *The Sheepstealers:* Violet Jacob's own first novel, set in the Anglo-Welsh borders, and published in 1902.
21. Nandia, the holy bull: the god Shiva's bull-mount, his chamberlain and musician. Also associated with fertility.
22. hamadryad: large poisonous Indian snake of the cobra family.
23. Ganesh, the elephant god: one of the most popular Indian deities, represented as a short, pot-bellied man with four arms and an elephant's head bearing a single tusk. Ganesh is a son of Shiva and Parbati.
24. Mr Ernest Barnes: of the Indian Army. First appointed as Political Assistant, Third Class, 21st April 1896. He had attained the rank of Major by 1905, when he was awarded the Kaisar-I-Hind Medal for Public Service In India. He was proficient in several languages of the region.
25. Gwalior Fort: the city of Gwalior is famous especially for its huge and ancient fort, whose history goes back over a thousand years. It was taken over by the British several times, and in 1858 some of the final and most dramatic events of the Indian Mutiny took place here.
26. Mr Waterfield: Mr Harry Gordon Waterfield, Assistant to the Agent to the Governor-General in Central India in the Criminal Branch. Appointed 1895.
27. the *Sahibzada* Wahid-ud-din: a member of the Indore royal family.
28. Captain Stewart: W.H.M. Stewart, appointed 19th June 1889 as Political Agent in Bhapawar, Southern States of Central India.
29. Shadrach, Meshach and Abednego: in the Old Testament (Daniel 3), these three companions of Daniel, who all held high office, refused to worship King Nebuchadnezzar's golden image. They were therefore cast into a fiery furnace, but were miraculously delivered; the king was thus convinced of the power of their God.
30. A.D.C.: Aide-de-Camp to the Viceroy in India.
31. the Jain god Parasnath: the ancient Jain religion stresses reverence for all living things. Many legends surround Parasnath or Parssva (?872-?772 B.C.), whose symbol was the hooded serpent, and whose followers were probably the first of the white-clad monks of Jainism.
32. Dewas: a small Hindu state bordering the state of Indore, ruled by two Maratha Rajahs.

1. Two Rajahs: Violet Jacob appears to have made a mistake about the two Rajahs of Dewas; in fact, the younger man represented the Junior branch, the older man, the Senior. Dewas Junior was Malhar Rao Puar, born 10th August 1877, who succeeded on adoption on 23rd May 1892, and died in 1934. His wife was Lelita Rani.

2. the wife of the other Rajah: Dewas Senior was Rajah Krishnaji Rao Puar II (1849-99), who ruled from 1860 to 1899. His first wife, Tara Raje of Gwalior (sister of Scindia), died in 1891. His second wife, the one described here, was Tara Raje of Kolhapur. Krishnaji died childless, and was succeeded in 1899 by his nephew, Tukoji Rao Puar III, who assumed the throne at the age of 11, and gained full powers in 1908. Tukoji Rao was the Rajah of Dewas for whom E.M. Forster worked as secretary.

3. *cabochon* emeralds: gems which have been polished but not faceted.

4. John Company India: 'John Company' was the Honourable East India Company, which was formed in 1599 and governed British India from 1833 to 1858.

5. Mrs Vansittart: the name has several precedents in the history of colonial activity in India in the 18th century. In the 19th century, Lt. Col. Eden Vansittart was the author of Handbooks for the Indian Army, and this is the most probable reason for Violet Jacob choosing such an apparently unlikely name for the character in her anecdote.

6. Shiva and Parbati his spouse: Parbati is the goddess in her kind and gentle form, pictured as a beautiful woman.

7. M.K.: not identified, but apparently the wife of an army officer, possibly Lieutenant W.H. Kay of the Royal Artillery. Violet Jacob dedicated *The Good Child's Yearbook* to 'Mamie Kay' — possibly the same woman.

8. Simrole: in Mhow *pargana* or district, in Indore State.

9. the colour *mezereum*: as in the plant *daphne mezereum*.

10. *datura*: a toxic solanaceous plant.

11. The Fourth Bombay Rifles: a regiment of the Indian Army which arrived in Mhow, 20th December 1896.

12. the Linnaean System: Carl von Linné, best known as 'Linnaeus' (1707-1778), was a Swedish doctor and botanist whose system of naming and classifying plants, 'the Linnaean system', is of lasting significance, although it has been considerably updated and improved.

13. Royal Irish: The Royal Fusiliers were replaced in Mhow by the 2nd Battalion of the Royal Irish Regiment.

14. sounder of pig: (archaic) herd of wild swine.

15. the sun-descended house of Udaipur: the Rajput royal family of Udaipur

(a sizeable state now part of Rajasthan) traditionally called themselves 'the race of the sun'.

16. Captain Newmarch: Lindsay Sherwood Newmarch of the Indian Army, appointed as Political Agent at Bhopal, May 1897.

17. a military funeral: Arthur Napier was formerly a captain in the Indian Army.

18. the Bayleys: the Honourable Mr C.S. Bayley, I.C.S., C.S.I., afterwards became the Agent to the Governor-General in Central India.

19. Forbes-Mitchell: William Forbes-Mitchell was the author of *Reminiscences of the Great Mutiny 1857-59* (London, 1893).

20. Nairne's *Flowering Plants of Western India*: this was *The Flowering Plants of Western India* by A.K. Nairne (London, 1894).

21. Bhopal: situated 105 miles north-east of Indore, this Muslim city takes its name from the legendary 11th century founder, Raja Bhoj. Capital of the state of Bhopal in the Central India Agency, it is famous for the fort, built in 1728, and several mosques, including the Jamma Musjid, mentioned here, built in 1837 by Qudsia Begum.

22. Secundra Begum: a former (woman) ruler of Bhopal during the time of the Mutiny. She died in 1868, and was succeeded by Shah Jehan Begum, whom Violet met here.

23. Violet's French is at fault here. This should read:
'Mais oui – en voila un – . J'ai oublié son nom, mais je me rappelle de lui – il nous a donné une collection de tableaux et de chansons obscènes.'

24. Shah Jehan Begum: born in 1837, she was pronounced ruler of Bhopal at the age of ten, but abdicated in 1860 in favour of her mother. She reigned from 1868 until 1901, when she was succeeded by her daughter, Sultan Jehan.

25. the Sanchi Tope: the largest of the many stupas erected in the 3rd century B.C. by the Emperor Ashoka.

26. The *Gulistan* of Sadi: Sa'di, Muslih-Al-Din, Shaikh (born Shiraz, 1194, died 1282 or 1292), was an important Persian poet and writer, whose *Gulistan* (1258), in rhymed prose, has a significant place in Persian literature.

27. P.M.: unidentified, but might be 2nd Lieutenant P.G. Mason of the 20th Hussars.

28. 'the horns of Elfland faintly blowing': a quotation from the song between Books 3 and 4 of Alfred Lord Tennyson's poem 'The Princess' that begins 'The splendour falls . . .'.

29. Kumaun lakes: an area of lakes in the Kumaun hills, in the north-west of the state now called Uttar Pradesh.

1899: DIARIES AND LETTERS

1. Cawnpore: a major site of the Indian Mutiny of 1857. The British garrison at Cawnpore was besieged by mutineering Indians; those British who survived were allowed to go free in boats, but while leaving they were again attacked at the *ghat*. The remaining women and children were massacred within a few more weeks, and the bodies thrown down a well.

2. Naini Tal: a hill-town, and once the summer capital of Uttar Pradesh.

3. Crooke's *North Western India* and *Religion and Folklore of Western India*: William Crooke (1848-1923) served in the North West Provinces and Oudh as magistrate and collector, and his many books about India, including the ones mentioned here, had some currency in their time.

4. Corvus: a Southern constellation.

5. Brandis' *Trees*: Sir Dietrich Brandis authored several books about Indian trees and flora in the late 19th and early 20th centuries, including the one mentioned here, presumably his *Indian Trees*, although this did not appear in London until 1906.

6. Mallowa Tal: a lake.

7. Sir Samuel Baker: Sir Samuel White Baker (1821-1893) was a traveller and sportsman, and author of many books, including *The Albert N'Yanza, great Basin of the Nile, and exploration of the Nile Sources* (two volumes, London, 1866), *Eight Years' Wandering in Ceylon* (London, 1855), and others.

8. the Shwe Dagon temple: in fact, this pagoda is in Rangoon, not Mandalay.

9. as many arms and hands as Kali: the goddess is generally depicted as having four arms.

10. The Transvaal: the war of the South African Republic (Transvaal) and the Orange Free State against Great Britain (popularly known as the Boer war) lasted from 1899 to 1902.

11. Col. Irwin: Lieutenant Colonel W.J. Irwin, Commanding Officer of the 20th Hussars in Mhow.

12. the god Krishna: popular Hindu deity, the eighth incarnation of Vishnu, and object of devotional worship known as *bhakti*. As an adult, Krishna is the epic hero of the *Mahabharata*, and preacher of the *Bhagavad Gita*.

13. B., the new commanding officer: Lieutenant Colonel H.G.P. Beauchamp.

14. the Little Man: Colonel Irwin.

15. Alan Goring: a lieutenant in the 20th Hussars.

16. Sir John Malcolm: (1769-1833). Son of a Borders farmer, Malcolm's long career in India combined political and military experience. He was at one time Governor of Bombay, also of Central India, where he was the founder of the Mhow Cantonment in 1818. Also author of *Memoir of Central India*, 2 vols (London, 1832), which Violet read.

17. Lily Edwards: may be the wife of an officer in the 20th Hussars, G.T.G. Edwards, who, as Lieutenant Colonel, commanded the regiment in the First World War; or of Assistant Adjutant General, District Bombay Command, F.J.M. Edwards, based in Mhow, 1895-1901.
18. Ram (or Rama): Ramachandra, the god Vishnu's seventh incarnation. Rama is worshipped throughout India.
19. pi-dog: homeless dog.
20. Sir George White and the garrison of Ladysmith: Ladysmith was a South African town held by the British and besieged by the Boers during the war of 1899-1902. In fact, the British resisted, under the command of Field Marshal Sir George Stewart White (1835-1912), a Scot, and the town was not taken; British relief arrived on 15th February 1900. The rumours heard by Violet Jacob were, therefore, misleading.
21. the village: this is the village of Mandu. The buildings of Mandu are divided into three groups; the 'Village Group' buildings include the Jamma Musjid and Hoshung's tomb, mentioned by Violet. The 'Royal Enclave' includes the Jahaz Mahal or 'Ship Palace', also mentioned here. Further south is the 'Rewa Kund' group of buildings.
22. the hill: this is the hill that gave its name to E.M. Forster's *The Hill of Devi*. Forster lived at Dewas in 1912-1913, and again in 1921, when he acted as temporary Private Secretary to Tukoji Rao Puar III, Maharajah of Dewas State Senior.
23. the embracer: presumably her husband's favourite mistress.

Bibliography of Works published
by Violet Jacob

The Baillie MacPhee (a poem), by Walter Douglas Campbell and Violet Kennedy-Erskine (Edinburgh and London, 1888); with illustrations by Violet Kennedy-Erskine.

The Sheepstealers (London, 1902).

The Infant Moralist (verses), by Lady Helena Carnegie and Mrs Arthur Jacob (Edinburgh and London, 1903; reprinted 1926); with illustrations by Mrs Arthur Jacob.

The Interloper (London, 1904).

The Golden Heart and Other Fairy Stories (London, 1904).

Verses (London, 1905).

Irresolute Catherine (London, 1908).

The History of Aythan Waring (London, 1908).

Stories Told by the Miller (London, 1909).

The Fortune Hunters and Other Stories (London, 1910).

Flemington (London, 1911).

Songs of Angus (London, 1915).

More Songs of Angus and Others (London and New York, 1918).

Bonnie Joann and Other Poems (London, 1921).

Tales of My Own Country (London, 1922).

Two New Poems: 'Rohallion' and 'The Little Dragon' (Edinburgh, 1924).

The Northern Lights and Other Poems (London, 1927).

The Good Child's Year Book (London, 1928); with illustrations by Violet Jacob.

The Lairds of Dun (London, 1931).

The Scottish Poems of Violet Jacob (Edinburgh, 1944).

The Lum Hat and Other Stories: Last Tales of Violet Jacob, edited by Ronald Garden (Aberdeen, 1982).

Glossary

Anna: Unit of currency, the sixteenth part of a rupee

Attar: Fragrant essential oil of roses and other flowers

Ayah: Indian maid-servant or nanny

Bahadur: Champion, hero

Banana-wallah: Artisan. The affix 'wallah' usually denotes 'doer', person who does something.

Bazaar: Market-place

Begum: Title for Muslim women of high rank; feminine of 'Nawab'

Betel: The leaf of the betel vine is chewed with other ingredients as a mild intoxicant and savoury. Sometimes called 'pan'; reddish-brown in colour.

Bheesti: Domestic servant who supplies family with water, carrying it in a goatskin slung on his back

Bhil: Race inhabiting the hills and forests of the Vindhya, Malwa and North-western Deccan

Bhiru or *Bhairon:* One of the twin sons of Kali

Borah: A trader or man of affairs

Brahmin: Member of Hindu priestly caste

Brinjara: Grain-carriers, dealers in grain and salt, who move about in parties with cattle, carrying their goods to different markets

Budmash: Rogue, rascal

Bund: Artificial embankment, dam, dyke, causeway

Cardamom: Aromatic spice

Charpoy: Common Indian bedstead

Chatri: Domed building such as a cenotaph; an umbrella

Chatti: Globular earthen vessel

Chik: Screen or blind made of split bamboo sticks

Chota: Small

Chowkidar: Watchman, sentry, guard

Cummerbund: Sash or belt

Dâk: Post

Dâk bungalow: Government rest-house and staging-post

Dâk or *Dhâk tree:* Small bushy tree (*Butea frondosa*) with deep orange flowers used in preparing *Holi* powder

Dalli: Basket of fruit and vegetables; a present for visitors

Dandy: A kind of open litter or sedan chair used for carrying people in the mountains

Dhaman: A kind of serpent, said to suck cows, but harmless

Dhobi: Washerman

Dhoti: Loose loincloth worn by caste Hindus

Dhurri: Rough cotton rug

Diwalli: Hindu festival of lights, a happy occasion, held for five days in October-November

Diwan: Prime Minister or principal officer in a princely state (Hindu or Muslim)

Dusera: Major Hindu religious festival, the nine-nights' (or ten-days') festival in October; also called *Durga-puja*

Fakir: Originally a Muslim who has taken a vow of poverty, but also applied to Hindu devotees and ascetics

Fez: Type of hat worn by men

Gadi: Cushion or throne of royalty

Ghat: Quay, path or place of descent to a river; a mountain path; name of a mountain range (Ghats or Ghauts); Hindu funeral pyre

Ghi: Clarified butter

Goldmohur: Caesalpinia pulcherrima or 'peacock-flower'

Gram: Grain or pulse fed to horses, especially *chana* or chick-pea

Haar: Tinsel ceremonial garland

Jaghir: Hereditary estate of land given by government or ruler

Jats: An agricultural caste of Upper India

Jawari-fields: Fields of crops, either Indian millet or maize

Khud: Precipitous hillside, deep valley, chasm

Koel: Bird of the cuckoo family; its name derives from its cry during the breeding season

Krait: Small but extremely venomous snake

Kulang: Crane

Log: People, folk

Lota: Small, usually brass, pot, used by Hindus for drinking and sometimes for cooking

Maharajah, Maharana, Maharao: The highest of Hindu hereditary rulers; masculine of 'Maharani'

Maharani: Hindu queen; feminine of 'Maharajah'

Mahli: Gardener

Mahout: Elephant-driver

Mahseer: Large river fish

Mahunt: Hindu lay Archbishop

Maratha or *Mahratta:* Name of a famous Hindu race

Memsahib: Polite title used by Indians for addressing European women; female form of 'sahib'

Mohurrum: Period of fasting and public mourning during the first month of the Muslim lunar year, in commemoration of the nephews of the Prophet, Hassan and Houssein

Munshi: Interpreter, secretary, writer

Mussulman: Muslim, Mohammedan

Nautch: Kind of dance performed by women; a stage entertainment

Nautch girls: Hindu professional dancing girls

Nawab: Title of Muslim ruler; masculine of 'Begum'

Nazir: Indian official, inspector

Nullah: A watercourse (often a dry one)

Pagari: Turban

Palanquin: Box-litter for holding a traveller, carried on poles borne on four (or six) men's shoulders

Pan: Betel vine and other ingredients for chewing

Pariah: Originally the name of a low Hindu caste in Southern India, sometimes applied to other low caste or casteless people; also used of dogs

Patel: Headman of a village; one controlling village affairs and communicating with Government officers

Peepul: Indian fig tree

Pir: Muslim holy man, religious teacher, saint

Puja: Hindu ceremony or act of worship

Punkah: In the original sense a portable fan; often refers to a large swinging fan suspended from the ceiling of a house

Purdah: Literally 'a curtain', especially one screening women from the sight of men; the practice of keeping women secluded

Rajah: Hindu ruler of high rank, but below that of 'Maharajah' (also: *Raj, Rana, Rao* etc.); masculine of 'Rani'

Rajput: Literally 'king's son'; a Hindu of the warrior caste in Central and Western India, from one of the 'royal' clans. Hence, 'Rajputana': country of kings' sons.

Ramadan: The ninth month of the Mohammedan year, a time of fasting, when Muslims may not eat between dawn and sunset

Rani: Hindu woman of high rank; feminine of 'Rajah'

Rupee: Standard unit of currency

Sadhu: Hindu holy man

Sahib: Polite title used by Indians for addressing European men or high-born Indians; female form is 'memsahib'

Sahibzada: One genteelly born, a young gentleman

Salaam: Form of salutation

Sambhar: A kind of stag

Sarus crane: type of bird

Sepoy: In Anglo-Indian use, an Indian soldier in British service

Shigram: A kind of carriage

Sirdar: In India, a chief, leader or military officer

Su'ar: Hog, pig; brat, whelp, puppy; a form of abuse

Suttee: Hindu widow who burns with her dead husband; hence the practice of widow-burning

Syce: A groom

Taboosh: Type of hat; a fez

Tank: Reservoir of water

Tatti: A light screen or mat made of grass, hung in door or window openings

Thakur: Local chief; title of respect applied especially to Rajput nobles

Tonga: A type of small, light two-wheeled vehicle, pulled by a horse or a man

Tope: Grove or orchard; an ancient Buddhist monument in the form of a solid dome

Topē or *Topee:* A hat

Tulsi: A plant; basil (*Ocymum sanctum*)

Zenana: Women's quarters

Index

Akbar, 53
Akolia, 75, 96, 174
Anderson, Dr, 132

Baker, Major Lewis Hyde, 156–67
Baker, Sir Samuel, 161–2
Bala Sahib, 31, 32, 40, 45
Baneria, 103
Bannerman, Captain Arthur D. G., 49, 51
Bannerman, Captain Pat, 8, 81, 83–5, 91
Barnes, Ernest, 8, 90
Barnes, Eugénie, 8, 90, 91, 101, 135, 139–42
Barr, Colonel (later Sir) David, 8, 30, 51–2, 78, 101–2, 129–30, 184, 193
Barr, Evelyn, 8, 12, 51, 78, 90–2, 94–7, 184, 193
Barr High School, Jaora, 8
Barwai, Maharajah Holkar's palace, 94–5
Bayley, Hon C.S., 134–5
Baz Bahadur, king of Mandu, 68–9
Beauchamp, Col H.G.B., 176
Bercha, 62, 63, 132, 173
Bhim Tal, 153, 160
Bhiru, 58
Bhopal, 13, 138–43
bird life, 25–6, 38, 40, 169
borahs, 54
Brinjara people, 148–9
Burton, Captain C. Fowler, 62–3, 77

Caldecott, Dr Randolph, 8, 30–1, 45, 51
Cawnpore, 151–2

Central India Agency, 3–4
Chambal river, 60, 116
Chatri Bagh, 73, 76, 105, 137
chatris, 84
climate, 38, 41, 75–82, 126–8
Cooper, Mrs, 104
cricket match, 175

Daly College, Indore, 29
Degararia (Deva Garya), 70–2
Depalpur, 103–4, 144
Dewas state, 13, 105–9, 188–92
Dhar, 4, 63–4, 69–70, 74–5, 120–121
Dhar, Maharajah of, 11–12, 64, 120–1, 132
disease/illness, 37, 86–9, 180
Diwalli, 182
Doughty, Marian, 8, 50, 56, 58–9, 70, 76
Dusera procession, 45–6

Edwards, Lily, 181–4
Elgin, Lady, 12, 48–9
Elgin, Victor, 9th Earl, 7, 12; viceregal visit to Indore, 47–8
Erskine, David, 13th Laird of Dun, 1
Erskine, Sir Joh, 5th Laird of Dun, 1

Flemington (1911), 16
flora, Dhar, 64: Indore, 73; Jamli, 87, 90, 143; Kumaun lakes, 152–63, 167–72; Mhow, 27, 33–44, 56, 72, 74, 79, 81, 87, 131; Simrole, 113–15
Forbes-Mitchell, William, 135
Forster, E. M., 4, 13
Fortune Hunters and Other Stories, The (1910), 9